Shadow Banking in China

Shadow Banking in China

An Opportunity for Financial Reform

EDITED BY
ANDREW SHENG
NG CHOW SOON

WILEY

Registered office
John Wiley & Sons Ltd, The Atrium, Southern Gate, Chichester, West Sussex, PO19 8SQ, United Kingdom

For details of our global editorial offices, for customer services and for information about how to apply for permission to reuse the copyright material in this book please see our website at www. wiley.com.

Library of Congress Cataloging-in-Publication Data

Names: Sheng, Andrew, editor. | Ng, Chow Soon, editor.
Title: Shadow banking in China : an opportunity for financial reform / Andrew
    Sheng, Ng Chow Soon.
Description: Hoboken : Wiley, 2016. | Includes index.
Identifiers: LCCN 2016004493 (print) | LCCN 2016011405 (ebook) |
    ISBN 9781119266327 (hardback) | ISBN 9781119266358 (ePDF) |
    ISBN 9781119266341 (ePub)
Subjects: LCSH: Nonbank financial institutions—China. | Finance—China. |
    BISAC: BUSINESS & ECONOMICS / Finance.
Classification: LCC HG187.C6 S53343 2016 (print) | LCC HG187.C6 (ebook) |
    DDC 332.10951—dc23
LC record available at http://lccn.loc.gov/2016004493

A catalogue record for this book is available from the British Library.

ISBN 978-1-119-26632-7 (hardback)   ISBN 978-1-119-26635-8 (ebk)

ISBN 978-1-119-26634-1 (ebk)   ISBN 978-1-119-26639-6 (obk)

Cover design: Wiley
Cover image: © Liufuyu/Getty Images

Set in 11/13.5pt TimesLTStd-Roman by Thomson Digital, Noida, India
Printed in Great Britain by TJ International Ltd, Padstow, Cornwall, UK

CONTENTS

FOREWORD

The Fung Global Institute (FGI) was established in August 2011 to create a dialogue on global issues from Asian perspectives. Its research agenda covered a wide range of global issues, such as global trade and supply chains, development growth models, finance and the environment. This study on shadow banking in China comprises the third of three major FGI studies on China. Our first report comprised a major study undertaken with the China National Development Research Council on the story of Foshan and how a city could be a prototype for the evolving growth model for China to tackle a wide range of social and developmental issues. The second report was a major review of the issues and challenges of RMB internationalization, providing a road map on China's way forward. This study on shadow banking looks at the emergence of shadow banking and its opportunities and challenges for the reform of the financial sector in China.

This book puts recent developments in China's shadow banking sector into perspective. Currently, there is much debate and confusion over the potential risks of Chinese shadow banks, with some commentators even suggesting that it could trigger the next Chinese financial crisis.

Specifically, this study sheds light on the scale of shadow banking in China by clarifying definitional issues to address the problems of double counting and under counting associated with a simplistic aggregation of different products and assets of shadow banking activities, which created errors of double counting and under counting. Working in partnership with Oliver Wyman, the leading global financial and strategic consultant, the FGI has built upon the official definition and estimation of China's shadow banking activities to derive a more realistic estimate of the scale of shadow bank risks.

The book also seeks to identify the Chinese characteristics or factors underpinning the rapid growth of Chinese shadow banks. Chinese shadow banks arose from a market response to limitations in the current banking business model to meet real sector needs for access to credit, combined with market demand for higher-yielding saving/investment products by China's household and corporate high savers.

The book delves into Chinese data sources and research studies, many not available in English. Using China's recently available national balance sheet and flow of funds data, the authors drill down into the interconnectivity and relationships between the different components of shadow banking and formal banking through a stock-flow approach. Fresh insights on the interconnectivities and vulnerabilities at the sectoral level (external sector, household sector, central government, local government, non-financial corporate, and financial sector) are offered.

The comprehensive assessment of the scale of risks of Chinese shadow banking considers carefully the quality of its assets. The ultimate credit exposures of the Chinese banking system (including shadow banks) fall mainly on four major categories of borrowers: large state-owned enterprises (SOEs); private sector small- and medium-sized enterprises (SMEs); real estate companies; and Local Government Financing Platforms (LGFPs). The authors assess the quality of these four different classes of banking assets to provide an indication of the potential risks of such assets becoming non-performing loans (NPLs), as well as the likely impact on the formal banking sector and broader financial system. China's financial system also suffers a structural maturity mismatch because its long-term investments have been funded largely through short-term borrowing from the banking/shadow banking system. At the same time, there is a structural debt/equity mismatch as most investments are funded by debt rather than equity.

By looking at shadow banking risks at the product, institution and system levels, the authors develop the likely scenarios for shadow banking NPLs for selected industries, based on different assumptions on the level of economy-wide stress. Going a step further, shadow banking is categorized into three different risk layers based on its connection with the formal banking system. Between 20–40 percent of such NPLs could be 'transferable' to the formal banking system and may drive banking NPLs towards ~7 percent under the "disaster" scenario.

With the economy still growing at 6–7 percent per annum, low fiscal deficit, a high savings rate and very large foreign exchange reserves, the book concludes that a systemic financial meltdown is unlikely as China has adequate resources and policy flexibility to address what is essentially a domestic debt problem with no direct global implications.

Nevertheless, the combination of slower world growth and trade, plus the threat of a domestic real estate price adjustment, could create the conditions for an escalation of domestic financial risks, with indirect, contagion effects on foreign banks and investors. All these underscore the need for prompt action to resolve the shadow banking issues to preempt any contagion effects. Whilst the emergence of shadow banks poses some risks, there is a golden opportunity to utilize the time available to implement major structural reforms so that in the long term, China's financial system will be able to support efficiently, stably and equitably, the needs of the real economy.

The book concludes that instead of introducing more regulations and piecemeal reforms, the reform of the shadow banking sector offers the opportunity to expedite financial reform on a system-wide basis. Building on officially announced reforms, it offers a comprehensive financial system blueprint (with detailed immediate, medium- and longer-term policy recommendations) to address the potential risks of shadow banking and diversify China's bank-dominated financial sector to address structural maturity and debt-equity mismatches to promote a more sustainable and inclusive financial system.

It is hoped that the book will be useful for policy makers, investors, analysts and those interested in China's continued transformation and engagement with the global economy.

On July 1, the FGI was inaugurated as the Asia Global Institute at The University of Hong Kong. Its research agenda will continue to focus on global issues with Asian perspectives.

Dr Victor K. Fung
Founding Chairman, Fung Global Institute and
Chairman, Advisory Board, Asia Global Institute,
The University of Hong Kong
October 1, 2015

FOREWORD

This book considers the sources of gains, losses and risks associated with the Chinese shadow banking industry from a historical and public policy perspective. While the scale of China's shadow banks is still relatively small by international comparison, their rapid growth in recent years requires careful attention by policymakers and the industry to ensure that the problem is properly managed. In identifying the Chinese characteristics or factors that led to its rapid growth, this book helps to highlight the underlying problems in the shadow banking industry in China.

Mr Andrew Sheng, in his role as former President of the Fung Global Institute (FGI) and the Chief Adviser to the China Banking Regulatory Commission (CBRC), has been doing research on this emerging issue with his FGI team to understand the scope, size and nature of Chinese shadow banks and their complex interconnectedness with and implications on the rest of the financial system and the economy in China. The results of their research are reflected in this book, which offers an objective and comprehensive assessment of the scale and possible impact of China's shadow banks on the domestic and external markets.

The book contends that the best means of responding to the threat represented by shadow banking is to adopt a two-pronged approach with two key procedural mechanisms: (a) careful monitoring and supervision of all shadow banking activities to mitigate their interconnected risks that could lead to unintended consequences, including crisis; and (b) expedite the reform and restructuring of the financial services industry to serve the real economy in a more efficient and effective way.

Given the centrality of financial institutions and markets to real economic growth and societal well being, it is exceedingly important for all of us to act swiftly and decisively, in order to ensure that matters do not take a turn for the worse. The recommended financial reforms will enable China to face the current environment of increased volatility and uncertainty in financial markets, both in China and abroad, and go a long way toward achieving the dream of a vigorous and successful China.

Liu Mingkang
former Chairman, China Banking Regulatory Commission;
Professor and Distinguished Fellow,
Institute of Global Economics and Finance,
The Chinese University of Hong Kong, Hong Kong
Honorary Dean, Lingnan (University) College,
Sun Yat Sen University, Guangzhou, China

ACKNOWLEDGMENTS

This book had its origins in a board meeting of the Fung Global Institute, when board member Stuart Gulliver, Group CEO of HSBC Holdings PLC, suggested that the FGI should undertake a more comprehensive study of shadow banking in China due to the many divergent guesstimates and forecasts on the size of the shadow banking problem in China. This book could not have been possible without the generous contributions and support from FGI's corporate partners in its financial studies, particularly from HSBC, China Development Bank, Japan Post Bank and AIA. The book also benefited from their helpful comments and insights, but responsibility for the opinions, views and errors and omissions remain solely with the authors and editors.

Oliver Wyman has been a major partner and collaborator on this project, led by Christian Edelmann and Cliff Sheng, with support from their Asia-Pacific Chairman, Rafael Gil-Tienda. Working with their team was a pleasure because the book had the benefit of their global skill sets and on-site China experience.

The book also owes its completion to the unstinting support of FGI Chairman Dr Victor Fung, Academic Council Chairman and Nobel Laureate Michael Spence, Distinguished Fellow Liu Mingkang, President Dr Bill Overholt, Barbara Meynert and other board members who gave their moral and critical support at all stages of its production. Nobel Laureate Myron Scholes, and other anonymous reviewers, gave valuable comments and insights for the improvement of the book. Dr Xiao Geng and Eva Yi also provided helpful comments that kept the book on its focus on ground conditions in China.

The book could not have been completed without the hard work and dedication of its principal contributors, Ms Jodie Hu, Ms Wang Yao, Mr Li Sai Yau and Ms Cathleen Yi Tin. They read all the available literature on the subject, especially original Chinese research and sources not available in English, and meticulously compiled all the data, tables and drafts. Comments on the Chinese translation were provided by Ms Zhang Liang and Dr Li Chen. Tremendous support was received from Yvonne Mak, Arian Hassani, Galvin Chia, Jenny Chan, Jillian Ng, Warren Lu and Thomson Ng. Sarah Wong provided all the coffee, tea and biscuits to keep the team going.

Events are moving very rapidly following the A-share turmoil in June–September 2015. Whilst recent events did not negate the findings and recommendations of this book, the authors are embarking on a new book on the A-share market and its role in the reform and development of the Chinese economy. This will be forthcoming in 2016.

We would like to acknowledge the unstinting help and comments from various individuals in CBRC, People's Bank of China, universities and other research institutes who provided valuable comments on how to look at these complex issues. Finally, this book benefited from many helpful comments from friends, colleagues and experts in China, Hong Kong and elsewhere. They made this book more meaningful and less incomplete, but responsibility for any errors and omissions remain with the authors and editors.

Andrew Sheng and Ng Chow Soon

ABOUT THE EDITORS

Andrew Sheng is Chief Adviser to the China Banking Regulatory Commission; former Chairman of the Securities and Futures Commission, Hong Kong; and former Deputy Chief Executive in HKMA. Uniquely, he sits on international advisory councils of the China Investment Corporation, China Development Bank, China Securities Regulatory Commission, Securities and Exchange Board of India, and Shanghai Municipality for Shanghai as an International Financial Centre. He is Board Director of Khazanah Nasional Berhad of Malaysia, and adjunct Professor to Tsinghua University School of Economics and Management and the WuDaoKou School.

Ng Chow Soon is former Director of the Governor's Office, Bank Negara Malaysia and a Harvard Mason Fellow.

EXECUTIVE SUMMARY

While China has weathered the Global Financial Crisis (GFC) with continued economic growth, it now faces new headwinds in the form of a slowing domestic and global economy and weaker world trade. As the economy adjusts to a new normal of slower growth where reliance on export-driven growth may no longer be viable, questions are being raised about the sustainability of the Chinese growth. Some commentators have suggested that China's "Lehman moment" is imminent and that the Chinese shadow banking sector could become the cause of the next systemic global financial crisis.

This book seeks to bring the explosive growth in China's shadow banking credit into the light as there is much confusion over the potential risks of Chinese shadow banks due to definitional, methodology and measurement issues. Using China's national balance sheet data, the study assesses that the size of its shadow banking risk assets (at RMB 30.1 trillion or 53 percent of GDP and 27 percent of formal banking system credit assets in 2013) is still manageable, based on current fairly favorable conditions, as China has adequate resources and policy flexibility to deal with what is an essentially domestic debt problem.

However, time is of the essence in implementing remedial measures. This is because national balance sheet data only provide a top-down, snapshot view of the situation in China and a review of current conditions. They do not attempt to forecast dynamic changes in the Chinese economy and its interactions with global conditions. Conditions could well change dramatically for the worse if growth falters or property prices collapse due to some unforeseen shock. While modeling of these dynamics could offer additional insights and predictive value, such analysis is highly complex and data intensive (which requires the cooperation of regulators) and is beyond the scope of this book.

Nevertheless, this national balance sheet analysis reveals that the problem should not be underestimated, as the nexus of shadow banks, the formal banking system and inter-enterprise credit could be highly vulnerable to further economic slowdown and property price adjustments. This became evident with the turmoil in the A-share stock market in June–September 2015, where shadow banking institutions provided some of the margin financing for investors that made the markets more volatile and fragile.

While China's shadow banking risks are unlikely to trigger a worldwide systemic crisis, any further slowdown could affect market confidence and have indirect, contagion effects on foreign holdings of China's bonds and securities. The risks of contagion will grow as China already plays an increasingly significant role in global growth, trade and investments, as the world's second largest economy. If not properly managed, a series of defaults by shadow banks or their clients can affect domestic as well as foreign confidence.

Hence, prompt policy action is urgently required to preempt any escalation in shadow banking non-performing loans (NPLs) that could trigger wider contagion effects. Given the risks of slower world growth, a property market correction in China, as well as prospects of higher interest rates in the long term, any delays could make the problem more intractable.

The book concludes that introducing more regulations and piecemeal reforms is not enough and calls for a comprehensive financial system blueprint to diversify China's bank-dominated financial sector, in order to address structural maturity and debt–equity mismatches to improve financial intermediation and stability in China. As the current financial system provides short-term debt when the real sector needs long-term finance, especially equity to reduce leverage risks, the development of the capital/equity markets and institutional investors as a more sustainable source of long-term finance has become more urgent and critical. The immediate-term priority is to enhance transparency and address the moral hazard and bundling of risks between the shadow banks and the formal banking sector. There is also a need to untangle the inter-enterprise credit, which, bundled with shadow banking debt, increases contagion risks through evergreening and cross-guarantees.

This calls for speedy implementation of the legal entity identifier initiative (LEI), a bank resolution/exit mechanism, and greater clarity of regulatory roles and cooperation, as well as rapid implementation of the deposit insurance scheme announced in 2014. Early restructuring of failing enterprises and problem debt situations will prevent recurrent worsening of contagion effects. Development of a strong credit culture and discipline is essential for a more modern and resilient financial system that is market-based and globally integrated. Equally important are measures to further enhance corporate governance and corporate social responsibility as the basis of a sound and more inclusive financial services industry.

The present financial system was designed to serve a largely state-owned production environment – based on investment and manufactured exports – that has reached its limits due to excess capacities, pollution and rising labor costs. The financial system needs to reform to meet China's changing needs as it rapidly shifts to a mass consumption and service-driven and market-led economy that is closely integrated with the world economy. Financial reforms are particularly important as China is undergoing profound change, moving into middle-income, urbanized consumption and production that is not only more broad-based, but is technologically knowledge-based and services-driven, mobile Internet friendly, more inclusive and ecologically green.

There is global concern that China may experience its own subprime crisis through the explosive growth in shadow banking credit. This was predicated on Chinese debt/GDP ratio of over 200 percent, rising more than 70 percent since 2008.

China's shadow banks comprise non-bank financial intermediaries (NBFIs) that came into prominence when they packaged wealth management products (WMPs) in order to sell to investors at higher than official interest rates, whilst at the same time fulfilling credit demand at non-official lending rates. In the last ten years, two broad groups of NBFIs began to perform bank-like activities in fund raising and lending. One group, commonly called Chinese shadow banks, comprising trust companies, moneylending and microfinance entities, served both depositors seeking higher returns and small borrowers who had limited access to bank funding. Internet financial platforms, on the other hand, used the gap between logistics and e-commerce business and the payments function to enter into funds transfer, wealth management and, increasingly, lending business.

These two groups responded to fundamental changes in the Chinese supply chain production, distribution and consumption and savings patterns, whilst addressing the genuine needs of the real sector and exploiting regulatory and interest rate arbitrages not addressed by the official banking system.

While the explosive growth in new and less understood products gives rise to regulatory concerns, it is important to recognize that they represent opportunities to reform processes and systems made obsolete by technology and market competition. However, closer regulatory attention is warranted to curb shadow banking activities that involve significant moral hazard, especially where the promoters are merely looking for quick profits (for example, in "Ponzi" or "get-rich-quick" schemes), exploit the poor and hide risks. Hence, the challenge for policy makers is to promote orderly financial market innovations to improve the allocation of capital and meet real sector needs while controlling the negative effects of shadow banking.

KEY FINDINGS AND POLICY RECOMMENDATIONS

1. Shadow banks or NBFIs are not fearsome, toxic creations that must be regulated out of existence. Globally, they are an integral part of the financial system, providing financial services to underserved sectors. While advanced country shadow banks contributed to the global financial crisis (GFC), those in China are smaller and less complex, with lower risk. However, some Chinese shadow banks share the weaknesses of their foreign counterparts in promoting opaque, usurious lending, financialization and Ponzi schemes that complicate credit risks due to the moral hazards of linkages with the formal banking system. Whilst not all of the international experience is applicable, there can be no complacency in dealing with the emerging shadow banking risks that have unique Chinese characteristics. An example is the underregulated P2P platforms that provided margin finance credit to stock market speculators, which contributed to the A-share market vulnerabilities.

2. The rapid growth of Chinese shadow banks can be seen as part of a market response to circumvent tight bank lending quotas and interest rate regulations to meet a real sector (especially SMEs) need for access to credit, and a concurrent demand for higher-yielding saving/investment products by China's household and corporate savers. Shadow banks also expanded because the formal banking model is skewed toward short-term lending, whilst structural issues create demand for liquidity where enterprises are willing

to pay higher interest rates than official rates. Under these circumstances, shadow banks can be seen as a "roundabout" channel for financial innovation and development that regulators did not initially discourage.

3. Unfortunately, like elsewhere, financial innovations are sometimes accompanied by greed and motivation for quick profits through financialization, usurious lending, Ponzi schemes, fraud and outright abuse of controls and regulations. The Ponzi aspects in China involve cross-guarantees and tying shadow banking credit with formal bank involvement so that the credit quality of the formal system may be called into question. It is these areas that demand closer and immediate regulatory attention to curb their negative effects and moral hazard issues.

4. There is much debate (and confusion) about the potential risks in China's shadow banks, due to a lack of clarity in definition, terminology and measurement. Market estimates of the size of Chinese shadow banking assets range from 14 to 70 percent of GDP. Apart from definitional differences, the wide range of estimates also reflects the problems associated with a simplistic addition of different products and assets of shadow banking activities with specific characteristics, which introduces an element of under counting, as well as double or even triple counting. Adding banks' WMPs to other shadow banking assets held by other financial intermediaries (OFIs) results in double counting when banks package OFI assets, for example trust loans, as their off-balance sheet WMPs and the trust company still reports the loan as a trust loan on their balance sheet. However, if both the bank and trust company treat the loan off-balance sheet, the loan is not reported and there is under counting.

5. To address this problem, FGI has adopted the PBOC's definition of China's shadow banking activities, supplemented by the three criteria in Yan and Li (2014) to arrive at a more realistic estimate (with a focus on systemic risks). Specifically, our estimate of the scale of China's shadow banking sector is based on our calculations of the scale of trust companies, microcredit companies, pawnshops, private/informal lending, P2P Internet lending and guarantors, banks' WMPs and two kinds of interbank assets (entrusted loans and undiscounted bankers acceptances).

6. After netting out possible double counting, our study suggests that at the end of 2013, the scale of Chinese shadow banking risk assets

was RMB 30.1 trillion[1] or 53 percent of GDP and 27 percent of formal banking system credit assets. Based on latest published stock data on PBOC's Total Social Financing, our estimates suggest that the total shadow bank risk assets rose to RMB 32.2 trillion or 51 percent of GDP at the end of 2014. At this level, Chinese shadow banks have not yet reached crisis proportions, but the speed of recent growth and the complicated interrelationships leave no room for complacency. Some commentators have suggested that it could take at least ten years to resolve losses of this scale if problems break out into wider defaults.

7. Placed within the global context, shadow banking in China appears small relative to the global average of 120 percent of GDP. It has no direct global systemic implications, since China is a net lender to the world and very few foreigners hold Chinese shadow banking assets. However, any deterioration in shadow banking problems could undermine market confidence, with possible contagion effects on foreign holdings of China's bonds and securities. As shadow banks are also driven by a rush for quick profits, they warrant closer regulatory oversight to curb exploitation and excessive financialization that do not serve the needs of the real sector.

8. China's national balance sheet showed that at the end of 2013, China's public sector had net assets of RMB 103 trillion (162 percent of GDP), even after taking into consideration gross liabilities of RMB 124 trillion or 195 percent of GDP. With the economy still growing at 6–7 percent per annum, low fiscal deficit and a high savings rate, a financial meltdown on the scale of the GFC is unlikely as China has adequate resources and policy flexibility to address what is essentially a domestic debt problem. Nevertheless, the combination of slower world growth and trade, plus the threat of domestic real estate price adjustment, could create conditions for an escalation of domestic financial risks, with indirect, contagion effects on foreign banks and investors. All these underscore the need for prompt action to resolve the shadow banking issues to preempt any contagion effects.

---

[1]FGI and Oliver Wyman jointly published a report on shadow banking in January 2015, in which estimates were slightly higher at RMB 31.2 trillion, based on earlier PBOC data. Details on the differences are explained in Chapter 4 (section 4.2).

9. In some cases, the central government may need to step in to restructure a few local government debts to return them to stability and productive growth. The other area of concern is the rapid growth in inter-enterprise debt, which requires comprehensive financial reform to enhance private sector (especially SME) access to financing (especially equity finance).

10. In analyzing the implications of risks inherent in shadow banking at the product, institution and system levels, we estimated the NPL ratio for the shadow banking sector. Working closely in collaboration with Oliver Wyman, our NPL estimation methodology involves three distinct features. Firstly, it uses industry credit ratings as a proxy indicator of credit asset quality to estimate NPLs. Secondly, it is industry specific by estimating the shadow banking credit rating for each industry. Thirdly, it is scenario based on notching down different levels of credit ratings and considering the possibility of fast deterioration of credit asset quality of selected industries.

11. Based on our analysis, the NPL ratio for the shadow banking sector was 4.4 percent in the Optimistic Scenario, 10 per cent for the Base Scenario, 16.1 percent for the Pessimistic Scenario and 23.9 percent for the Disaster Scenario, based on different assumptions on the level of economy-wide stress.

12. Furthermore, by categorizing shadow banking into three different risk layers based on the connection with the formal banking system, we found that about 20–40 percent of such NPLs could be "transferable" to the formal banking system and will drive banking NPLs towards ~7 per cent under our Disaster Scenario. However, we cannot discount the possibility of a much larger transfer (up to 50 percent) of shadow bank NPLs to the formal banking sector, in the event of a sudden shock or collapse in confidence.

13. A comprehensive assessment of the scale of risks of Chinese shadow banking must consider the quality of assets. The ultimate credit exposures of the Chinese banking system (including shadow banks) fall mainly on four major categories of borrowers – large state-owned enterprises SOEs, private sector SMEs, real estate companies, and Local Government Financing Platforms (LGFPs). Assessment of the quality of these four different classes of banking assets provides an indication of the potential risks of such assets becoming NPLs, as well as the likely impact on the formal banking sector and broader financial system. The risk analysis must also consider the maturity mismatch because China has funded

long-term investments largely through short-term borrowing from the banking/shadow banking system. At the same time, there is a structural debt/equity mismatch as most investments are funded by debt rather than equity.

14. Because the stock market is largely accessible only by SOEs or large corporations, there is a shortage of equity for private sector SMEs, which also lack access to formal bank credit. Hence, inter-enterprise credit of RMB 51 trillion is even larger than enterprise loans from the banking system of RMB 39 trillion at the end of 2011. In other words, the rise in shadow banking credit represents a "roundabout" channel of funding for the private sector and local governments to finance their large investments in real assets, but at higher costs and with hidden risks and moral hazard implications.

15. In order to reduce the shadow banking and banking credit risks, it is important not only to price the risks properly (market-based interest rates), but also to deleverage their borrowers and therefore enhance their ability to absorb risks. The solution lies in taking a holistic assessment of the way the shadow and formal banking sector interacts and provides funding for the real economy. This calls for a comprehensive financial sector blueprint to improve transparency, promote financial diversification, and strengthen the corporate governance and credit culture and discipline as the basis for a modern, sound and stable financial system.

16. The greatest risks to the current financial system are a sharp slowdown in growth, sudden spike in interest rates and collapse of real estate prices. Given global low interest rates and fundamental demand for residential and commercial real estate from continued (albeit slower) urbanization, there is some policy space to provide central bank liquidity and manage property prices through improving buyer affordability, as well as debt/equity swaps through project restructuring. Closer supervision is important to ensure that shadow banks and their moral hazard issues do not become a source of risk to financial stability.

17. In the immediate term, the priority is on policy measures to address the lack of transparency and bundling of shadow banking risks with the financial sector, including putting in place a safety net and exit mechanism for failed institutions:

   ▪ Expedite implementation of the deposit insurance scheme and bank restructuring/exit mechanism. This is urgently needed to address any potential build-up in shadow banking NPLs and facilitate the orderly resolution of any shadow bank failures. It would also clarify public misperceptions about the implicit guarantee and reduce moral hazard about state bailout of troubled shadow banking products.

- Establish an inter-agency task force to sort out the inter-enterprise credit problem and improve credit accountability, removing the joint-guarantee, joint credit system. This is closely related to the underlying problem of real sector funding for long-term investments.
- Implement the FSB's Legal Entity Identifier (LEI) initiative to clarify who owes what to whom and untangle the bundling of risks between shadow and commercial banks. This is urgently needed to prevent further evergreening of loans and to expose Ponzi and fraudulent credit schemes. At the same time, the establishment of a nationwide property registry will help to clarify property rights.
- Set up a market-oriented credit bureau and promote financial consumer education to strengthen the credit culture in China as the basis for a sound and stable financial system.
- Strengthen corporate governance and credit culture by improving corporate social responsibility and through higher disclosure and regulatory enforcement against corporate abuses.
- Strengthen public–private dialogue to increase consumer awareness of the risks of shadow banking. This will build public buy-in for the regulators' future plans to rein in the excesses of shadow banking to protect the public from exploitation and fraud.
- Clarify the roles of regulatory authorities, including through legislative amendments, to strengthen inter-agency cooperation and minimize supervisory gaps.
- Continue with the orderly process of financial liberalization to reduce the opportunities for regulatory arbitrage.

18. Over the longer term, China's reform agenda needs to focus on measures to diversify away from the bank-dominated financial system to address the structural mismatches in the economy, including the maturity and debt–equity mismatches:
    - Develop the capital/equity market, and long-term pension and insurance funds to reduce the overreliance on short-term bank lending to finance long-term development. This will enhance efficient allocation of capital, address the maturity and structural capital (debt/equity) mismatch as well as meet the social security needs of an aging population.

- Promote private equity and equity funds to inject capital into innovative enterprises and to deleverage the borrowers.
- Improve the management of state assets and separate the role of the state from ownership toward improving competition and efficiency in spearheading innovation and efficient resource allocation to maintain long-term inclusive growth.
- Control and manage the property market risks among local governments, including via the fiscal revenue sharing reforms that are being currently considered and development of the long-term municipal bond market and creation of secondary mortgage markets.

19. The key to addressing China's shadow banking and financial issues rests on China's ability to grow out of its internal debt problem and restructuring of such debt to sustainable levels. This requires careful balancing in providing sufficient liquidity in the financial system to support China's economic transformation without sparking off inflation. China has an inherent advantage to do this through progressively releasing the liquidity currently frozen in statutory reserve requirements. Another way of providing quantitative easing Chinese-style is for the PBOC to lend directly to fund long-term infrastructure, such as the financing of shanty town redevelopment via the China Development Bank.

20. Effective reforms require innovations in the financial and real sector, so that growth in profits and value creation exceeds growth in losses and value destruction. Here, the role of government is important in facilitating institutional, process and product innovation. The emergence of e-commerce and e-finance has enabled China to achieve scale and productivity in logistics and finance ahead of many emerging markets. However, regulators will have a key role to reduce the high risks and moral hazard concerns in e-finance/ shadow banking by addressing prudential concerns, especially the lack of disclosure, capital and provisioning standards. Closer regulation is also warranted to curb financialization and usurious shadow banking practices that exploit the poor and SMEs, and hide risks. The financial services industry, both incumbents and foreign players, will also need to adapt their business models and strategies to meet the challenges posed by mobile and Internet technology and the rise of e-finance.

21. Because e-finance platforms are encroaching into the banking system's core businesses, domestic banks and NBFIs need to adapt, cooperate and move rapidly in this area, improving their mobile banking capabilities and cybersecurity, and become the trusted partner in finance for retail and business customers. Global banks and financial institutions need to learn from China's breakthrough in e-commerce and e-finance and reverse engineer their own online strategies abroad using China's experience. At the same time, they can help improve the credit culture and offer innovative products in the growing China market in wealth management.

22. In conclusion, China's shadow banking problem is still manageable, but time is of the essence and a comprehensive policy package is urgently needed to preempt any escalation of shadow banking NPLs, which could have contagion effects. This is a golden opportunity for a holistic solution to address the structural imbalances in the Chinese economy and financial system. The key is to improve the allocation of capital, promote higher returns (and growth) and minimize the risks of a debt-fueled financial meltdown. In the process, this will ensure that the financial system meets China's changing funding requirements as the economy moves into middle-income, urbanized consumption and production that is not only more broad-based, but is technologically driven, mobile Internet friendly and more inclusive and ecologically sustainable.

23. The realization of a more market-driven and efficient Chinese economy will require a more proactive role of the state in rationalizing loss-making SOEs in obsolete industries and those suffering from over-capacity. Regular dialogues with key stakeholders, including the top leadership and the public at large, will be crucial in building the buy-in and public support to sustain the momentum for reforms as well as to obtain feedback on the implementation process.

24. Like all market innovations, shadow banking must be brought into the light so that all its opportunities and risks are properly evaluated and managed for China to emerge stronger and more stable in its path to an advanced economy.

CHAPTER 1

Introduction

Andrew Sheng

Before the stock market turmoil of June–September 2015, China appeared relatively unscathed from the global financial crisis of 2007–8 (GFC). Supported by ample liquidity and credit growth, the Chinese economy continued to grow. RMB internationalization increased, with its growing acceptance as a global trade and payment transaction currency. Such advances have also faced new headwinds in the form of a slowing global growth and trade environment. The World Bank (2015) has downgraded its global economic projections and cautioned that the global outlook is clouded by weak commodity prices, divergent monetary policies across key economies, volatile financial markets and a decrease in world trade.

Of particular concern is the structural decline in world trade, which is becoming less responsive to changes in global income. The IMF (2015a) also lowered its global growth forecasts, noting that positive factors such as lower oil prices will be more than offset by persistent negative forces, including lower investment and slower potential growth in many countries. A key concern of the IMF (2015b) is the risk of a "new mediocre" – a prolonged period of low growth. As the Chinese economy adjusts to a new normal of slower growth, questions are being raised about the sustainability of the Chinese model and its dependence on ongoing credit "fuelling." Some commentators have suggested that China's "Lehman moment" is imminent and that the Chinese shadow banking sector could become the cause of the next systemic global financial crisis.

However, a GFC-type crisis is unlikely, given China's still favorable fundamentals and policy space. At this juncture, Chinese shadow banking is also relatively small by global standards and essentially a domestic debt problem without any direct global implications. Prompt policy action is, however, urgently needed to deal with potential shadow bank failures and preempt any escalation of contagion risks. The problem should not be underestimated, as the nexus of shadow banks, the formal banking system and inter-enterprise credit could be highly vulnerable to further slowdown and property price adjustments. While China's shadow banking risks are unlikely to trigger a worldwide systemic crisis, any further slowdown could affect market confidence and have indirect, contagion effects on foreign holdings of China's bonds and securities. Corporate loan defaults (which include foreign currency debt), such as the recent default of a Chinese property developer's bonds, suggested that a domestic problem can spill over to foreign banks and investors, as China becomes increasingly integrated with the global financial system. The fact that global financial markets reacted negatively to the announcement of a devaluation of 1.9 percent of the RMB in August 2015 indicated that global investors recognize the contagion risks of China's role in global growth, trade and investments. If not properly managed, a series of defaults by shadow banks or their clients can affect foreign banks and investors, as well as domestic confidence.

Furthermore, closer regulatory supervision is needed to tackle the moral hazard implications of shadow banking financialization, Ponzi and get-rich-quick schemes, and usurious lending that exploits the poor.

Overall, barring any sudden shocks, we envisage that China's shadow banking problem is still manageable, although the central government may need to step in to restructure some of the local government debts and return them to stability and productive growth. While most local government debt is manageable, since the local governments have a fairly high level of assets, local government finances need to be reformed through greater transparency, appropriate sharing of fiscal revenue between central and local government and also clarity of rules on issuance of local government debt. The other area of concern is the rapid growth in corporate leverage, particularly in inter-enterprise debt, which requires comprehensive financial reform to enhance private sector (especially SME) access to bank credit and equity finance.

There is much misunderstanding of the role of shadow banks in an economy, including in China. They are not stand-alone, high-risk entities that should be regulated out of existence. Historically, entities such as microcredit companies, money lenders and pawn shops, for example, form an intrinsic part of the financial system that integrates finance with the real economy, notably in providing access to credit to marginalized sectors that may not qualify for loans from the formal banking industry due to lack of credit history or collateral, onerous regulations, lending requirements and gaps and overlaps in regulatory coverage. Shadow banks do fulfill market needs for longer-term financing that is not provided by the formal banking sector, which is biased towards short-term lending as longer-term loans attract higher capital and other regulatory requirements. Unfortunately, some shadow banking activities involve Ponzi or get-rich-quick schemes, while others exploit SMEs and the poor by charging usurious interest rates, and these require closer supervision.

Since 2007, the Group of 20 (G-20) has tasked the Financial Stability Board (FSB) to focus on too-big-to-fail (TBTF) financial institutions and on shadow banks in order to curb the systemic and institutional risks that precipitated the GFC.

The FSB recognized that there were gaps in financial regulation in advanced economies (AEs) that underestimated the role of shadow banks in the run-up to the GFC. While the international experience in dealing with shadow banks offers a useful guide to China, there is no one-size-fits-all solution to regulate banks and shadow banks "on a global level playing field." In particular, China's approach to shadow banking will need to "fit" domestic conditions and address risks that are peculiar to China.

In August 2014, the FSB Regional Consultative Group for Asia took the view that not only is there no uniform definition of shadow banks in Asia, but also their non-bank financial institutions (NBFIs) do not present systemic risks like those in AEs and are subject to adequate regulation, based on country-specific circumstances.

In a globalized, complex and highly interconnected financial system, diversity is a source of strength and resilience. Shadow banks exploit information, regulatory, price and tax arbitrage opportunities that fall beyond the purview of national financial regulators. The result is a global network of financial institutions, interconnected through complex and sometimes toxic financial derivatives and highly leveraged products that are not transparent to investors, operators and regulators alike.

Similarly, at the national level, the segmentation (and therefore fragmentation) of supervision of different financial products and institutions results in regulatory gaps and overlaps that enable new and unregulated institutions to emerge to meet market needs that were underserved because of obsolete policies and regulatory processes.

This is true of moneylenders and microcredit providers as well as Internet finance platforms that provide financial services to market segments not served by the formal banking system.

Bringing shadow banks into the light by understanding their mode of operations, appreciating their systemic risks and putting them within the context of the whole ecosystem of real sector economic demand and supply of financial services would suggest that policy makers should look at the opportunity of inculcating the right environment for stable, efficient and inclusive growth between banks and NBFIs (notably e-finance) in supporting the real economy. This calls for a comprehensive policy approach that goes beyond the introduction of more regulations to control shadow banking risks.

The purpose of this book is to bring the explosive growth in China's shadow banking credit into the light and explore the potential implications for financial stability in China, and also for fundamental structural reforms in the Chinese financial sector that have key implications for the real economy.

The study takes a broader view of shadow banks to include Internet finance providers, identifying both groups not just as potential sources of chaos due to quick-profit and high-risk activities, but also as areas of profound change in the real economy that must be met by structural changes in the financial sector.

China is undergoing profound change, as the economy and society moves into middle income, urbanized consumption and production that is not only more broad-based, but also technologically driven, mobile Internet-friendly and more inclusive and ecologically green. The present financial system was designed to serve largely a state-owned production environment, based on investment and exports. The financial system needs to reform to meet China's changing needs as it rapidly shifts to a mass consumption-driven and market-led economy that is closely integrated with the world economy.

Just as the explosive growth in Internet finance and e-commerce reflects fundamental changes in Chinese supply chain production, distribution and consumption patterns, so do microfinance, moneylending and wealth management products reflect the growing complex, diverse and specialized needs of different segments of the Chinese market and society.

Of course, such explosive growth in new, opaque products gives rise to regulatory concerns of personal privacy, cybersecurity, usury, greed, moral hazard and system failure, which warrant prompt and careful management to curb the negative aspects of shadow banking and e-finance. But they are also opportunities to address the genuine needs of the real sector and to reform the present antiquated financial structure and processes.

This book argues that to understand Chinese shadow banks, we must understand the current financial system with Chinese characteristics and look into how a better system can be evolved, through rigorous and fundamental financial reforms.

This is because more regulation per se will not resolve China's shadow banking problem, given its complicated interlinkages and opaque bundling of risks with the formal banking system and the real sector. Indeed, there is much confusion on the measurement of shadow banking risks, which has been constrained by the problems of double counting (and underreporting) of assets as liabilities in wealth management products (WMPs).

A comprehensive assessment of the scale of risks of Chinese shadow banking must consider the quality of assets or net assets at risk (non-guaranteed assets). At the same time, the rapid growth in inter-enterprise credit (a characteristic quite unique to China in terms of its size and complexity) represents another source of risk, which needs to be monitored and managed carefully. The solution lies in taking a holistic assessment of the way the shadow and formal banking sector interacts and provides funding for the real economy. This calls for a comprehensive financial sector blueprint to improve transparency, promote financial diversification, and strengthen corporate governance, the credit culture and financial discipline as the basis for a modern, sound and stable financial system. The financial services industry, both incumbents and foreign players, will also need to change to meet the challenges posed by advances in technology and the rise of e-finance.

This book is organized as follows:

Chapter 2. Shadow Banking in the Global Context. This chapter reviews the evolution of shadow banking in the global context, including a survey of developments across selected countries. The attendant challenges in measuring shadow banking (given the lack of a common definition) are discussed, as well as the factors underpinning the industry's recent growth. This chapter also highlights the complex interconnections and feedback loops between shadow and commercial banks as a potential source of fragility in the financial system. The chapter highlights that there is a divergence of views over the role of shadow banks in the emerging markets vis-à-vis the advanced countries and therefore the issue of risks and supervisory oversight will be different from those in the advanced markets.

Chapter 3. Shadow Banking within the National Balance Sheet. This chapter analyzes the interconnectivity and relationships between the different components of shadow banking and formal banking through a stock-flow approach. Financial stability in a large economy suffers from risk concentration at the product level, the institutional level and also the geographical/regional level. Traditional economic analyses through flow accounts (national income, trade, investments) do not reveal these vulnerabilities. Recently published Chinese national balance sheet and flow of funds accounts, based on the *China National Balance Sheet Report 2013* and its latest update in 2015 published by the Chinese Academy of Social Sciences (CASS), offer revealing insights on the interconnectivities and vulnerabilities by sector.

Whilst useful from a systemic perspective, national balance sheet data represents a top-down, snapshot view of the situation in China and a review of current conditions. This study does not attempt to forecast dynamic changes in the Chinese economy and its interactions with changing global conditions. Conditions could well change dramatically for the worse if growth falters or property prices collapse due to some unforeseen shock. While a bottom-up approach and modeling of the dynamics between shadow banks, the real economy and China's risks as a whole could well offer additional insights and predictive value, such analysis is constrained by data limitations. Hence, the rapid growth in shadow banking credit warrants closer monitoring and management to preempt any escalation of risks and contagion effects.

By comparing leverage and where it is located within the national balance sheet, it would be possible to detect an economy's state of robustness or its fragilities, particularly at the sectoral level. Based on the national balance sheet approach, we conclude that a systemic crisis is unlikely in China, as its sovereign balance sheet shows a net asset position of RMB 103 trillion at the end of 2013 (162 percent of GDP) even after accounting for all gross liabilities, with ample net assets at the national, household and central government levels. Even if we were to exclude all its natural resource assets, the sovereign government's financial position remains solvent to avoid any potential liquidity problems. As China is a net lender to the rest of the world, any emerging debt problem will therefore be a domestic one without any direct global systemic implications. However, indirect contagion effects cannot be discounted, if market confidence in foreign holdings of China's bonds and securities is affected. We conclude that China's shadow banking problem is manageable under current conditions.

Time is of the essence in implementing remedial policies, as the national balance sheet analysis represents a snapshot or static view of the shadow banking situation at a point in time. The situation may change at short notice, due to some unexpected shock, as the shadow banks interact dynamically with the real sector and China's risks as a whole. The sooner the shadow banking risks are properly managed, the lower will be the risks of systemic vulnerability to changes in domestic confidence and contagion.

Some commentators have suggested that it is often difficult to distinguish, ex-ante, between a liquidity and a solvency issue. The solvency issue is closely tied to the management of liquidity, which is critical to the stability or fragility of different sectors. If real interest rates rise sharply due to sudden bouts of tight liquidity, rapid asset sales and panic demand for liquidity can cause significant damage to any economy with tight interconnectivity in terms of bank-shadow bank-enterprise credit risks. A liquidity crisis can precipitate a solvency crisis. This was the lesson of the Asian financial crisis of 1997–99.

China is almost unique because of its high level of foreign exchange (FX) assets relative to external debt. However, since such FX assets were funded by high reserve requirements, domestic liquidity is totally within the control of the central bank in terms of capacity to adjust the reserve requirements. In other words, China has a structural liquidity "trapped" through its monetary/foreign exchange policy that can be released judiciously without affecting confidence in the exchange rate. This option is not open to emerging markets with high net foreign currency debt.

Management of domestic liquidity during this period of structural adjustments to the "New Normal" of slower growth requires careful balancing of liquidity release by the central bank, without fueling a revival in inflation or speculative asset bubbles. This requires a combination of judicious monetary easing with tight regulation against abuses in credit allocation.

At the same time, as some overleveraged state-owned enterprises and local governments need to restructure their debt, the central government may need to step in to restructure such debt in order to reduce overcapacity and return them to stability and productive growth. It is important to note that most local government debt is still manageable, since the local governments have fairly high levels of assets that can be used to offset their debt. Of course, local government finances should be reformed through greater transparency, appropriate sharing of fiscal revenue between central and local government and also clarity of rules on issue of local government debt.

The key area of concern is the rising level of corporate leverage, which is not just confined to the banks, but also inter-enterprise debt, which is already high by international standards. However, concerns about high Chinese corporate debt/GDP ratios should be tempered by the large amount of deposits held by Chinese corporates. It is the rising level of cross-guarantees in the bank-shadow bank credit to enterprises that creates risks of contagion and moral hazard.

The national balance sheet approach reveals that fundamental reforms should be undertaken in the funding of corporate balance sheets, since they are currently too reliant on debt to fund their high levels of inventory and fixed assets. This means that the deepening of capital markets and getting more equity into SMEs and more efficient use of resources at the state-owned enterprise (SOE) level, could improve their profitability, ability to innovate and invest in high risk-high growth areas and therefore enhance resilience to shocks. Measures to further strengthen corporate governance and corporate social responsibility will also be important.

Chapter 4. Shadow Banking with Chinese Characteristics. Chapter 4 reviews the Chinese characteristics of shadow banks, including the factors behind the rapid growth in its key components, such as the trust companies, loan guarantee companies, wealth management products (WMP) and interbank credit. This chapter reviews the wide range of projections from official and market sources, including FGI's own estimate of the potential size of the Chinese shadow banking industry.

The rise of shadow banking in China can be traced to two key trends: firstly, as a "roundabout" market response to real sector funding needs, arising from special characteristics of the bank-dominated system that tend to lend more to the SOE sector than to private sector entities; and secondly, the search for yield, as households and the corporate sector sought higher returns on their savings than official capped deposit rates. These two forces combined to create the circumstances that allowed shadow banks to arbitrage/circumvent tight financial regulations in the formal banking sector.

Regulatory arbitrage also played a part. Given the strict bank lending quotas and the 75 percent loan-to-deposit ratio cap, shadow banking in China is largely an alternative form of off-balance sheet credit provision by banks to enterprise customers. At the same time, as there were caps also on deposit interest rates (since more liberalized), wealth management products (WMPs) evolved as deposit-substitutes for corporate and retail investors.

Chinese shadow banking is not as leveraged or sophisticated as shadow banking in advanced economies. However, it shares some of their weaknesses such as financialization, lack of transparency, weak corporate governance, and fraud and Ponzi schemes that make risk assessment more complicated than usual. Apart from definitional differences, the wide range of market estimates on the size of shadow banking assets reflects the problems associated with a simplistic addition of different products and assets of shadow banking activities with specific characteristics, which introduces an element of undercounting, as well as double or even triple counting. Adding banks' WMPs to other shadow banking assets held by other financial intermediaries (OFIs) will certainly lead to double counting when banks package OFIs' assets, for example trust loans, as their off-balance-sheet WMPs. If the trust company still reports the loan as a trust loan on their balance sheet, adding the two counts the same asset twice. On the other hand, if both the bank and trust company treat the loan as off-balance sheet, the loan does not appear anywhere (except as collateral for WMPs owned by investors) and there is undercounting. Furthermore, undercounting will occur if the officially reported data had underestimated the scale of exposure.

To address this problem, FGI has adopted the People's Bank of China's (PBOC) definition of China's shadow banking activities, supplemented by the three criteria in Yan and Li (2014) to arrive at a more realistic estimate (with a focus on systemic risks). Specifically, our estimate of the scale of China's shadow banking sector is based on our calculations on the scale of trust companies, microcredit companies, pawnshops, private/informal lending, peer-to-peer (P2P) Internet lending and guarantors, banks' WMPs and two kinds of interbank assets (entrusted loans and undiscounted banker's acceptances).

Based on our flow of funds approach to address these overlaps, we estimate the size of China's shadow banking market at RMB 30.1 trillion in 2013, significantly lower than the outcome of a "plain vanilla" product aggregation approach, which leads to about RMB 57 trillion.

WMPs should be correctly seen as deposit substitutes, which were created in order to offer clients higher interest rates. Because these were treated as off-balance sheet items previously, the credit risks were shifted to investors, who may have treated WMPs bought from banks as being covered under the implicit deposit insurance for bank deposits. Hence, the moral hazard in Chinese shadow banking is whether credit risks inherent in shadow banking products are ultimately borne by the state or borne by the market.

Chapter 5. Inherent Risks in Chinese Shadow Banking. This chapter examines in greater detail the implications of risks inherent in shadow banking at the product, institution and system levels. We estimate the non-performing loan (NPL) ratio for the shadow banking sector by estimating the NPL ratio of the funding obtained from shadow banking for each industry and computing the average NPL ratio across the industries weighted by the size of funding they get from shadow banking.

The next step was to downgrade the credit rating for bank loans to a lower quality level for shadow bank loans. We benchmarked shadow banking exposures in China against those of other Asian countries. In particular, we found that Korea had the most similarities with China since interest rate differences between bank and non-bank financing were largely the same. The credit ratings for shadow banking exposures in Korea were on average at least three notches lower than banking-related exposures. We therefore assumed for our optimistic case scenario that shadow banking exposures should be downgraded by three notches compared to the related banking exposures. In the other three scenarios, namely, a Base Scenario, a Pessimistic Scenario and a Disaster Scenario, we applied the credit ratings for shadow banks by downgrading their ratings by 4 notches, 4 to 5 notches, and 5 notches, respectively. The distinction of downgrading reflected the different severities of the asset quality problem of the shadow banking sector across different scenarios. By mapping the resultant credit rating for shadow banks to the corresponding NPL ratios, we derived a proxy for the shadow banking NPL ratios for each industry.

The shadow banking asset distribution across industries was based on estimates from Morgan Stanley research. Using the asset size as weights, we calculated the weighted average of shadow banking NPL ratios across the industries and obtained an estimation of the NPL ratio for the whole shadow banking sector. The results showed that the NPL ratio for the shadow banking sector was 4.4 percent in the Optimistic Scenario, 10 percent for the Base Scenario, 16.1 percent for the Pessimistic Scenario and 23.9 percent for the Disaster Scenario.

Based on the risk profiles, we divided the shadow banking industry into three segments. The first layer is the formal banks' off-balance sheet lending, including WMPs, banker's acceptances, securities firms' AMPs, and bank–trust cooperation. The linkage between the off-balance sheet funding layer and the formal banks is tight as many of these can switch from being a contingent liability to a realized liability for banks, given that the implicit guarantees for investors persist in the market.

The second layer is the non-bank credit enhancement to facilitate lending, including guarantees. Banks are subject to risk when credit enhancers fail to repay for defaulted corporate loans. The last layer is the non-banking lending; for example, P2P and microfinancing. Usually there is no risk spillover to banks from this layer of shadow banking.

Each of the three risk layers comes with a different transferability of risks into the banking system. Hence, we calculated which share of NPLs was likely to be transferred from the shadow banking to the formal banking system.

We estimated the impact of shadow banking non-performing assets on banks' NPLs in two tracks. One is to load the shadow banking NPLs on the base of the formal banks' current NPL ratio. Under the Base Scenario with 33 percent of shadow bank NPLs transferred to banks, banks' NPL ratio will rise from the current level of 1.5 percent to 2.5 percent, which is still under the coverage of existing NPL provisions. In the Disaster Scenario, banks' NPL ratio will rise to 4.9 percent, slightly higher than the banking system's current provisioned levels of 4.6 percent of risk-weighted assets.

The other track is to sum up banks' current NPL ratio and the additional provision first and take it as the base of banks' NPL. This is to cover the concern that the NPL ratios reported by banks underestimate the real problem. Under the Base Scenario, the banks' NPL ratio remains under 5.1 percent, while in the Disaster Scenario, it can go up to 7.2 percent. As China is a net lender to the world, any financial crisis will not escalate into a foreign exchange crisis.

At this point in time, three factors suggest that a financial crisis remains unlikely as China has the policy space to manage any emerging risks: (1) China is still a fast growing economy with growth at 6–7 percent per annum, which would allow it to grow out of rising NPL or credit losses; (2) China's high domestic savings will enable the household sector to absorb a significant amount of shocks; and (3) Total government debt is still manageable, even taking into consideration potential losses from the shadow banking system. Furthermore, China's high foreign exchange reserves, exchange controls and low external debt enable policy makers to avoid a foreign exchange crisis from external sources.

Nevertheless, a combination of slower world growth and trade, plus the threat of domestic real estate price adjustment, could create conditions for an escalation of domestic financial risks. While China's shadow banking risks are unlikely to trigger a global crisis, any further deterioration could affect market confidence and have indirect, contagion effects on foreign holdings of China's bonds and securities. The risks of contagion will grow as China plays an increasingly significant role in global growth, trade and investments. All these underscore the need for prompt action to resolve the shadow banking issues to preempt any contagion effects.

The official treatment of shadow banking in China divides institutions into three categories – those that are fully regulated, those that are partially regulated (such as those for disclosure or registration purposes, but not for prudential purposes) and those that are largely unregulated (such as pawnbrokers and microlenders). As the Chinese authorities induced the banks to bring WMPs onto the balance sheet, the size of the WMPs began to increase but this was largely a shift between deposits and quasi-deposits. What is more relevant from the risk perspective is the quality of assets of the banks and shadow banks.

There are four key risk exposures for banks and shadow banks. These are essentially lending to four key sectors – the property sector, the state-owned enterprises (SOEs), local government financing platforms (LGFPs) and the private sector, largely small and medium enterprises (SMEs).

Such loans are complicated by three intertwined practices that affect the quality of the credit and therefore an accurate assessment of the true exposure to the banking system. These are "evergreening," "inter-enterprise credit" and a further element of fraud arising from corruption that cannot be ruled out.

Evergreening occurs when a borrower begins to borrow from different banks using different legal entities, escaping detection when it borrows outside the formal banking system by funding from shadow banks, often at usurious interest rates.

Inter-enterprise credit occurs through borrowing directly from other enterprises in the form of trade credit or packaged credit sold to cash-rich enterprises, which seek higher deposit rates. This binds the credit risk of cash rich enterprises with weaker, illiquid borrowers. Evergreening merely postpones the debt problem and is unsustainable, while bundling of risks via inter-corporate guarantees and corporate purchases of WMPs that contain other corporate risks leads to a tangled web of risks that are not easily identifiable by a single bank. Effective debt resolution must include assignment of losses to the parties involved, be it the corporate sector, households or government. This exercise will require on-site examination and identification of risk, which will inevitably take time and require greater transparency in the process.

Chapter 6. Impact of Technology on China's Financial System. This chapter discusses the flip side of the "credit" and "risk" perspective of the Chinese shadow banking sector: the emerging Internet revolution. China has one of the fastest technology adaptation rates and a fast growing community of customers able and willing to use new technologies. The rise of e-finance platforms will have implications for regulators, particularly in creating a conducive enabling environment (including appropriate disclosure, capital and prudential standards on a level playing field) while managing any negative effects of cybersecurity, identity theft and fraud.

This emerging trend also has strategic implications for incumbent Chinese players and international financial services institutions. Specifically, this chapter considers the rise of Alibaba and the impact of technological innovations on the financial system. It examines recent developments in e-commerce and e-finance that have facilitated a transformation of the business model of SMEs and the distribution and production industry, as well as made inroads into the payments, credit and wealth management business of the banking sector by leveraging on technology and partnerships between e-commerce and e-finance networks.

The Chinese economy is also benefiting from the productivity gains and access of SMEs to a new production, distribution and payments model using e-commerce and e-finance (the "clicks" business model). At the same time, there is creative destruction of the conventional business model offered through "bricks and mortar" branches (bank branches and retail shops). SMEs discovered that they are able to reach different market segments through the Internet, and obtain trade credit and payments with online convenience. At the core is a fundamental competition between the "clicks" and the "bricks" business models that will rapidly converge. However, an effective response to the new competition will require not only changes in the business model of Chinese banks, but also a re-think of the whole approach to financial regulation and development. The aim is to encourage healthy financial innovation and competition while maintaining financial system stability and avoiding excessive risk taking and exploitation/fraud. The banking industry (both incumbents and foreign players) will need to adopt different strategies to meet the challenges of e-commerce and e-finance.

Chapter 7. Implications for Reform Agenda. Chapter 7 discusses the need for shadow banking reforms across the three risk layers we have identified and then considers China's options for its overall financial reform agenda. This includes immediate, medium and longer-term measures to address the potential risks of shadow banking and promote a more sustainable and inclusive financial system. The priority in the short term is to expedite the implementation of the recently announced decisions to establish a deposit insurance and exit mechanism to deal with problem banks. This is because the re-regulation of the financial sector and introduction of more market-based interest rates and exchange rates will have implications for the survival of weaker financial institutions and their exit.

At the same time, priority should be accorded to implementing the Legal Entity Identifier (LEI) to clarify who owes what to whom. This will disentangle the problem of evergreening, inter-enterprise credit and fraud. After the failure of Lehman Brothers, the FSB noted that the market and the regulators did not know who transacted with whom (especially SPVs) and who is responsible for what debt. Hence, there is a drive for a global LEI initiative, which should be implemented at the national level. This is an excellent opportunity for China to clarify the data standard for determination of credit obligations by each legal entity. Without LEI clarity, there is no clarity of who owes what, enabling evergreening and Ponzi schemes to occur without adequate credit controls. Credit culture cannot be built without a uniform data standard.

Looking beyond the shadow banking issue, it is opportune to consider the formulation of a comprehensive financial sector blueprint to ensure that the financial system is aligned to China's long-term policy objectives to promote sustainable and inclusive development. In essence, the overreliance of developmental funding on the banking system should be addressed through the promotion of longer-term institutional investors such as pension, insurance and private equity asset managers. Deeper equity markets (including private equity and cloud equity funding for SMEs) would reduce the overdependence on debt and leverage that exposes the financial system to sharp liquidity shocks and systemic risks. At the same time, financial deepening would also improve the allocation of capital, increase returns for savers/investors and minimize the risks of a debt-driven financial meltdown.

Given the profound changes in the real sector and the need to provide inclusive finance and finance for long-term structural change, including funding for urbanization, innovation and ecological sustainability, a whole raft of legislative and institutional changes will be necessary. This would include reform of the financial legislation to clarify the roles of regulatory authorities and NBFIs, promote financial inclusion, consumer protection, corporate governance and a stronger credit culture as the basis for a modern, sound and stable financial system in China. Regular dialogues with key stakeholders, including the top leadership and consumers are important to garner support and obtain feedback on the reform process.

Chapter 8. Conclusion. This chapter notes that the Chinese authorities have already taken a number of preemptive measures to address the shadow banking problems. What is needed is more careful management of the potential rise in shadow banking NPLs, moral hazard and exploitation/fraud risks. Greater clarification of the roles and responsibilities of different agencies in dealing with the issues of regulatory arbitrage and gaps and overlaps will be important. The rapid growth in shadow banking and lack of clarity in credit accountability raises potentially damaging moral hazard implications for the economy as a whole, which must be resolved through greater transparency and accountability.

Implementation of the LEI initiative to untangle the opaque bundling of risks between enterprises, shadow and commercial banks is a necessary but not sufficient condition to restore China's credit culture and accountability. The key lies in introducing greater clarity and transparency of property rights, corporate governance, credit discipline, and allowing failed enterprises and weak banks to exit in an orderly manner without huge moral hazard consequences.

Although certain aspects of shadow banking can pose contagion and moral hazard risks, it offers a historic opportunity to address the need to build a strong credit culture to utilize China's precious savings more efficiently, inclusively and sustainably for its long-term development. A holistic methodology using the national balance sheet approach helps to refine the analytical comparatives and interrelationships to examine how to develop the financial sector in the long term. Whilst providing a systemic overview, the limitations of any assessment based on national balance sheet data are that it does not attempt to forecast dynamic changes in the Chinese economy and global conditions, which would have data requirements outside the scope of this study. Conditions could well change dramatically for the worse if growth falters or property prices collapse due to some unforeseen shock. Hence, time is of the essence in implementing the necessary reforms to manage the shadow banking risks and, more importantly, to ensure that the financial sector is transformed in tandem with China's changing requirements.

In the second decade of the 21st century, China is facing new 21st century challenges of moving beyond the "middle income trap." One opportunity is to harness technology and the changing consumer tastes and lifestyles to generate new products and services. The other is to change the way the transformation of the new business model is funded. Given high risks and unpredictable black swans, the way forward is to provide innovative companies with higher capital cushions and less leverage. In other words, the risks would be shared through an equity-based financing model rather than in a bank-based, debt model with high concentration of risks in borrowers with high leverage and huge maturity mismatches.

The opportunity of China's transformation cannot be missed, as risks are building up both externally as the world market slows and internal fragilities are surfacing. Time is of the essence, and the sooner these risks are confronted, the sooner China will break through the middle income trap.

REFERENCES

IMF. 2015a. World Economic Outlook Update (July 2015). http://www.imf.org/external/pubs/ft/weo/2015/update/02/.

IMF. 2015b. Lagarde: Prevent "New Mediocre" from Becoming "New Reality" April 2015. http://www.imf.org/external/pubs/ft/survey/so/2015/new040915a.htm.

World Bank. 2015. Global Economic Prospects, 2015. http://www.worldbank.org/en/publication/global-economic-prospects?cid=EXT_FBWB_D_EXT.

Yan, Qingmin, and Jianhua Li. 2014. *Research of China Shadow Banking Supervision*. China Renmin University Press.

CHAPTER 2

Shadow Banking in the Global Context

Cathleen Yi Tin

2.1 INTRODUCTION

The global financial system has undergone enormous transformation over the last few decades through globalization, financial liberalization and innovations. Advances in information and communication technology have also led to an increasingly borderless financial system, where banks and non-bank financial institutions or intermediaries (NBFIs) can exploit information, regulatory, price and tax arbitrage opportunities created off-balance sheet and/or offshore that are beyond the purview of national financial regulators. The result is a global network of highly intercon-nected financial institutions, interlinked through complex and often toxic financial derivatives and highly leveraged products.

The global financial crisis (GFC) in 2007–2008 demonstrated how problems in one financial system could spread contagion across the global economy. Shadow banking was identified as one of the factors leading to the crisis. Since then, there has been increased policy attention on the excessive leverage and systemic fragility and the risks posed by the shadow banking activities that precipitated the GFC.

It is important to note that not all "shadow banking" activities are toxic. Many (such as pawnbroking, moneylending and microfinance) perform a valuable function in providing access to credit to market segments that are underserved by the traditional banking system. Historically, non-bank financial intermediaries have always been an important and integral part of the financial system, in both the advanced and developing economies. Of course, certain shadow banking operations engage in activities that warrant regulatory oversight, such as cheating, fraud and those that create systemic risks and pose moral hazard issues.

The definition, nature and characteristics of shadow banking differ across economies, due to their different legal and financial histories. While the shadow banking system in China has its distinctive characteristics, this chapter provides an overview of the global context. It reviews the global shadow banking system in terms of its definition, size and factors for its growth.

2.2 WHAT IS SHADOW BANKING?

The term "shadow banks" was first coined by PIMCO analyst Paul McCulley to refer to the entire range of leveraged non-bank investment channels and structures used by banks in advanced countries to keep opaque and complicated securitized loans off their balance sheets (McCulley, 2007). Since then, the term "shadow banking" has been broadly applied to a variety of financial instruments, ranging from relatively common financial products (such as money market mutual funds, asset-backed securities, and real estate investment trusts) to the more exotic varieties of hedge funds, structured finance vehicles and leveraged derivative products, usually funded by investment banks and large institutional investors.

Globally, the term "shadow banking" can mean different things to different jurisdictions. The Financial Stability Board (FSB, 2013) broadly defines shadow banking as *"credit intermediation involving entities and activities outside the regular banking system or non-bank credit intermediation in short."* To further capture the elements of non-bank credit intermediation where important risks are most likely to emerge, the FSB offered a narrower definition, suggesting that regulators should focus on credit intermediation outside the regular banking system that raises "(i) systemic risk concerns, in particular by maturity/liquidity transformation, leverage and flawed credit risk transfer; and/or (ii) regulatory arbitrage concerns." (FSB, 2012).

The New York Federal Reserve's Pozsar et al. (2013) defined shadow banks as financial intermediaries that undertake maturity, credit and liquidity transformation without any explicit recourse to central bank liquidity or credit guarantee by the government.

The International Monetary Fund, on the other hand, views shadow banking as a large part of the financing in today's economy that is intermediated in wholesale money markets through banks and other financial intermediaries and lent in the capital markets (IMF, 2014a).

Within Asia, the Financial Stability Board Regional Consultative Group for Asia's *Report on Shadow Banking in Asia*, published in August 2014, noted that there is no uniform definition for shadow banking in Asian jurisdictions (FSB, 2014). They preferred to use the terms "non-bank financial intermediaries" (NBFIs) and "other financial intermediaries" (OFIs), which cover all financial institutions excluding banks, insurers, pension funds and public financial institutions.

According to Kodres (2013), there are four key aspects of intermediation in shadow banking activities:

1. *Maturity transformation*: mobilizing short-term funds to invest in longer-term assets.
2. *Liquidity transformation*: using cash-like liabilities to purchase assets such as loans.
3. *Leverage*: borrowing money to buy assets to magnify the potential gains on an investment.
4. *Credit risk transfer*: transferring the risk of a borrower's default from the originator of the loan to another party.

Historically, NBFIs have been in existence for many years, although many did not fall under the formal regulatory framework. For example, money market mutual funds are regulated for disclosure and conduct but not for prudential purposes. In many markets, pawn shops/money lenders in the developing world are registered but not supervised by bank regulators.

Interest in shadow banking arose during the GFC when many bank-linked special purpose vehicles in advanced economies encountered problems and brought down the traditional banks with them (Borst, 2014). This arose because there were gaps in the regulation of banks that allowed leverage and risks to be hidden in derivative transactions and counterparties through off-balance sheet and offshore activities.

Many derivative transactions are booked off-balance sheet and netted out and therefore not counted for regulatory capital compliance purposes. However, in a liquidity crisis, it is the demand for return of gross liabilities that causes systemic failure. Because of the practice of netting and offshoring, the GFC revealed that bank regulators ignored off-balance sheet and offshore transactions with shadow banks at their peril, because of the high degree of interconnectivity and interdependence with the regulated financial system.

2.3 SIZE OF THE GLOBAL SHADOW BANKING INDUSTRY

Estimating the size of the shadow banking system is particularly challenging given its evolving and fluid nature. Information is also scarce and patchy given the lack of transparency, as most shadow banks operate outside the regulatory framework. The differences in the definition of shadow banking inevitably reflect a divergence in the scope, coverage and methodology used in estimating shadow banking activities.

In the wake of the GFC, the Group of 20 (G-20) has called for better understanding of the global shadow banking system and recommendations to enhance its regulation and surveillance. The Financial Stability Board (FSB) has been conducting annual global data mappings of the global shadow banking system since 2011. Using the "macro-mapping" as a primary focus of the estimation which is based on national flow of funds and sector balance sheet data, the FSB looked at all non-bank financial intermediation to ensure that data gathering covers the areas where shadow banking-related risks to the financial system might potentially arise.

The FSB's *Global Shadow Banking Monitoring Report 2014* contained end-2013 data from 25 jurisdictions and the euro area, covering 80 percent of global GDP and 90 percent of global financial system assets (FSB, 2014). The report indicated that the global shadow banking system, conservatively proxied as the sum of the total assets of "other financial intermediaries" (OFIs), grew by US$5 trillion in 2013 to reach US$75 trillion, accounting for about 25 percent of total global financial assets and 50 percent of banking system assets. The overall non-bank intermediaries' assets grew by 7 percent in 2013 with growth trends differing considerably across different countries, ranging from –6 percent in Spain to +50 percent in Argentina.

As shown in Figure 2.1, the size of OFIs had increased sharply in the years prior to the crisis. Their assets grew from US$26 trillion in 2002 to

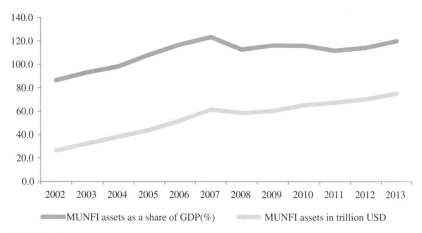

FIGURE 2.1 Estimation of global shadow banking between 2002 and 2013. *Note:* MUNFI refers to the "Monitoring Universe of Non-Bank Financial Intermediation" as defined by FSB in its 2014 update of the *Global Shadow Banking Monitoring Report.*
Source: FSB, *Global Shadow Banking Monitoring Report 2014.*

US$62 trillion in 2007. After a crisis-induced decline to US$58 trillion in 2008, OFI assets increased further to reach US$75 trillion by the end of 2013. The non-bank financial intermediation was equivalent to 120 percent of GDP at the end of 2013, compared to its peak level of 125 percent in 2007. Moreover, the share of non-bank financial intermediation in total financial intermediation has been relatively steady in the post-crisis period, at around 25 percent, down from its peak at 27 percent in 2007 (FSB, 2014). These patterns were relatively stable in post-crisis years.

As shown in Figure 2.2, global shadow banking activities are most prevalent in the advanced economies. By country, the U.S. had the largest share of the assets of non-bank financial intermediaries of US$25 trillion at the end of 2013, followed by the euro area (US$25 trillion), the UK (US $9 trillion) and Japan (US$4 trillion).

Figure 2.3 shows that the growth in shadow banking between 2012 and 2013 differed considerably across countries. Despite growing from a relatively small base, the emerging market economies experienced the most rapid increases in non-bank intermediation, with Argentina registering the highest growth rate of 50 percent, followed by China (33 percent), Turkey (25 percent) and South Africa (20 percent).

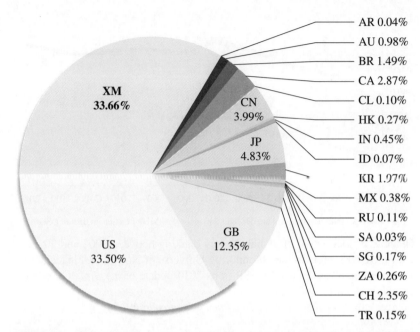

FIGURE 2.2 Share of assets of non-bank financial intermediaries (20 jurisdictions and euro area, end-2013).
Notes: AR = Argentina; AU = Australia; BR = Brazil; CA = Canada;
CH = Switzerland; CN = China; CL = Chile; DE = Germany; ES = Spain;
FR = France; GB = United Kingdom; HK = Hong Kong; ID = Indonesia;
IN = India; IT = Italy; JP = Japan; KR = Korea; MX = Mexico;
NL = Netherlands; RU = Russia; SA = Saudi Arabia; SG = Singapore;
TR = Turkey; US = United States; XM = Euro Area; ZA = South Africa.
Source: FSB, *Global Shadow Banking Monitoring Report 2014.*

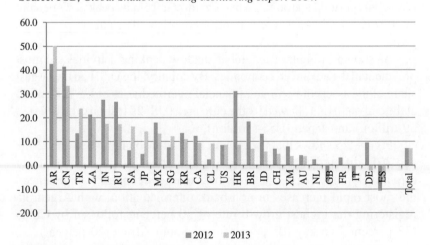

FIGURE 2.3 Annual growth of shadow banking system by country (%).
Source: FSB, *Global Shadow Banking Monitoring Report 2014.*

2.4 FACTORS FOR THE RISE IN GLOBAL SHADOW BANKING

While it is difficult to quantify the relative magnitudes of each factor, there are some broad drivers that have individually and collectively fueled the rise of the global shadow banking system. The cumulative effect of these interacting factors was the build-up of high and unsustainable gross leverage and higher systemic fragility that was underestimated by the market and regulators.

2.4.1 Regulatory Arbitrage

Regulatory arbitrage is often cited as an important driver of the growth in shadow banking (Tobias and Ashcraft, 2012; Gorton and Metrick, 2010). Arbitrage involves transactions or strategies designed to exploit differences or gaps within or between regulatory regimes.

Given regulatory constraints on banks' on-balance sheet activities, particularly the capital requirements they are subjected to, they shifted increasing amounts of their activities off balance sheets in order to conserve capital. Evidence suggested that liquidity-enhancing guarantees were structured to minimize regulatory capital (Acharya et al., 2012). Using shadow banking activities such as holding structured finance vehicles, banks were able to boost their expected returns by circumventing stringent capital requirements to achieve higher leverage than permitted under prudential regulations. Moreover, the off-balance sheet vehicles (special investment vehicles (SIVs) and conduits) also enabled banks to evade disclosure and accounting requirements, disguising the economic reality of risks being taken.

The divergences in the regulatory and legal structures across different economies meant that leverage and risks not only increased through off-balance sheet transactions, but also offshore activities, with the incentive to avoid tax, capital, accounting and regulatory requirements. While regulations remain confined to national borders, shadow banking operations are embedded across borders on a global scale.

The prevalence of shadow banking activities in many lightly-regulated tax havens and offshore financial centers gave rise to a global collective action trap. No single national government can regulate global money and risks created from offshore and off-balance sheet shadow banking activities.

After the GFC, more stringent regulations and capital requirements were imposed on traditional banks, whereas regulatory reforms relating to shadow banking remain a work in progress. Ironically, tighter and more capital requirements and bank regulations create new regulatory arbitrage opportunities, further increasing complexity and risks in the financial system.

While securitizations have become less prominent since the crisis, the perceived higher counterparty risks gave rise to more collateral-based activities with NBFIs. Overall, global shadow banking is still expanding, increasing from US\$58 trillion in 2008 to US\$75 trillion in 2013 (FSB, 2014).

2.4.2 Demand-side Drivers

In addition to regulatory arbitrage, two main demand-side drivers are securitization and collateral intermediation.

Securitization caters to two main drivers. The first is the demand for safe and liquid assets by corporations and the asset management industry to manage their liquidity. Large corporations discovered that they need higher-quality products with good liquidity to manage their global cash flow. Products such as money market funds and asset-backed securities grew substantially to meet such demand, enhanced by credit insurance and synthetic credit enhancements (Claessens et al. 2012).

The second driver of securitization was the demand from traditional banks for securitized debt to use as collateral to boost repo funding which increased their leverage and returns. Instead of holding long-term mortgages funded by short-term deposits, securitization enabled banks to reduce capital charges by holding securitized debt through SIVs, enhancing their capital efficiency. On paper, securitization appeared to transfer risks from the banking sector to investors in order to disperse financial risks across the economy. Because banks became major market-makers in such ABS and through their contingent commitments to buy back such paper, the liquidity and credit risks remained largely with the banks, and ultimately generated the systemic risks that contributed to the GFC.

Another function of shadow banking is collateral intermediation, making liquid and more fungible what were previously illiquid assets, such as mortgages, student loans and junk bonds. Dealer banks such as the failed Lehman Brothers were at the heart of this process, where they source collateral and pledge to other parties to obtain funding or to support other contracts. Use and re-use of collateral amplified pro-cyclicality and increased the fragility in the financial system. Moreover, collateral intermediation became a source of systemic risks when the dealer banks also used some of the same collateral for their own funding, making them vulnerable to the withdrawal of collateral by their customers (Claessens et al. 2012).

Another major driver for shadow banking products is the search for yield by investors, given the decline in global interest rates and higher household and corporate savings. This demand arose as the supply of high quality assets (such as U.S. Treasury Bills) became smaller than demand. In addition, the prolonged period of historically low interest rates also encouraged investors to search for alternative private investment assets with more attractive yields (Turner, 2009). The shadow banks simply manufactured structured vehicles that were perceived as "safe" assets that provide equity-like returns with bond-like volatility (Pozsar, 2014).

2.4.3 Financial Innovation and Technology

Rapid advancements in financial innovation and financial technology also facilitated the growth of shadow banking. A liberal but sanguine regulatory attitude towards financial innovation prior to the GFC allowed enormous complexity to emerge in global financial markets without the information and tools that were needed to manage the risks.

Studies such as those by Boz and Mendoza (2010) showed that overconfidence about the riskiness of financial products was one of the central factors behind the U.S. credit crisis in 2007. Former FSA Chairman Adair Turner also argued that financial innovations in the credit and money creation process generated large negative externalities (Turner, 2012). While certain types of financial innovations were beneficial, most of the innovation in the run-up to the GFC was not aimed at strengthening the role of the financial sector in meeting its social objectives (Stiglitz and Levine, 2010).

For example, securitization was one of the major financial innovations in recent decades. Unfortunately, the "originate-to-distribute" model became more leveraged and non-transparent as the banks at the core of the financial system became more and more reliant on interbank market funding based on securitized assets as collateral. The GFC demonstrated that the "safe and risk-free" assets that securitization had meant to create, proved to be risky and fragile, due to the fundamental flaws in the securitization process and the build-up of "tail risks." Other significant financial innovations such as money market mutual funds, derivatives and repos have collectively and individually added to the accumulation of leverage and systemic risks.

Another significant factor was the emergence of financial technology, such as automated asset allocation algorithms and high-speed (proprietary) trading. Today, high-speed trading accounted for more than half of the U.S. stock trading volume. The costly investments in technology and the edge it gives those that have the platform and the know-how have given a few traders a huge market advantage, but led to greater market concentration and higher market volatility.

Given that profits from equity trading dropped significantly from US $4 billion in 2009 to US$1 billion in 2012, high-speed trading is moving to seek profits from other markets such as bonds, currencies and derivatives (Massoudi and Mackenzie, 2013). These new platforms compete actively with traditional banking and also pose significant regulatory challenges because investors are usually outside the regulatory net. High-speed trading gives rise to flash crashes and dark pools (of liquidity outside formal regulation) that heighten concerns of system and operational stability, market volatility and the potential for market manipulation and insider trading.

Furthermore, new financial institutions such as financial technology platforms (Alibaba, eBay, etc.) have begun to offer payments, credit and transactions convenience to retail customers that represent direct competition to the payment, deposit and wealth management function of banks. This study has included such new activities in its analysis of shadow banking, because the rise of e-commerce and e-finance is a factor that cannot be ignored in the evolution of Chinese finance as it carries both positive (increased competition and innovation) and negative (high risk, fraud and systemic spillover) implications.

2.5 INTERCONNECTEDNESS BETWEEN SHADOW BANKS AND THE FORMAL BANKING SECTOR

Shadow banking does not exist as a stand-alone financial system. It is an integrated part of the national and global financial system that has complex interconnections with the regulated banking sector through ownership and financial interlinkages. Regulated banks continue to engage significantly in shadow banking activities. In the U.S., for example, financial derivatives trading is dominated by four large Federal

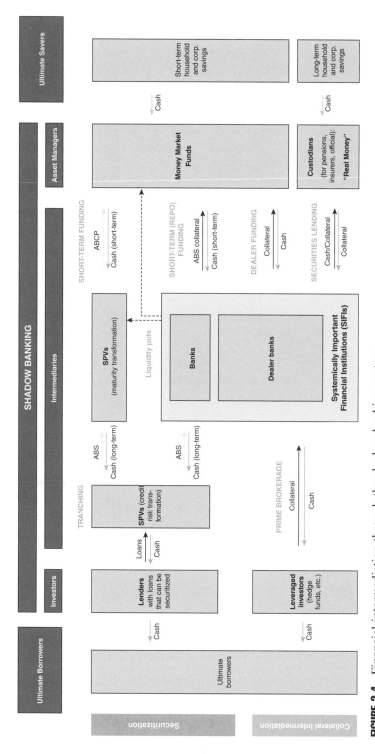

FIGURE 2.4 Financial intermediation through the shadow banking system.

Notes: ABS = asset-backed securities; ABCP = asset-backed commercial paper; SPV = special-purpose vehicle.

Source: Reproduced by permission of IMF. Claessens et al. (2012).

Deposit Insurance Corporation (FDIC)-insured commercial banks, representing 93 percent of the national industry (OCC, 2013).

The shadow banking activities that connect both banks and NBFIs have led to an opaque, overleveraged and highly complex financial system, with high interconnectivity and interdependence. There are complex and dynamic feedbacks between the links and hubs across borders, which are still not fully understood.

As shown in Figure 2.4, the shadow banking system is a complex ecosystem, which combines a web interconnecting banks and NBFIs through the securitization and collateral chains. The long, complex and opaque credit intermediation process is inherently fragile because it embeds high and unsustainable levels of system leverage.

Interconnectedness involves both direct and indirect linkages. Direct linkages occur when shadow banking entities form part of the bank intermediation and securitization chain. Indirect linkages occur when both share common counterparties or invest in similar assets. Both types of linkages create contagion channels where systemic risks are transmitted (FSB, 2013).

Ultimately, the interconnectivity effectively linked the retail savers, investors and borrowers/issuers, exposing a range of financial market participants to potential systemic risks and vulnerabilities (Claessens et al. 2012). Shadow banking entities effectively bundled their risks with the formal banking sector and the real sector.

This means that the shadow banking–banking nexus is an ecosystem with a hierarchy and structure and cannot be examined independently in its parts. It must be examined holistically through both its flows and stocks. Consequently, this study uses national balance sheets and flow of funds accounts to examine the linkages and interrelationships between banks and shadow banks in China.

2.6 THE NATURE OF SHADOW BANKING DIFFERS ACROSS COUNTRIES

Given the fundamental differences in the nature of financial markets, shadow banking systems differ across countries in terms of key actors, compositions and drivers. Typically, the shadow banking system is relatively simple in emerging economies, compared to advanced economies, particularly in terms of sophistication of financial markets and instruments. Advanced systems have a wider range of institutions that

TABLE 2.1 Shadow banking system in China and the U.S.

	Shadow banking in China	Shadow banking in the U.S.
Size	End 2012 – US$3.6 trillion (43% of GDP) (FGI estimation)	End 2012 – US$26 trillion (167% of GDP) (FSB, 2013)
Main Products	Wealth management products (WMPs) Trust products Entrusted loans	Money market mutual funds (MMMFs) Securitization (Structured investment products and CDOs)
Product Structure and Characteristics	Simple in terms of structure and involves one layer of securitization Backed by risky loans (Trust products) Invests in interbank market	Complex financial verticals Securitization (Pooling and tranching) Involves several financial institutions with multiple layers of securitization
Main Investors	Retail investors Non-financial cooperates	Institutional investors Financial institutions
Main Selling Platforms	Traditional banks	Capital markets

(continued)

TABLE 2.1 *(Continued)*

	Shadow banking in China	Shadow banking in the U.S.
Sources of Risks	Evergreening – banks issue new WMPs to cover the losses of old ones	Systemic risks generated from the interlinkages between shadow banking entities, traditional banks and capital market
	Moral hazard – even without explicit guarantee, investors view WMPs as bank fixed deposits where banks will bear the losses	Financial stability risks due to high level of complexity and opacity in the financial system from the shadow banking activities
	Risk bundling and moral hazard – SOEs, LGFVs, and banks are the main shareholders and also investors in WMPs, thus there is a strong incentive for the state to intervene during default	Moral hazard – systemically important financial institutions (SIFIs) expect the state to intervene during defaults

Source: FGI.

provide alternative sources of financing to the economy (Ghosh et al. 2012).

For example, the FSB regional shadow banking study found that NBFIs play a significant role in economic development in Asia. Asian regulators stressed the importance of fit-for-purpose regulations on shadow banks, based on country-specific circumstances and the level of risk (FSB, 2014b).

Table 2.1 compares and contrasts the shadow banking system in the U.S. and China to illustrate the differences in financial development.

With a well-developed non-bank asset management industry and open financial system, the U.S. shadow banks established their footprint in the capital markets decades ago. Their evolution came with financial deregulation in the 1970s, facilitated further by waves of rapid advancements in financial innovation and technology. The U.S. shadow banking system comprises a complex set of activities, markets, contracts and institutions, with enormous information asymmetry and embedded leverage (Figure 2.5).

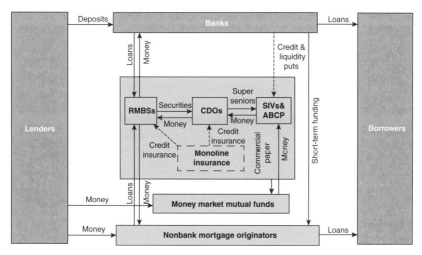

FIGURE 2.5 U.S. shadow banking system.
Note: This is a simplified schematic of the pre-crisis U.S. financial sector showing the flow of funds from lenders to borrowers and the interlinkages between them and shadow banks. Securitization vehicles include asset-backed commercial paper (ABCP) conduits, collateralized debt obligations (CDOs), residential mortgage-backed securities (RMBSs) and structured investment vehicles (SIVs).
Source: Reproduced by permission. IMF (2014b) *Global Financial Stability Report.*

In contrast, shadow banking in China is relatively much smaller in terms of absolute size and global share, simpler by product type and domestic in terms of ownerships and participants. There are, however, some similarities in underlying problems, such as the opaque bundling of credit risks with the formal banking sector, which create moral hazard for the system as a whole. Like all under-regulated financial activities, Chinese shadow banks also suffer from get-rich-quick schemes, fraud and usurious lending that exploit the poor and small borrowers. These issues do require regulation on a level playing field with the formal banking system.

The key systemic issues confronting China's shadow banks will be discussed in detail in the subsequent chapters.

REFERENCES

Acharya, Viral V., Philipp Schnabl, and Gustavo Suarez. 2012. Securitization without Risk Transfer. *Journal of Financial Economics*, NBER Working Paper 15730.

Borst, Nicholas. 2014. Flying Blind: Monitoring Shadow Banking in Emerging Markets. Peterson Institute of International Economics China Economic Watch, 4 April. http://blogs.piie.com/china/?p=3844.

Boz, Emine, and Enrique Mendoza. 2010. Financial Innovation, the Discovery of Risk, and the U.S. Credit Crisis. IMF Working Papers 10/164, International Monetary Fund. https://www.imf.org/external/pubs/ft/wp/2010/wp10164.pdf.

Claessens, Stijn, Zoltan Pozsar, Lev Ratnovski, and Manmohan Singh. 2012. Shadow Banking: Economics and Policy. IMF Staff Discussion Note 12/12. https://www.imf.org/external/pubs/ft/sdn/2012/sdn1212.pdf.

FSB (Financial Stability Board). 2012. Global Shadow Banking Monitoring Report 2012. http://www.financialstabilityboard.org/publications/r_121118c.pdf.

FSB (Financial Stability Board). 2013. Global Shadow Banking Monitoring Report 2013. http://www.financialstabilityboard.org/publications/r_131114.pdf.

FSB (Financial Stability Board). 2014a. Global Shadow Banking Monitoring Report 2014. http://www.fsb.org/2014/11/global-shadow-banking-monitoring-report-2014/.

FSB (Financial Stability Board). 2014b. Report on Shadow Banking in Asia. Financial Stability Board, Regional Consultative Group for Asia. http://www.financialstabilityboard.org/publications/r_140822c.pdf.

Ghosh, Swati, Ines Gonzalez del Mazo, and İnci Ötker-Robe. 2012. Chasing the Shadows: How Significant is Shadow Banking in Emerging Markets?

Economic Premise, 88, World Bank. http://siteresources.worldbank.org/
EXTPREMNET/Resources/EP88.pdf.

Gorton, Gary, and Andrew Metrick. 2010. Regulating the Shadow Banking
System. *Brookings Papers on Economic Activity*, 261–97.

IMF (International Monetary Fund). 2014a. Mapping the Shadow Banking
System Through a Global Flow of Funds Analysis. IMF Working Papers
WP/14/10. http://www.imf.org/external/pubs/ft/wp/2014/wp1410.pdf.

IMF (International Monetary Fund). 2014b. Global Financial Stability Report.
Risk Taking, Liquidity, and Shadow Banking. Curbing Excess While
Promoting Growth, October 2014. https://www.imf.org/external/pubs/ft/
gfsr/2014/02/pdf/text.pdf.

Kodres, Laura E. 2013. What is Shadow Banking? *Finance & Development*,
50 (2). International Monetary Fund. http://www.imf.org/external/pubs/ft/
fandd/2013/06/pdf/basics.pdf.

Massoudi, Arash, and Michael Mackenzie. 2013. Markets: In Search of a Fast
Buck. *Financial Times.* http://www.ft.com/intl/cms/s/0/037522b0-7a7e-
11e2-9c88-00144feabdc0.html#axzz3G0tki2Jk.

McCulley, Paul. 2007. Teton Reflections. PIMCO Global Central Bank Focus,
September 2007. McCulley coined the term "shadow banking" to refer to
"the whole alphabet soup of levered up non-bank investment conduits,
vehicles, and structures" used by banks in advanced countries to keep
opaque and complicated securitized loans off their balance sheets. http://
www.pimco.com/en/insights/pages/gcbf%20august-%20september%
202007.aspx.

OCC (Office of the Comptroller of the Currency). 2013. OCC's Quarterly Report
on Bank Trading and Derivatives Activities, Fourth Quarter 2013. U.S.
Department of Treasury. http://www.occ.treas.gov/topics/capital-markets/
financial-markets/trading/derivatives/dq413.pdf.

Pozsar, Zoltan. 2014. Shadow Banking: The Money View. Office of Financial
Research, Working Paper 14-04, U.S. Department of Treasury. http://www.
treasury.gov/initiatives/ofr/research/Documents/OFRwp2014-04_Pozsar_
ShadowBankingTheMoneyView.PDF.

Pozsar, Zoltan, Tobias Adrian, Adam Ashcraft, and Hayley Boesky. 2013.
Shadow Banking. *Economic Policy Review*, 19 (2), 1–16, Federal Reserve
Bank of New York. "Shadow banks are financial intermediaries that
conduct maturity, credit, and liquidity transformation without explicit
access to central bank liquidity or public sector credit guarantee." http://
www.ny.frb.org/research/epr/2013/EPRvol19no2.pdf.

Stiglitz, Joseph, and Ross Levine. 2010. Financial innovation. Most of the financial
innovation in the run-up to the GFC "was not directed at enhancing the ability
of the financial sector to perform its social functions." *The Economist.* http://
www.economist.com/debate/days/view/471/CommentKey:483033.

Tobias, Adrian, and Adam B. Ashcraft. 2012. Shadow Banking Regulation. *Annual Review of Financial Economics*, Annual Reviews, 4 (1), 99–140, October.

Turner, Adair. 2009. The Financial Crisis and the Future of Financial Regulation. The Economist's Inaugural City Lecture, Financial Services Authority, 21 January. Speech. http://www.fsa.gov.uk/pages/Library/Communication/Speeches/2009/0121_at.shtml.

Turner, Adair. 2012. Securitization, Shadow Banking and the Value of Financial Innovation. The Rostov Lecture of International Affairs School of Advanced International Studies (SAIS), Johns Hopkins University, 19 April. Lecture http://www.fsa.gov.uk/static/pubs/speeches/0419-at.pdf.

CHAPTER 3

Shadow Banking within the National Balance Sheet

Jodie Hu and Andrew Sheng

3.1 INTRODUCTION

As indicated earlier, historically, shadow banking is not a stand-alone system, but highly integrated with the formal financial system. No analysis of shadow banking and its interrelationship with the formal banking system can be complete without examining the interconnectivity and relationships between the different components of shadow banking and formal banking with the real economy through a stock-flow approach. This is best achieved through a set of national balance sheet and flow of funds accounts, which previously was only available in the advanced economies.[1]

Financial system fragility arises from product concentration, institutional/counterparty concentration or geographical concentration. If too many resources or too much credit are concentrated in one activity, counterparty (financial or non-financial) or geographical region, its failure could lead to failure of another activity, counterparty or region. Hence, it is important not just to look at flow accounts, but also balance sheet accounts, compiled to reveal commonalities or concentrations at the product, institutional or geographical levels. The quality of such accounts

---

[1]See for example, the Federal Reserve Board of Governors' quarterly flow of funds accounts, available at http://www.federalreserve.gov/releases/z1/current/

would reveal where the risks lie in the whole set of financial accounts, both on a flow and stock basis.

In December 2013, the Chinese Academy of Social Sciences (CASS) published for the first time a comprehensive *China National Balance Sheet Report*, with data up to 2011. This was subsequently updated with more recent data up to 2013 in an extended study published in 2015.[2] In the past, most economic analyses have focused on flows, such as gross national product accounts, annual trade, investments or savings. Balance sheet data, in contrast, reveal stocks outstanding at a point of time. By comparing leverage and where it is located within the national balance sheet, it would be possible to detect an economy's state of robustness or its fragilities, particularly at the sectoral level.

It should be noted that there are inherent difficulties in compiling national balance sheets because there are serious valuation problems regarding the use of book, historical or market values, and also methodological, reporting and coverage issues. Many of the sectoral data are based on sample surveys, except where the regulatory data are reasonably reliable and cross-checked (for consistency) against other data, such as financial institutions' balance sheets and profit and loss accounts. However, it is the broad trends and comparative ratios that are revealing on the relationships, pattern and context of change.

Because the national balance sheet reveals the sectoral balance sheets of the central government, local governments, the non-financial corporate sector and the financial sector as well as the external sector, the accounts are able to shed light on the considerable interrelationships and inter-dependencies between the different elements of the financial sector and the subsectors in the real economy.

It should also be noted that national balance sheet data only provide a top-down, snapshot view of the situation in China and a review of current conditions at a particular point in time. It does not attempt to forecast dynamic changes in the Chinese economy and its interactions with changing global conditions. Conditions could well change dramatically for the worse if growth falters or property prices collapse due to some unforeseen shock. While modeling of these dynamics could offer additional insights and predictive value, such analysis is highly complex and

---

[2]See Li Yang and Zhang Xiaojing, 2013, "China's Sovereign Balance Sheet and Implications for Financial Stability." In Das US, Fietcher J and Sun T, eds. *China's Road to Greater Financial Stability: Some Policy Perspectives.* IMF Press.

data intensive (which requires the cooperation of regulators) and is beyond the scope of this book.

Despite the data limitations, interpretation of China's national balance sheet relationships, especially in comparison with the U.S., which has the most comprehensive data, is quite illuminating on the broad trends and patterns within the Chinese economy and financial system.

3.2 OVERVIEW OF THE CHINESE NATIONAL BALANCE SHEET

The first distinguishing feature of the Chinese national balance sheet is that the state still owns a large portion of national assets. While the household sector accounted for just under half of national net assets, the central and local governments accounted for a quarter and the enterprise sector the balance. This is in sharp contrast to the U.S. situation, where the household sector accounted for 95 per cent of U.S. net assets (Table 3.1).

The state sector in China had net assets equivalent to 23 percent of the national total, whereas in the U.S., the state sector (Federal plus state government) was a net borrower to the tune of 4 percent of GDP. In China, the local governments had many more net assets (17 percent of national net assets), compared with the U.S. local government sector (9 percent of national total), whilst China's central government had another 6 percent of total net assets (Table 3.1.).

In addition to a large share of state ownership in net assets, the state also accounts for a considerable proportion of gross debt in the economy. The total liabilities of the central and local governments in China amounted to US$8 trillion or nearly one fifth of total liabilities in the whole economy in 2013, whereas the non-financial enterprises sector accounted for 72 percent. The major sources of government debts are the bonds issued by the central government and the borrowings by local government financing platforms (LGFPs).

The liabilities in the US are concentrated in the federal government and household sector, which accounted for 21 percent and 18 percent of the national total, respectively. In contrast, the Chinese household sector only accounted for 8 percent of the total liabilities (Table 3.2).

On top of central government and local government, the state sector in China also participates in the economy through state-owned enterprises (SOEs). The total assets of SOEs were estimated to be 34 percent of the total assets of the non-financial enterprise sector, or RMB 104 trillion

TABLE 3.1 Net assets by sector – China vs. U.S.

China	USD TN			%GDP			%Total*		
	2007	2011	2013	2007	2011	2013	2007	2011	2013
National net assets	22	47	57	624	644	619	93	94	85
of which: Households	12	23	32	335	315	344	50	46	47
Non-financial enterprises	6	12	20	165	204	218	25	30	30
Central govt	1	3	4	32	38	42	5	6	6
Local govt	5	9	11	135	129	123	20	19	17

US	USD TN			%GDP			%Total		
	2007	2011	2013	2007	2011	2013	2007	2011	2013
National net assets	80	71	84	574	475	499	100	100	100
of which: Households	67	64	79	478	425	472	83	90	95
Non-financial enterprises	12	10	8	82	65	48	14	14	10
Federal govt	−5	−10	−11	−33	−63	−67	−6	−13	−13
State/local govt	7	7	8	49	43	45	8	9	9

Note: China's national net assets are not equal to the sum of sectoral net assets because there is methodological discrepancy in compiling balance sheets at different levels due to data availability and technical issues.
Data sources: Li et al. 2015, FRB 2015, authors' calculations.

TABLE 3.2 Total assets and total liabilities by sector – China vs. U.S.

China

USD TN	Year	Total	% GDP	Household	Non-financial enterprises	Central/Federal govt	Local/state govt
Total assets	2007	33	930	12	12	2	7
Total liabilities	2007	10	278	1	7	1	2
Total assets	2013	107	1165	35	49	7	16
Total liabilities	2013	40	439	3	29	3	5

% Total	Year	Total	% GDP	Household	Non-financial enterprises	Central/Federal govt	Local/state govt
Total assets	2007	100	930	37	37	6	20
Total liabilities	2007	100	278	7	67	8	19
Total assets	2013	100	1165	32	46	7	15
Total liabilities	2013	100	439	8	72	8	11

(*continued*)

39

TABLE 3.2 *(Continued)*

US

USD TN	Year	Total	% GDP	Household	Non-financial enterprises	Central/Federal govt	Local/state govt
Total assets	2007	141	1004	81	46	3	10
Total liabilities	2007	60	429	14	34	8	4
Total assets	2013	160	942	93	50	5	13
Total liabilities	2013	77	456	14	43	16	5

%Total	Year	Total	% GDP	Household	Non-financial enterprises	Central/Federal govt	Local/state govt
Total assets	2007	100	1004	58	32	2	7
Total liabilities	2007	100	429	24	57	14	6
Total assets	2013	100	942	58	31	3	8
Total liabilities	2013	100	456	18	55	21	6

Source: Li et al. (2013, 2015), FRB (2015) authors' calculations.

(Li et al., 2015, 90). The total liabilities of SOEs were roughly RMB 67 trillion, estimated by multiplying the total assets with SOEs' leverage ratio of 64 percent. Hence, the state sector, including central government, local government, and SOEs, accounted for 37 percent of the national total assets and 46 percent of total liabilities in China.

While the state sector takes up nearly half of the total credit in the economy, its contribution to GDP is disproportionately smaller. From the production perspective, the state accounted for only 30–35 percent of GDP, including the SOEs' contribution of about 24 percent (Natixis, 2015), and government-sponsored institutions' contribution of 5–10 per cent[3]. In terms of expenditure, central and local government purchases accounted for an even smaller proportion (only 14 percent) of GDP. Hence, there is significant scope to enhance the productivity of the state sector and ensure greater efficiency in the allocation and utilization of resources.

The second distinctive feature is that the bulk of Chinese net worth lies in real assets, particularly housing, fixed investments and land, whereas U.S. net wealth is mostly in the form of financial wealth. Chinese gross real assets were 591 percent of GDP in 2013, compared with the U.S. equivalent of 428 percent of GDP (Table 3.3). This is due to the exceptionally high level of fixed-asset investment in recent years by Chinese households, enterprises and local governments. Due to the fast rate of urbanization of the population and the rise of the (lower) middle class, the household sector in China has invested heavily in residential housing, whereas the local governments have invested heavily in infrastructure, such as roads, railways, airports and public utilities.

Although there are inherent problems in making accurate valuations of such real estate, equipment and infrastructure, the fact that most of Chinese investment in fixed assets were made in recent years means that the cost numbers are not grossly out of line with market values. This does not mean that these numbers are not vulnerable to sharp real estate valuation falls in the event of sharp increases in interest rates or a sudden slowdown in the economy due to various factors. Under conditions of broad political and global stability, the numbers suggest that whilst real estate values in individual cities or regions may suffer some corrections, the overall net asset situation appears generally adequate to cushion the

---

[3]Estimation by Zhong Yi Ageing Development Centre, available at http://zyac .mca.gov.cn/article/llyj/201203/20120300292545.shtml

TABLE 3.3 Assets and liabilities – China vs. U.S.

	China						US					
	USD TN			%GDP			USD TN			%GDP		
	2007	2011	2013	2007	2011	2013	2007	2011	2013	2007	2011	2013
Non-financial assets	21	45	54	596	610	591	68	62	72	470	402	428
Real estate	12	23	29	331	309	315	53	46	54	366	294	322
Financial assets	17	40	57	475	545	624	142	147	171	981	948	1018
Total assets	37	85	112	1071	1155	1215	210	210	243	1451	1350	1445
Financial liabilities	16	37	55	447	511	596	130	139	161	897	894	956
Net financial assets	1	2	3	28	34	28	12	8	10	84	55	62
Net assets	22	47	57	624	644	619	80	71	82	554	458	489
Net assets excl real estate	10	25	28	293	335	304	27	26	28	188	164	167
GDP	3	7	9	100	100	100	14	16	17	100	100	100

Source: Li et al. (2013, 2015); FRB (2015); authors' calculations.

economy from modest falls (of, say, up to 30 percent) in real estate values. (For a more detailed analysis on the real estate sector, see Chapter 5, Inherent Risks in Chinese Shadow Banking.)

A third feature is the high level of financialization of the U.S. economy compared with China, with the former having financial assets equivalent to 1,018 percent of GDP, two-thirds more than that in China (624 percent of GDP). Obviously, the U.S. has an advanced, sophisticated and deep financial system, which is capital market-dominated; whereas the Chinese system is more bank-dominated, with relatively shallow long-term pension and insurance institutions. The higher level of financial assets indicates that the U.S. system is more liquid relative to China. In the event of need, therefore, U.S. entities would be able to encash their financial assets more readily than their Chinese counterparts, where real assets make up the majority of total assets.

U.S. financial assets comprise mostly debt instruments and equities, whereas Chinese financial assets are mostly held in bank deposits and bonds, with nearly half of GDP in holdings of foreign exchange reserves. U.S. financial assets held in equities were 133 percent of GDP at the end of 2013, significantly higher than the 35 percent equivalent in China (IMF, 2015). The underdevelopment of China's equity markets meant that Chinese enterprises were more debt-dependent and highly leveraged. Furthermore, since the bulk of the equity market capitalization comprised listed SOEs, the private sector SMEs were further constrained as to their equity funding.

Most concerns with China's shadow banking center on the rapid increase in domestic debt, particularly since the 2008 stimulus package that loosened credit conditions. Chinese non-financial assets have remained relatively stable at around 590–610 percent of GDP over the period 2007–2013, whereas financial assets have grown from 475 percent of GDP to 624 percent of GDP, an increase of 149 percentage points of GDP in six years (Li et al., 2015). Financial liabilities also rose rapidly from 447 percent of GDP to 596 percent of GDP, or by 149 percentage points of GDP.

China's foreign exchange reserves rose from 45 percent of GDP in 2007 to 49 percent of GDP by the end of 2011 but declined slightly to 47 percent of GDP by the end of 2013. The Chinese financial system is almost unique in having such high foreign exchange assets relative to other assets. The acquisition of such foreign exchange reserves carried a cost to the central bank, sterilizing the monetary creation through increases in statutory reserve requirements on the commercial banks, which effectively "froze" their lending capacity in the absence of such requirements. The full implications of such reserve requirements will be discussed later, but the bottom line is that the Chinese financial system is neither vulnerable to foreign exchange shortages, nor a sudden withdrawal of foreign funds, because of its currently favorable fundamentals, including a strong reserves position.

The concern is China's rapidly increasing domestic debt, which amounted to over 214 percent of GDP by September 2012 (Mann et al., 2013). According to the latest national balance sheet data, total financial liabilities in the form of loans and bonds amounted to 218 percent of GDP in 2013, comprising 165 percent of GDP in loans and 53 percent of GDP in bonds. This was mostly due to the increase in loans between 2007 and 2013, which amounted to 52 percentage points of GDP (Li et al., 2015, 13).

The real question (from a systemic risk management perspective) is who are the major borrowers and whether they are vulnerable to default risk. In other words, it is not just about the *size of liabilities* and the *speed of their increase*, but also about the *quality* of assets and *equity* (net assets) that underpin such debt.

As the CASS 2015 study indicated, "from the data and gross asset point of view, the period 2000–2007 was a period of 'private sector advance, public sector retreat.' But from 2010, there was a 'public advance, private retreat' trend" (Li et al., 2015, 91).

3.3 WHO OWES WHAT IN CHINA'S NATIONAL BALANCE SHEET?

The borrowers in any economy are the households, the non-financial corporate or enterprise sector, the government (divided into central and local government), financial sector and external sector (the rest of the world). In most economies, the households are the major savers, and the government and corporate sectors are the major borrowers.

Prior to the GFC, the financial sector was not a major area of concern because it performed its intermediary role with very small net exposure. However, the GFC revealed that large gross borrowing by the financial sector could be a concern, because highly leveraged financial institutions are vulnerable to contagion, liquidity runs and systemic failure. A collapse of systemically important financial institutions, including shadow banks, can lead to system failure.

The national balance sheet gives a good overall view of the structural funding issues in China.

The big picture is that China is a net lender to the rest of the world and the debt problem is therefore a domestic issue without any direct global systemic implications. At the end of 2013, China's net international investment position totaled US$2 trillion – 21 percent of GDP – with gross foreign exchange reserves totaling just under US$4 trillion.[4] In contrast, the U.S. owed the rest of the world 32 percent of its GDP. At the end of 2014, the Chinese net position declined somewhat to US$1.78 trillion or 17 percent of GDP, whereas the U.S. net position worsened to a negative position of US$7.0 trillion or 40 per cent of GDP.

Given China's favorable reserves position, it is unlikely to face a foreign exchange or national insolvency crisis anytime soon. This being the case, China's shadow banking issues are not a global threat, since foreigners do not have much direct exposure to Chinese shadow bank liabilities.

However, indirect contagion effects cannot be discounted, as market confidence in foreign holdings of China's bonds and securities can be affected by a severe deterioration in the shadow banking problems. As the market turbulence in China and major financial markets showed in June–September 2015, concerns over a possible hard landing in China are real.

Overall, China's issues with shadow banks and credit growth are largely a domestic debt problem. Is it sustainable and what are the downside risks?

Structurally, because the financial system is still largely state-owned,[5] it has tended to lend mostly to state-owned enterprises (SOEs) and local governments. Since 2008, SOEs and so-called local-government financing platforms (LGFPs) have been using bank loans to fund massive fixed-asset investments, as local governments have only recently been permitted to access the bond market on a limited basis. On

---

[4]SAFE (State Administration of Foreign Exchange), 2015. *"The Time-Series Data of International Investment Position of China, Annual,"* Last modified 9 September, 2015.

[5]The central government through Central Huijin owns two-thirds of the equity of the largest banks, and also at least one-third of the equity of the listed joint-stock banks and city banks, insurance companies and securities companies. The policy banks are fully state-owned, as are the exchanges. According to CASS, at the end of 2010, the state owned 53.8 percent of the equity of the Chinese banking system.

the other hand, because private sector enterprises have limited access to stock market funding, bond markets and bank loans, they have borrowed at higher interest rates – often from the shadow banking sector – to finance their investments and their cash flow needs. Quite a lot of their investments have been in real estate development, because of the high returns on such investments as property prices rose as a result of both fundamental commercial and residential requirements and speculative demand.

This excessive dependence on bank credit stems from the lack of access to funding relative to demand and the relative underdevelopment of China's equity markets, with market capitalization amounting to only 35 percent of GDP, compared to 133 percent of GDP in the U.S. in 2013 (IMF, 2015). The debt of non-financial enterprises amounted to 113 percent of GDP in China, compared to 72 percent in the U.S. and 99 percent in Japan (Sheng and Xiao, 2014).

Given that the largest enterprise borrowers are either state-owned or local government entities, their debts are essentially domestic sovereign obligations. The good news is that the sovereign government balance sheet is still healthy, with net assets of RMB 103 trillion, of which RMB 51 trillion was net equity in SOEs (Li et al., 2015, 29). Even if we were to exclude all its natural resource assets,[6] the sovereign government's financial position remains solvent to avoid any potential liquidity problems. Much of this could be used to help restructure local government finances and SOE debt. With China's total central and local government debt to GDP ratio amounting to only 53 percent – much less than the U.S.'s 80 percent and Japan's 226 percent – there is sufficient policy space to undertake debt–equity swaps to tackle the internal debt problem (Sheng and Xiao, 2014).

Furthermore, since the local government sector has net assets equivalent to 123 percent of GDP, as against liabilities of 48 percent of GDP, there are sufficient gross assets in the local government sector to pay for their rapid increase in debt (Li et al., 2015, 50). In addition, the central government has recently passed a law to increase the revenue sharing between the central and local governments and to enable local

---

[6]While it is difficult to accurately measure all of China's natural resource endowments, some estimates suggest it could be as high as RMB 52 trillion (Li et al., 2013). It is recognized that forest reserves and mineral ores in the ground (coal, iron ore, rare earths, petroleum, etc.) may not be very readily useable in a crisis, but their availability does provide an indication of long-term sustainability.

governments to issue municipal debt. As assets held by local governments (such as land) may be difficult to dispose of quickly in a crisis without incurring substantial discounts, the question arises as to whether local governments would be willing or able to sell such assets to pay for the debt in times of need. Individual local governments may have liquidity problems, but the overall solvency picture suggests that the situation is stable and manageable, based on current conditions.

Nevertheless, the national balance sheet numbers suggest that China's high investment stock, funded largely by debt, will require deeper capital markets to increase the equity element in order to make the system less vulnerable to excessive leverage and more resilient to shocks. The high real estate numbers also means that the system as a whole is vulnerable to deflation in the event of a property market collapse.

These questions are examined in detail at the sectoral level in the following section.

3.4 ZOOMING IN ON CHINA'S SECTORAL BALANCE SHEETS

This section examines China's balance sheet developments in relation to the external sector (rest of the world), household sector, non-financial corporate sector, central government, local government and the financial sector.

3.4.1 External Sector – Net International Investment Position

As indicated above, China is a net lender to the world, with US$3.8 trillion of official foreign exchange reserves in 2013, equivalent to 41 percent of GDP. The net international investment position of China was US$2 trillion or 22 percent of GDP. In contrast, the U.S. owes the rest of the world US$6 trillion or 34 percent of GDP (Table 3.4). At the end of November 2014, China held US$1.3 trillion or 20 percent of total foreign holdings of U.S. Treasury securities of US$6.1 trillion (U.S. Treasury, 2015). China was the largest holder, ahead of Japan (US$1.2 trillion).

It should be noted that the gross foreign investment position includes inward foreign direct investments, so that China has more than sufficient foreign exchange reserves to manage not only short-term outflows, but also long-term outflows.

TABLE 3.4 Net international investment position – China vs. U.S.

	China				U.S.		
	USD TN 2007	USD TN 2013	% GDP 2013	%Total assets 2013	USD TN 2013	% GDP 2013	%Total assets 2013
Net position	1	2	22	33	−6	−34	−34
A. Assets	2	6	65	100	17	100	100
Foreign exchange	2	4	41	64	0	0	0
B. Liabilities	1	4	43	67	21	126	126

Source: Li et al. (2013, 2015); FRB (2015); authors' calculations.

3.4.2 Household Sector

The total assets of the household sector in China amounted to RMB 215 trillion at the end of 2013, rising substantially from RMB 94 trillion at the end of 2007 (Table 3.5). Non-financial assets accounted for 60 percent of the total household assets in 2013, with the bulk being held in real estate, totaling RMB 118 trillion or 207 percent of GDP. By comparison, real estate comprised only 30 percent of U.S. household total wealth, and amounted to US$22 trillion or 133 percent of GDP at the end of 2013. In other words, relatively speaking, Chinese households held double the amount of real estate by value than their U.S. counterparts.

In contrast, U.S. households have more than double the ratio of financial assets (387 percent of GDP) compared with Chinese household financial assets of RMB 86 trillion or 151 percent of GDP. RMB 45 trillion or 52 percent of total Chinese household financial assets were in bank deposits, with only RMB 6 trillion or just 7 percent in equities. By comparison, U.S. households held only US$7 trillion or 8 percent of their financial assets in bank deposits.

What is remarkable is the low level of Chinese household debt. Total liabilities of the Chinese household sector were only RMB 20 trillion or 35 percent of GDP, compared with US$14 trillion or 82 per cent of GDP for U.S. households. Chinese household financial liabilities represented 10 percent of total net wealth of RMB 196 trillion and less than half of total bank deposits. Consequently, unlike many middle-income countries, the Chinese household sector does not have a debt overhang.

TABLE 3.5 Balance sheet of households – China vs. U.S.

	China				US		
	RMB TN 2007	RMB TN 2013	%GDP 2013	%Total assets 2013	USD TN 2013	%GDP 2013	%Total assets 2013
Total assets	94	215	379	100	93	552	100
Non-financial assets	61	129	227	60	28	165	30
Real estate	57	118	207	55	22	133	24
Of which: Urban	50	100	175	46	n/a	n/a	n/a
Rural	7	18	32	8	n/a	n/a	n/a
Automobiles	2	8	15	4	5	29	5
Fixed assets for rural production	1	3	6	1	n/a	n/a	n/a
Financial assets	34	86	151	40	65	387	70
Currency	3	5	9	2	1	6	1
Deposits	18	45	78	21	7	44	8
Debt securities	1	0	1	0	4	22	4
Equities	5	6	10	3	12	74	13
Investment fund shares	3	1	2	0	7	43	8
Securities company client margins	1	0	0	0	n/a	n/a	n/a
Insurance reserves	3	9	16	4	1	7	1

(continued)

TABLE 3.5 (*Continued*)

	China				US		
	RMB TN 2007	RMB TN 2013	%GDP 2013	%Total assets 2013	USD TN 2013	%GDP 2013	%Total assets 2013
WMP	n/a	10	17	4	n/a	n/a	n/a
Trust products	n/a	11	19	5	n/a	n/a	n/a
Financial liabilities	5	20	35	9	14	82	15
Consumption loans	3	13	23	6	n/a	n/a	n/a
Short-term	0	3	5	1	n/a	n/a	n/a
Mid-/long-term	3	10	18	5	10	57	10
Proprietorship loans	2	7	12	3	n/a	n/a	n/a
Short-term	1	4	8	2	n/a	n/a	n/a
Of which: rural	1	n/a	n/a	n/a	n/a	n/a	n/a
Mid-/long-term	1	3	4	1	n/a	n/a	n/a
Net financial assets	28	66	117	31	51	305	55
Net assets	89	196	344	91	79	469	85

Data sources: Li et al. 2015, FRB 2014, authors' calculations.

For example, the mortgage indebtedness, that is, the mid- and long-term liabilities of the household sector, of RMB 10 trillion was less than 10 percent of the value of household ownership of real estate of RMB 118 trillion. This is because over 80 percent of urban and rural households own their own residential property and many were bought at levels before the recent property price increase (Rothman, 2014). Thus, even though individual households may be vulnerable to a sharp drop in house prices, the risk of widespread residential mortgage default is very small. Most Chinese households would prefer to cut household expenditure in order to service their mortgages, rather than to lose their homes. Residential subprime mortgages are not a major risk in China. Furthermore, residential mortgages in China are with recourse to borrower, whereas they are without recourse to borrower in the U.S., with the default risks falling mostly on the banks.

It is noteworthy that proprietorship loans, most of which are small and medium enterprise (SME) or micro-enterprise credit, amounted to RMB 7 trillion, since households form the bulk of micro-enterprises. Given the high level of household savings and net wealth, the overall credit risk of the household sector is unlikely to be big.

3.4.3 Non-financial Corporate Sector

In contrast to the household sector, the liabilities of the Chinese non-financial corporate sector are large and still rising. In 2013, the sector's total liabilities amounted to RMB 181 trillion or 318 percent of GDP. In comparison, U.S. non-financial corporate debt was only 218 percent of GDP.

The *China National Balance Sheet Report, 2013*, contained a detailed breakdown of the assets and liabilities of the non-financial corporate sector as of the end of 2011. However, the 2015 update contained fewer details. Consequently, the following analysis on the non-financial corporate sector is still based on the 2013 Report with data at the end of 2011.

There are several distinguishing factors in comparing corporate debt in China with the rest of the world. The first is the high level of state ownership, which technically implies that some corporate debt could be reclassified as sovereign debt. The largest enterprises in China are mostly state-owned enterprises (SOEs), although a number of privately owned enterprises is beginning to emerge. Related to this is the distribution of credit to the corporate sector. In 2011, large enterprises – mostly SOEs, which enjoy considerable financial subsidies and privileges of being in oligopolistic utilities with comfortable liquidity – accounted for 43 percent of total bank loans. Private sector SMEs, which contribute to more jobs and GDP growth, face higher borrowing costs, more competition and tighter liquidity, accounting for only 27 percent of bank loans (Sheng and Xiao, 2014).

The role of SOEs in the non-financial enterprises sector had been on the decline since 2000, reflecting the rise of private firms and the upgrading of the industrial structure in line with China's market reforms. The number of SOEs dropped from 191,000 in 2000 to 112,000 in 2007 and remained flat in 2008–2010 (Li et al. 2015, 90). However, the trend reversed after 2010, with the number of SOEs increasing steadily to 155,000 in 2013. Consequently, the growth rate of the total assets of SOEs has also accelerated since 2011.

The second distinguishing feature is the high level of corporate deposit holdings, which amounted to RMB 29 trillion or 60 per cent of GDP, compared with US$1 trillion or 6 percent of GDP for the U.S. corporate sector. This is partly due to the lack of sophistication in corporate asset-liability management in terms of insufficient financial products for investment. It is also due to a particular banking practice in China, whereby banks do not lend on a commitment basis, but debit the total loan immediately whilst crediting the borrower with an equivalent amount of bank deposit. This enables the bank to earn a higher level of interest on the loan, since the loan is not charged on a disbursement basis and deposit rates are significantly lower than lending rates. This practice increases the deposit base at the same time as bank lending activity rises, resulting in a faster increase in money supply as credit is expanded. The regulators are beginning to change this practice towards credit being on a drawdown or disbursement basis.

The third distinguishing factor is the high level of inter-enterprise credit. Due to the stringent controls on bank credit following the post-2003 reforms and lack of access by private sector borrowers to bank credit, the private sector (as well as SOEs with weaker credit ratings) tends to rely heavily on trade credit or inter-enterprise credit. The size of Chinese inter-enterprise liabilities was RMB 51 trillion or 109 percent of GDP in 2011, compared with RMB 39 trillion or 84 percent of GDP in bank short-term and long-term debt. In contrast, U.S. corporations borrowed from the banking system US$8 trillion or 52 percent of GDP, whereas they borrowed more from the capital market in the form of bonds and market instruments. U.S. corporations had US$3 trillion in trade payables (inter-enterprise debt), equivalent to 19 percent of GDP, or one-sixth the level in China (Table 3.6).

TABLE 3.6 Balance sheet of non-financial corporations – China vs. U.S.

	China				U.S.		
	RMB TN 2007	RMB TN 2011	%GDP 2011	%Total assets 2011	US$ TN 2011	%GDP 2011	%Total assets 2011
Total assets	93	197	416	100	30	192	100
Non-financial assets	62	126	265	64	15	98	51
Fixed assets	40	69	146	35	13	85	44
Inventories	14	37	78	19	2	13	7
Other non-financial assets	8	20	42	10	n/a	n/a	n/a
Of which: intangibles	3	9	18	4	n/a	n/a	n/a
Financial assets	31	71	151	36	15	94	49
Currency and deposits	12	29	60	14	1	6	3
Inter-enterprises credit	13	29	61	15	9	56	29
Notes receivable	2	6	12	3	n/a	n/a	n/a
Accounts receivable	5	13	28	7	n/a	n/a	n/a
Advances to suppliers	3	7	14	3	n/a	n/a	n/a
Other receivables	2	3	7	2	n/a	n/a	n/a
Long-term equity investment	4	7	15	4	4	29	15
Other	3	7	14	3	1	4	2

(continued)

TABLE 3.6 (*Continued*)

	China				U.S.		
	RMB TN 2007	RMB TN 2011	%GDP 2011	%Total assets 2011	US$ TN 2011	%GDP 2011	%Total assets 2011
Total liabilities	50	117	247	59	28	180	94
Short-term borrowings	10	19	41	10	2	11	6
Long-term borrowings	9	20	43	10	6	41	21
Inter-enterprises liabilities	21	51	109	26	3	19	10
Notes payable	2	5	11	3	n/a	n/a	n/a
Accounts payable	9	24	50	12	n/a	n/a	n/a
Advances from customers	5	14	29	7	n/a	n/a	n/a
Other payables	4	8	16	4	n/a	n/a	n/a
Long-term payables	1	1	3	1	n/a	n/a	n/a
Other financial liabilities	9	26	54	13	17	109	57
Net assets	44	80	169	41	2	11	6
Net financial assets	−18	−46	−96	−23	−13	−86	−45
Debt asset ratio	0.53	0.59			0.94		

Data sources: Li et al. 2015, FRB 2014, authors' calculations.

There are two major reasons why Chinese enterprises borrow significantly from inter-enterprise credit. Firstly, Chinese corporations grew up mostly as manufacturing concerns or distributors of manufacturing products, which rely largely on trade credit that is normally provided interest-free for short-term credit (Wignaraja and Jinjarak, 2015). Secondly, cash-rich SOEs may be willing to lend to customers at higher than bank deposit rates, because they believe that they understand their customers' credit risks better because of their business or supply-chain relationships. Such high inter-enterprise credit does mean that banks are not the only source of credit. However, the resolution of failed borrowers could be complicated in a system where bank debt is collateralized, whereas inter-enterprise credit is less secured. The failure of one inter-enterprise borrower could lead to a contagion failure in other enterprises due to the interconnectivity of inter-enterprise credit.

In the early 1990s, there was an earlier build-up of inter-enterprise credit called triangular debt. At its peak between 1991 and 1992, the size of triangular debt was estimated to be one-third of total banking credit. With rising cases of default and delays in repayment, the triangular debt caused a sharp rise in bank NPLs, since the state-owned banks were highly exposed to SOEs. Consequently, the resolution of SOEs required the Chinese government to clean up the triangular debt problem under the leadership of former Premier Zhu Rongji.

The level of inter-enterprise credit in 2011 had also risen significantly to be an important part of enterprise funding. Some of the inter-enterprise credit was actually channeled through shadow banking operations to obtain funding, sometimes through cross-guarantees. Although current inter-enterprise credit has evolved differently from the triangular debt problem, which was uniquely amongst SOEs, its high level of credit exposure has systemic implications that deserve closer attention of the government and financial regulators.

The fourth distinguishing factor is that in contrast with U.S. companies, which prefer to be "asset light," Chinese enterprises tend to invest heavily in fixed assets and inventory. Total corporate non-financial assets were 265 percent of GDP in 2011, two and half times the level of U.S. corporate holdings of real assets (98 percent of GDP). Holdings of inventory in Chinese corporates were 78 percent of GDP, compared with 13 percent in the case of U.S. corporations. They are less efficient in terms of inventory management and overreliant on bank funding for fixed and illiquid assets in China. These indicators suggest that Chinese enterprises still suffer from over-capacity in fixed assets and possibly obsolete inventory, which needed to be valued more realistically.

Thus, although the net asset position of Chinese enterprises appeared large at 169 percent of GDP in 2011, compared with only 11 percent in the case of U.S. corporations, the Chinese debt–asset ratio has risen steadily from 0.45 in 2000 to 0.59 at the end of 2011. A key reason why the leverage kept growing is that the capital market has not kept pace with the need to supply equity capital for the corporate sector. The bank funding model has constrained corporate governance improvements in China, as they are less subject to public scrutiny when enterprises borrow from banks.

The corporate gross leveraged position can be seen from the fact that the Chinese corporate sector has gross liabilities of RMB 117 trillion and net financial liabilities of RMB 46 trillion or 96 percent of GDP. Once liquidity conditions tightened, it was not surprising that the corporate sector began to borrow from the shadow banks in order to obtain liquidity.

Thus, even though their net equity may appear high at 169 percent of GDP, China's non-financial corporate sector is still vulnerable to financial shocks due to its high level of debt and less efficient use of assets.

To validate our observations on the above distinguishing features of the non-financial enterprises sector, we made a comparison against more recent data available for the industrial enterprises in China (Table 3.7). This group of industrial enterprises accounted for RMB 67.6 trillion of assets or 34.3 percent of total non-financial enterprise assets at the end of 2011. Total receivables were RMB 7.1 trillion or 10.5 percent of total assets, lower than the ratio of 14.7 percent for the national group. Fixed assets for the industrial enterprises accounted for 37.4 percent of total assets, compared with 34 percent for the national group.

What was interesting was that state ownership of industrial enterprises declined from 12 percent of total equity in 2007 to 8 percent in 2010, but climbed again to 9.7 percent in 2013. This suggested that the role of the state actually increased as a result of larger intervention after the 2008 stimulus package.

Ultimately, the overall vulnerability of the financial system will rest on the quality of total credit from banks and shadow banks to the SOEs, the SMEs, real estate companies, and the local government financing platforms (LGFPs). The sectoral distribution of such risks is discussed in Chapter 5.

TABLE 3.7 Balance sheet of Chinese industrial enterprises.

RMB TN	2007	2008	2009	2010	2011	2012	2013
Total Asset	35.3	43.1	49.4	59.3	67.6	76.8	87.1
Total Asset: Current	16.3	19.6	22.3	27.9	32.8	36.8	41.3
Total Asset: Current: Account Receivable	3.9	4.4	5.1	6.1	7.1	8.4	9.7
Total Asset: Current: Inventory	4.5	5.4	5.7	7.0	8.1	8.8	9.7
Total Asset: Fixed	14.7	17.9	20.7	23.8	25.3	28.4	31.6
Total Asset: Net Fixed	12.9	15.8	18.0	21.1	n/a	n/a	n/a
Total Liability	20.3	24.9	28.6	34.0	39.3	44.5	50.6
Total Liability: Current	15.8	19.0	21.4	25.8	29.9	33.8	38.1
Owners' Equity	15.0	18.2	20.7	25.1	28.2	32.1	36.1
Owners' Equity: Paid-in Capital	8.3	10.4	11.1	12.2	14.5	16.1	17.4
Owners' Equity: State Capital	1.8	2.3	2.1	2.0	2.3	2.9	3.5
Owners' Equity: HK, Macau & Taiwan Capital	0.8	1.0	1.0	1.1	1.1	1.9	1.2
Owners' Equity: Foreign Capital	1.5	1.7	1.8	2.0	2.0	2.1	2.2

Source: CEIC, authors' calculations.

3.4.4 Central Government

The Chinese central government held total assets worth RMB 45 trillion at the end of 2013, of which RMB 35 trillion are financial assets, as real assets amounted to only RMB 11 trillion in 2013. The bulk of the financial assets comprised equity in large SOEs and public agencies that had a combined net worth of RMB 28 trillion in 2013 (Tables 3.8 and 3.9).

TABLE 3.8 Balance sheet of the central government – China vs. U.S, 2007 and 2011.

	China				U.S.		
	RMB TN 2007	RMB TN 2011	% GDP 2011	% Total assets 2011	US$ TN 2011	% GDP 2011	% Total assets 2011
Total assets	14	26	55	100	4	23	100
Non-financial assets	2	3	6	11	2	14	62
Structures	2	3	6	11	1	9	40
Financial assets	12	23	48	89	1	9	38
Currency and deposits	2	1	3	5	0	1	4
Currency and transferable deposits	1	1	3	5	0	1	2
Securities and investment fund shares	11	21	45	83	0	1	3
SOE equity	9	17	36	67	0	0	2
Equity in institutions	2	3	7	13	n/a	n/a	n/a
Securities held by pension	0	0	1	1	n/a	n/a	n/a
Equity investment under public–private inv. program	0	1	1	2	0	0	0
Total liabilities and net worth	14	26	55	100	4	23	100
Liabilities	6	8	16	30	12	79	349
Debt securities	5	7	15	28	12	75	332
Treasury securities inc. savings bonds	5	7	15	28	10	67	297
Net worth	8	18	38	70	–9	–56	–249

Data sources: Li et al. 2015, FRB 2014, authors' calculations.

In the national balance sheet computations, SOEs were technically classified in the non-financial enterprises sector and the financial sector because of their dominant role in the economy. Implicitly, the state has the controlling power to dispose of the assets of SOEs as well as the responsibility to ensure a timely payback of the liabilities of SOEs, so

TABLE 3.9 Balance sheet of China's central government, 2013 and 2014.

	China			
	RMB TN 2013	% GDP 2013	%Total assets 2013	RMB TN 2014e
Total assets	45	80	100	51
Non-financial assets	11	19	23	12
Fixed assets	7	13	16	8
Ongoing projects	2	3	4	2
Inventories	0	1	1	1
Intangibles	1	2	2	1
Financial assets	35	61	77	38
Currency	3	5	6	3
Receivables	3	4	6	2
Investments	29	52	65	33
Non-financial SOE equity	12	20	26	13
Financial SOE equity	5	9	11	6
PBOC equity	0	0	0	0
Pension funds	1	2	2	0
Total liabilities and net worth	45	80	100	51
Liabilities	21	38	47	24
Borrowings	2	3	3	2
Payables	3	4	6	3
Bonds	9	15	19	10
Foreign debts	0	0	0	0
Net worth	24	42	53	27

Source: Li et al. (2015); authors' calculations.

a complete government balance sheet should also incorporate its investments in SOEs and reflect the stake and risks assumed by the government.

In the government balance sheet by CASS, the SOE investment was incorporated with the equity method under the standard accounting treatment. The same method was also applied to local government balance sheets for its incorporation of the local SOEs and local government financing platforms. It should be noted that following the methodology of the CASS study, the balance sheet of the central government did not include the gross assets and liabilities of SOEs controlled by the State-owned Assets Supervision and Administration Commission of the State Council (SASAC), which is classified under the non-financial enterprises sector instead. However, there is some ambiguity about the extent of the government's responsibility (if any) in the event of an SOE bankruptcy. As some backup by the government for the debt problems of SOEs is still expected by the market, the liability numbers here may be underestimated by the potential or contingent obligations. It is important that this issue of quasi-fiscal liability should be clarified in the reform of SOEs.

On the other hand, the bulk of central government liabilities are treasury securities, amounting to RMB 7 trillion or 15 percent of GDP. Taken together, the Chinese central government had net assets equivalent to 38 percent of GDP, compared with the U.S. federal government, which had a gross debt equivalent to 79 percent of GDP, with negative net assets of US$9 trillion or 56 percent of GDP.

It should also be noted that the central government net asset calculations do not include unfunded pension liabilities of Chinese citizens, which are subject to wide measurement errors, due to the uncertainty of longevity and size of pensions to be provided. These complexities of estimation are discussed specifically in Chapter 15 of the CASS National Balance Sheet study.

3.4.5 Local Government

By tradition, local governments from the rural county to provincial level hold the bulk of state-owned real assets in China, primarily because the state is legally the owner of all land and natural resources. The private sector only has user rights on land that are leases from the state and subject to expiry and renewal. In addition, local governments also own the net assets of local SOEs equivalent to RMB 19 trillion at the end of 2013. The total assets held by local governments accounted for 172 percent of GDP in China, whereas those held by U.S. state and local governments were 75 percent of GDP (Table 3.10).

TABLE 3.10 Balance sheet of local governments – China vs. U.S., 2007 and 2011.

	China				U.S.		
	RMB TN 2007	RMB TN 2011	% GDP 2011	% Total assets 2011	US$ TN 2011	% GDP 2011	% Total assets 2011
Total assets	50	90	190	100	11	72	100
Local SOE assets	13	29	62	32	n/a	n/a	n/a
Local state-owned non-corporate assets	4	7	15	8	n/a	n/a	n/a
Resources held by local govt.	31	52	110	58	n/a	n/a	n/a
Deposits at central bank	1	2	4	2	n/a	n/a	n/a
Liabilities	14	29	61	32	4	24	33
Direct explicit liabilities	0	1	2	1	n/a	n/a	n/a
Local govt. bonds	n/a	1	1	1	n/a	n/a	n/a
Municipal sovereign debts	0	0	1	0	n/a	n/a	n/a
Direct implicit liabilities	2	2	5	3	n/a	n/a	n/a
Contingent explicit liabilities	3	16	33	18	n/a	n/a	n/a
Debts guaranteed by local govt.	1	2	5	3	n/a	n/a	n/a

(continued)

TABLE 3.10 (*Continued*)

	China				U.S.		
	RMB TN 2007	RMB TN 2011	% GDP 2011	%Total assets 2011	US$ TN 2011	% GDP 2011	%Total assets 2011
Local public debts	2	13	28	15	n/a	n/a	n/a
Debts of local public institutions	1	2	4	2	n/a	n/a	n/a
Debts of LGFPs	1	11	24	13	n/a	n/a	n/a
Contingent implicit liabilities	9	10	20	11	n/a	n/a	n/a
Local financial institution NPLs	1	1	1	1	n/a	n/a	n/a
Local SOE debts	8	9	19	10	n/a	n/a	n/a
Net assets	36	61	129	68	8	48	67

Data sources: Li et al. 2015, FRB 2015, author analysis.

Chinese local government funding has a structural problem as it relies heavily on revenues from land and property sales, or 35 percent of revenue (Zhang and Shi, 2015) (Table 3.11). However, this created a perverse situation in which it has become more profitable for local governments to push development of high priced land and real estate in order to generate revenue. This generated a pro-cyclical rise in property prices and made residential property unaffordable for young workers and the lower income groups.

Until very recently, the central government tightly controlled the issue or incurrence of direct bank or bond debts by local governments. To circumvent this, local governments created local government financing platforms (LGPFs), essentially shell companies, to borrow from the banks and shadow banks to invest in infrastructure projects, such as toll roads and new development zones.

Although earlier liabilities of local governments were mostly with local government SOEs, more recent local government debt was accumulated through LGFPs. The debts of LGFPs were only RMB 1 trillion in 2007, but rose rapidly to RMB 11 trillion by the end of 2011. An audit by the National Audit Office revealed that not all such LGFP debts are explicitly acknowledged as the obligations of the local government. Since Chinese local governments have a net wealth of RMB 70 trillion, while their total liabilities are RMB 28 trillion in 2013, they should have sufficient solvency cushion to service their debt. From the fiscal flow perspective, annual fiscal revenue for local governments was RMB 11.7 trillion in 2013, equivalent to 40 percent of total liabilities stock, while the fiscal expenditure was RMB 12.1 trillion. In individual cases, some local governments may run into difficulties, but this could be sorted out with central government assistance.

In December 2013, the National Audit Office released an updated report entitled *Audit Findings on China's Local Governmental Debts,* which surveyed the local government debt position as of June 2013. According to their extensive investigations, the total debt of local governments amounted to RMB 18 trillion as of June 2013, compared with RMB 11 trillion at the end of 2011 (Table 3.12). Despite this increase in local government debt, however, debt servicing should remain manageable for the first- and second-tier cities, but third- and fourth-tier cities may have a problem. This will be solved on a case-by-case basis with help from the central government.

TABLE 3.11 Balance sheet of local governments – China vs. U.S., 2013 and 2014.

	China				US		
	RMB TN 2013	% GDP 2013	% Total assets 2013	RMB TN 2014e	USD TN 2013	% GDP 2013	% Total assets 2013
Total assets	98	172	100	108	13	75	100
Currency	4	7	4	5	0	3	3
Investments	20	35	20	25	0	2	3
Of which: SOE equity	19	34	20	25	n/a	n/a	n/a
Fixed assets	6	11	6	7	0	1	2
Ongoing projects	1	2	1	2	n/a	n/a	n/a
Inventories	0	1	0	0	n/a	n/a	n/a
Receivables	3	6	3	4	0	2	3
Land	62	109	64	65	n/a	n/a	n/a
Intangibles	0	0	0	0	0	1	1
Other	0	1	0	1	n/a	n/a	n/a
Total liabilities and net worth	98	172	100	108	13	75	100
Liabilities	28	48	28	30	5	31	41
Borrowings	14	25	15	15	0	0	0

Of which: Loans by LGFPs	10	17	10	10	n/a	n/a	n/a
Infrastructure trust loans	3	5	3	3	n/a	n/a	n/a
Insurance investments in infrastructure	0	1	0	0	n/a	n/a	n/a
Local government sovereign foreign debts	0	1	0	0	n/a	n/a	n/a
Bonds	4	7	4	5	3	17	23
Payables	3	6	3	4	1	5	6
Guaranteed debts	3	5	3	3	n/a	n/a	n/a
Bank NPLs	1	1	1	1	n/a	n/a	n/a
Pension liabilities	3	4	3	3	1	8	11
Other	0	0	0	0	n/a	n/a	n/a
Net worth	70	123	72	78	8	45	59

Data sources: Li et al. 2015, FRB 2014, authors' calculations.

TABLE 3.12 Channels of local government debt, June 2013.

RMB TN	Debt for which govt. has repayment responsibility	Debt guaranteed by govt.	Other relevant debt (govt. may rescue)
LGFPs	4.1	0.9	2.0
Govt. departments and institutions	3.1	1.0	0.0
Institutions with govt. subsidies	1.8	0.1	0.5
Govt-owned/ controlled corporations	1.2	0.6	1.4
Independent institutions	0.3	0.0	0.2
Public institutions	0.1	0.1	0.0
Others	0.3	0.0	0.2
Total	10.9	2.7	4.3

Source: NAO (2013).

3.4.6 Financial Sector

The total assets of the financial sector at the end of 2013 were RMB 123 trillion (US$20 trillion) or 215 percent of GDP, compared with U.S. financial assets of US$83 trillion or 492 percent of GDP (Table 3.13). As mentioned earlier, the distinctive feature of the Chinese financial sector was its high level of holdings of foreign assets and an overreliance on the banking system, which meant a fundamental maturity mismatch. There is also a capital structure mismatch, with high leverage in the non-financial corporate sector, especially private SMEs and non-bank financial intermediaries (shadow banks) relative to their risks.

In 2000, the Chinese banking sector had a negative capital of RMB 1 trillion, due to the legacy of non-performing loans to SOEs and local governments (Li et al., 2013, 119). After major reforms in the banking and SOE sectors in the first decade of the 21st century, the banking sector became much better capitalized with low levels of NPLs. The financial

TABLE 3.13 Balance sheet of the financial sector – China vs. U.S., 2007 and 2013

	China				US		
	RMB TN 2007	RMB TN 2013	% GDP 2013	% Total assets 2013	USD TN 2013	% GDP 2013	% Total assets 2013
Total assets	47	123	215	100	83	492	100
Loans	26	72	127	59	22	133	27
Securities and investments	8	21	38	18	45	266	54
FX	13	29	51	24	n/a	n/a	n/a
Total liabilities and equity	47	123	215	100	83	492	100
Deposits	39	104	183	85	16	94	19
Debt securities	1	1	1	1	13	77	16
Currency	3	6	10	5	n/a	n/a	n/a
Insurance reserve	2	5	9	4	23	137	28
Paid in capital	2	4	7	3	n/a	n/a	n/a
Net other	0	1	2	1	−1	−3	−1

Data sources: Li et al. 2015, FRB 2014, authors' calculations.

system is still largely dominated by the banking sector, as 85 percent of the total liabilities are bank deposits. Loans comprised RMB 72 trillion or 127 percent of GDP, in ratio terms slightly smaller than loans of US$22 trillion or 133 percent of GDP in the U.S.

What is distinctive is the high proportion of FX assets in the China financial sector, comprising RMB 29 trillion or 51 percent of GDP, compared with only a negligible amount for the U.S.

The national balance sheet data for 2011 may not have fully captured the size of the emerging shadow banking assets. There is also a slight difference in measurement of the size of the financial sector between the People's Bank of China (PBOC) and the China Banking Regulatory Commission (CBRC). The difference, mainly accounted for by the different non-bank financial intermediaries included within the scope of the financial sector, amounted to RMB 5 trillion or 9 percent of GDP in 2013 (Table 3.14). The PBOC and CBRC estimates were also much smaller than the market-estimated size of shadow banking.

As discussed in detail in Chapter 4, the market estimated size of shadow banking ranges from RMB 23 trillion (ANZ) to RMB 36 trillion (JPMorgan). This wide range in estimation arose because there are definitional differences and also some double counting and underreporting. As wealth management products (WMPs) reflect the liability side of

TABLE 3.14 Alternative estimation of the size of shadow banking.

		2007		2011		2013	
		RMB TN	**% GDP**	**RMB TN**	**% GDP**	**RMB TN**	**% GDP**
PBOC measure	**Total assets of other depository corporations**	54	203	114	241	153	268
CBRC measure	**Total assets of banking institutions excl. non-bank financial institutions**	52	196	111	234	147	259
	Difference in size	2	7	3	7	5	9

Source: PBOC (2014); CBRC (2013); authors' calculations.

the financial sector, and trust loans and entrusted loans reflect the asset side, simply summing up the asset size of different shadow banking institutions would lead to an overestimation of the size of risks in shadow banking activities.

There are three types of errors giving rise to confusion in the size estimation. The first type of error is double counting if the underlying asset (of loans or securitized assets) is counted in both the bank and shadow bank balance sheets, or counted twice in two different shadow banks. The second type of error is double underreporting, if both underlying asset and corresponding liability are reported below the line for both shadow bank and bank entities. The third reporting error is inter-enterprise credit, which is not included in shadow bank credit, but where credit defaults of one corporate borrower could lead to default to banks or shadow banks because of the inter-enterprise debt chain.

Such errors can only be sorted out with the adoption of a unique Legal Entity Identifier (LEI) initiative (FSB, 2012), assigning any asset or liability to the correct legal entity. This will also avoid cases where one entity borrows from different banks/lenders using different names, resulting in ambiguity as to the true extent of its leverage.

To put the above exposures in perspective, total loans of the financial sector amounted to RMB 72 trillion or only 59 percent of the assets of the financial system. A further 24 percent comprised foreign exchange assets (equivalent to lending to foreigners, but mostly held as FX reserves). Another 18 percent was in bonds and other securities (Table 3.13). In other words, the asset side of the financial sector in China is relatively simple, with 100 percent of assets in three categories – loans, FX assets and bonds/other securities.

On the liabilities or funding side, bank deposits accounted for RMB 104 trillion or 85 percent of the financial liabilities, and currency in circulation represented another RMB 6 trillion or 5 percent of total financial liabilities.

As indicated above, loans to the household and central government sectors have little risk due to the high household savings and low sovereign risk/low debt of the central government. The local government debt is essentially sovereign risk and local governments should have both the net assets and revenue (with reforms in tax revenue sharing with the central government) to deal with their rise in local government debt.

This leaves the credit exposure risk largely with the non-financial corporate sector. An examination of the balance sheet of the commercial banking sector revealed the risks shown in Table 3.15.

TABLE 3.15 China banking system credit risk.

	2007	2008	2009	2010	2011	2012	2013	2014
Total Assets	54	64	81	96	114	134	152	172
Claims on Central Government (ctr govt. bond)	3	3	4	4	5	6	6	7
Reserve Assets (cash in vault+deposits with PBOC)	7	9	10	14	17	20	21	23
Claims on Central Bank (PBOC bills)	4	4	5	4	2	1	1	1
Total sovereign backed assets	14	17	20	22	25	27	28	31
Assets "at risk"	40	47	61	74	89	107	124	141
Total liabilities	54	64	81	96	114	134	152	172
Core capital*	n/a	n/a	n/a	4.3	5.3	6.4	7.6	9.1
Total capital (core + supplementary)*	n/a	n/a	n/a	5.3	6.3	8.2	9.9	11.3
Core capital/"asset at risk" (%)	n/a	n/a	n/a	5.8	6.0	6.0	6.1	6.4
CAR (%)	8.4	12.0	11.4	12.2	12.7	13.3	12.2	13.2
NPL balance	1.3	0.6	0.5	0.4	0.4	0.5	0.6	0.8
NPL ratio (%)	6.1	2.4	1.6	1.1	1.0	1.0	1.0	1.2
Provisions	0.6	0.8	0.9	1.0	1.3	1.5	1.8	2.1

Note: *In 2013, CBRC started the implementation of the new measures for the capital of commercial banks. The core capital was replaced by net core tier-one capital, while total capital was replaced by net capital for 2013 and 2014.
Source: PBOC, CBRC, authors' calculations.

At the end of 2014, the commercial banks had total assets of RMB 172 trillion. Out of this, RMB 31 trillion or 18 percent are high quality, almost risk-free assets, being central government bonds, or deposits and statutory reserves with the central bank.

Out of the balance of risk assets of RMB 141 trillion, RMB 8 trillion comprised residential mortgages, which are considered safe (as discussed in section 3.4.2). Of the remainder, RMB 10 trillion comprised LGFP debts, which have some form of government backing. Two-thirds of the remainder was extended as loans to SOEs, which are quasi-government debt. Thus, the area of concentration of risk exposure lies in lending to the private sector, which amounted to RMB 43 trillion of their loan book.

Assuming that the state will provide some form of assistance to the resolution of credit problems of SOEs and LGFPs, the amount of capital and provisions against NPLs of the Chinese banks amounted to RMB 13.4 trillion, approximately 10 percent of total risk assets (less sovereign debt status assets) or 31 percent of private sector debt.

Since Chinese banks are still amongst the most profitable in the world, with a net interest margin of 5 percent in 2012 (Xu et al., 2013), there is sufficient domestic savings and fiscal space, including current profits, to deal with the system-wide credit risks. However, some individual banks or shadow banks could suffer from high concentration of high-risk assets and would require recapitalization or restructuring. Implementation of the recently announced deposit insurance scheme will help in the resolution of such problem financial institutions.

3.4.6.1 Central Bank

The PBOC is unique amongst large country central banks to have a balance sheet that comprises mostly foreign exchange assets. The bulk or 83 percent of the central bank's assets are foreign exchange assets (Table 3.16). Indeed, the central bank held RMB 32 trillion in assets at the end of 2013, equivalent to 26 percent of total financial sector assets or 56 percent of GDP. In terms of liabilities, the bulk comprised reserve money of RMB 27 trillion, of which RMB 6 trillion was currency in circulation, with RMB 21 trillion being deposits and statutory reserve requirements of banks and financial institutions. A further RMB 3 trillion comprised deposits of the central and local governments.

The combined balance sheets of the financial sector and the central bank revealed a structural "tightness" in liquidity within China that presented a unique challenge to the exercise of monetary policy, particularly in recent years. Between 2007 and 2013, China's money supply increased by 116 percent, whereas its foreign exchange reserves grew by

TABLE 3.16 Balance sheet of the People's Bank of China

Items	RMB TN 2007	RMB TN 2013	% GDP 2013	%total assets 2013
Foreign Assets	12	27	48	86
Foreign Exchange	12	26	46	83
Monetary Gold	0	0	0	0
Other Foreign Assets	1	1	1	2
Claims on Government	2	2	3	5
Of Which: Central Government	2	2	3	5
Claims on Other Depository Corporations	1	1	2	4
Claims on Other Financial Corporations	1	1	2	3
Claims on Non-financial Corporations	0	0	0	0
Other Assets	1	1	1	2
Total Assets	17	32	56	100
Reserve Money	10	27	48	85
Currency Issue	3	6	11	20
Deposits of Other Depository Corporations	7	21	36	65
Deposits of Financial Corporations Excluded From Reserve Money	0	0	0	0
Bond Issue	3	1	1	2
Foreign Liabilities	0	0	0	1
Deposits of Government	2	3	5	9
Own Capital	0	0	0	0
Other Liabilities	1	1	1	2
Total Liabilities	17	32	56	100

Source: Li et al. (2013); authors' calculations/

129 percent. The excess monetary creation was mopped up through statutory reserve requirements amounting to as much as 20 percent of bank deposits.

Seen from this perspective, China's financial system has lent out nearly 30 percent of its assets to foreigners, whereas the bulk of its savings are domestic savings, largely by households and corporations. The corporate sector and the government sector are large investors in fixed assets and inventory, and their funding has relied largely on the banking system. But since 30 percent of assets of the financial system are locked into foreign exchange reserves, the corporate sector is structurally "short" of liquidity. Furthermore, the corporate sector lends to itself in terms of inter-enterprise liabilities of RMB 51 trillion, larger even than the RMB 39 trillion borrowed from the banking system.

During the period when monetary and credit policy was loose due to China's RMB 4 trillion stimulus package, Chinese enterprises had little problem with liquidity as there was considerable credit creation through bank lending. However, once the central bank started tightening, the shadow banks emerged to borrow from banks (for on-lending to Chinese enterprises) through WMPs that were collateralized by either bank loans, shadow bank loans or corporate debt.

Thus monetary policy in China is today exercised through the release of the high statutory reserves kept with the central bank. As the balance of payments account is now broadly in balance, the impetus for monetary creation from increases in FX reserves becomes less of an issue. Selective release of liquidity by the central bank has the effect of ensuring that banks do not overly depend on foreign borrowing, which could push interest rates beyond usurious levels.

3.4.6.2 Insurance Companies and Securities Houses

In comparison with the commercial banks, the non-bank financial intermediaries (NBFIs) are not well developed in China. The total assets of the insurance companies amounted to only RMB 4.7 trillion, comprising mainly bonds (RMB 1 trillion), stocks (RMB 3 trillion) and miscellaneous assets. Securities companies, with assets of RMB 1.9 trillion, are even smaller in size in China, reflecting the lack of depth of the securities markets (Li et al., 2015, 113). With long-term institutional funds and asset managers lacking size and depth, it is not surprising also that enterprises in China rely more on debt rather than equity to fund their long-term investments.

3.5 SHADOW BANKS WITHIN THE NATIONAL BALANCE SHEET

The CASS study also faced considerable difficulties with the definition and compilation of data on China's shadow banks. They noted that estimates of its size ranged from official projections of RMB 15 trillion (29 percent of GDP) to market estimates of RMB 21 trillion (40 percent of GDP) at the end of 2012. Given these disparities, the CASS study cautioned against putting too much faith in these estimates, where accuracy could be affected by definitional differences, double counting and errors and omissions. Their best estimates were a size of RMB 13 trillion, or 25 percent of GDP and 14 percent of the total assets of the financial system.

3.6 EVALUATION OF THE NATIONAL BALANCE SHEET APPROACH

The development and compilation of national balance sheets in emerging markets is still at an early stage. In China, this is also a work in progress, and the CASS recognized that much remains to be done to improve the data estimation and identification of the gaps in coverage and analysis.

For example, the CASS report devoted special sections to examine the estimation of unrecorded retirement benefits and contingent debts in the national balance sheet. A further section studied the difficulties and problems encountered in the measurement and estimation of the residential property sector. The estimates showed that Chinese household residential property valuations and income affordability ratios were considerably higher than those in even some advanced countries. This was due to the low-income levels of Chinese households. Particular difficulties were encountered in the estimation of residential value of rural households. This was based on the estimated size of rural residential housing multiplied by the average price, estimated from the rural household surveys (see Li et al., 2013, Chapters 15 and 16).

Despite these deficiencies, the CASS study revealed that national balance sheets are vital and helpful in identifying potential risks within the financial and real sectors in three areas. First, the accounts helped identify three mismatches – currency mismatch, maturity mismatch and capital structure mismatch. The second benefit is the ability to identify trends and patterns in shifts of risks between sectors; particularly vulnerabilities within each sector and how these are transmitted through different channels (products, institutions and geographically). The third benefit is the identification of emerging medium and long-term trends (see Li et al., 2013, Chapter 6).

As explained earlier, the Chinese economy does not have a large currency mismatch, because it is a net lender to the foreign sector. The country is not likely to face a foreign currency crisis due to its high level of foreign exchange reserves and with minimal foreign exposure in shadow banking activities, any shadow bank crisis is unlikely to be globally systemic, unless it harms China's long-term growth that will affect the rest of the world through the trade, investment and other channels.

The national balance sheet revealed that China is exposed to both maturity and capital structure mismatches. The system is too reliant on the banking system and on short-term funding of long-term investments. To address this maturity mismatch, development of long-term institutional investors, such as pension and insurance funds, as well as municipal and secondary mortgage markets is becoming more urgent.

Furthermore, the fundamental capital structural mismatch is serious, with the system being overreliant on debt and not enough on equity. Between 2008 and 2013, only 3 percent of the total social financing comprised IPO funds for the corporate sector; the rest was raised through bank loans or debt. This showed that the private sector has inadequate channels for raising capital through the official financial system (stock market).

The capital market must be reformed to increase equity funding for SMEs and for innovation. Similarly, the development of institutional investors, such as pension and insurance funds, asset managers and private equity funds and the related market infrastructure is also urgently needed. In this regard, the creation of the New Third Board in China[7] is helpful, but this needs to be broadened, as currently only 2,800 enterprises are listed, whereas there are over 40 million registered businesses in China.

The second advantage in using national balance sheets is the identification of risk-shifts within the system as a whole. As explained earlier, there is a distinct trend of moral hazard appearing in shadow banking activities, with the private sector investors and borrowers

---

[7]The Chinese National Equities Exchange and Quotations, commonly known as the New Third Board, is a small, market-driven stock exchange, launched in 2006.

shifting their risks under the umbrella of state "insurance" through a variety of means. If private enterprises are short of funding, they can borrow through SOEs in the form of inter-enterprise liabilities or inter-enterprise guarantees, so that credit losses are passed to the state sector. In addition, retail investors treat WMPs sold by banks as quasi-deposits, which fall under the implicit deposit insurance coverage, meaning that default risks should be absorbed by the banks or the state. All these mean lack of clarity of property rights and liabilities.

The third area is the identification of medium- and long-term risks. As an emerging country, China faces a unique set of challenges over the medium and long term. These include the structural slowdown in the economy, population aging and the need for medicare and pension protection, RMB internationalization, the shift to a more inclusive and green economy, advancement into a service-oriented economy, etc. The national balance sheet approach provides policy makers with a more comprehensive tool to examine the interrelationships between the different sectors and how reform efforts would affect the various sectors in different ways. It is clear that there are large externalities in reform measures and therefore unintended consequences through these linkages. Indeed, the national and sectoral balance sheets enable the authorities to model the impact of different policy measures on different sectors. This improves the analytical quality as well as pushes for the refinement of data quality and more sectoral and regional compilations of data.

The national balance sheet approach also identified specific areas of risk that would require more research and policy attention. The first area of vulnerability is to assess the implications of asset price developments. China is fortunate that its stock market was for most of 2010 to 2014 at a historical low, so that there is less risk of a stock market bubble on top of a real estate bubble in parts of the country.

In terms of bank loans to real estate relative to total loans, the regulators have been careful to control the ratio within the 20 percent level. The average loan-to-value ratio has been kept at around 70 percent, which means that bank loans can absorb up to a 30 percent fall in asset value before risks of default arise.

Real estate, however, forms the bulk of collateral for other forms of lending. For example, according to the National Audit Office examination of local government debt, 38 percent of loans are based on land as collateral or on the prospect of land sales. The CASS study considered that as the total real estate value to GDP ratio in China is within the range experienced in more advanced countries, at roughly twice GDP, and that the current leverage problem lies in the corporate sector and local government sector, rather than in households and the central government, the risks are still manageable.

The second area of exposure in the medium term is the social security funding gap. Unfunded pension and social security liabilities are becoming a serious problem in aging advanced economies, particularly Japan, Europe and also the U.S. The pension funding gap for the Chinese urban population was estimated at RMB 2 trillion at the end of 2011 (Zheng, 2012). The real risk is difficult to estimate due to uncertainties in the size of benefits, the longevity risk and the actuarial methodologies used. CASS estimated that the retirement benefits in China amounted to 3 percent of GDP in 2010, at the lower level of emerging market benefits, and considerably lower than the Organisation for Economic Cooperation and Development (OECD) average of 8 percent. In aging advanced countries like Italy, Japan and U.S., they are as high as 15, 10 and 7 percent respectively. By 2050, the retirement benefits in China may reach as high as 12 percent of GDP. Clearly, considerable policy efforts will have to be made to ensure that the rapidly aging population in China is provided with sufficient retirement income and welfare benefits. This important issue is outside the scope of this book.

Whilst the national balance sheet approach revealed that the domestic or foreign solvency risks for the Chinese economy (other than high leverage in the corporate sector) are manageable because of the strong growth, high domestic savings and ample foreign exchange assets, the liquidity risks require skillful balancing.

Advanced countries with reserve currency status do not have solvency problems because they can borrow and devalue their currencies through quantitative easing. Liquidity provision by central banks at low interest rates ensures that the system is kept afloat with maturing debt being rolled over.

Smaller emerging market economies (EMEs) have both liquidity and solvency risks because they normally do not have sufficient foreign exchange assets to defend their exchange rate and if they engage in quantitative easing, domestic capital flight is possible if exchange rate devaluation leads to panic among domestic savers.

After the Asian financial crisis and the experience of the Japanese economy, China built up strong foreign exchange reserves and has been cautious in its capital account liberalization precisely to avoid such risks.

As former FSA Chairman Adair Turner has identified, however, a vicious circle of high real interest rates, deflating asset prices, tight liquidity and sudden exits was part of the reason why the Asian financial crisis (1997–1999) and the Great Recession (2007–2009) were precipitated (Turner, 2011). An EME central bank cannot totally control the emergence of high real interest rates when the system is over-leveraged at both domestic and foreign currency levels.

China has ample domestic savings and is a net lender to the rest of the world. However, it is unique in having substantial domestic savings "locked" into lending to the foreign sector, since the PBOC has imposed high reserve requirements of up to 20 percent of bank deposits in order to fund its holdings of foreign exchange reserves. Thus domestic liquidity is structurally constrained within China and the PBOC can unwind such liquidity through reducing the level of reserve requirements. It has been reluctant to do so for fear of sparking off inflation and imprudent lending by banks to fund speculative assets.

In other words, the management of liquidity in China is largely within the control of its central bank because it can judiciously release liquidity to avoid the sudden real interest rate spikes identified by Turner without sparking off a foreign exchange crisis. As the RMB becomes more internationalized and more flexible, the use of such monetary tools becomes more sophisticated. However, there is fear that further opening of the capital account would either lead to uncontrolled inflows of capital or sudden outflows that undermine domestic monetary policy.

The bottom line is that because of high domestic savings, relatively low central government debt and high external reserves, China has the fiscal and monetary space to manage its liquidity challenges, including those emanating from the shadow banking sector.

3.7 BASIC ANALYTICAL CONCLUSIONS AND POLICY RECOMMENDATIONS FROM THE NBS APPROACH

It may be useful to summarize some of the tentative conclusions and policy recommendations of the CASS studies in 2013 and 2015.

Firstly, the rapid development of the economy between 2007 and 2013 threw into focus the overuse of investment in infrastructure as a means of stimulating growth, which in the long term is unsustainable and creates funding and financial risks. This strategy relies on a government-led investment model that is overreliant on debt that creates systemic risks in a banking system with a structural maturity mismatch.

Secondly, the above strategy accentuates the role of the state in economic activities, particularly the role of SOEs, LGFPs, central bank and state-owned financial institutions. This raises the question of the sustainability of China's sovereign debt over the long term. As long as the growth rate in sovereign debt matches that of China's GDP growth, the debt level will be stable. But if debt grows substantially faster as real interest rates rise, the same problem of sovereign debt sustainability as experienced in Europe will arise.

Thirdly, the major source of the Chinese government's net assets is its equity holdings in SOEs. Excluding its SOE equity holdings, the net assets of the central government would drop from RMB 15.1 trillion to RMB 2.3 trillion. Given the important role of SOEs in contributing to the overall wealth of the central government, any SOE reforms should therefore be handled carefully.

Fourthly, the overall national debt to GDP ratio must also be closely monitored. At the end of 2014, China's non-financial corporate debt to GDP ratio had already reached 123 percent of GDP, higher than the Organisation for Economic Cooperation and Development (OECD) average of 90 percent of GDP (Li et al., 2015, 40). Although the household debt level remained low, it is the rapid growth in enterprise debt and local government debt that needs policy attention.

Fifthly, while the leverage of the whole non-financial corporate sector has increased steadily, the leverage of industrial enterprises remained flat, or declined slightly. This means the leverage accumulation is significant in the service sector, which is becoming an increasingly important contributor to China's economy. Historically, all financial crises had been related to debt crises. The full implications of the higher leverage in the service sector should be carefully studied.

In addressing the above issues, therefore, the first policy recommendation is to address the structural mismatches in the economy, including the maturity mismatch.

The second policy recommendation is to reduce the role of the state in economic activities by increasing the role of the market, particularly in reducing the resource allocation mismatches and reducing the debt/equity imbalance.

The third policy recommendation is to address directly the debt/ equity mismatch in the system, particularly reducing the overreliance on the banking system.

The fourth policy recommendation is to reduce the income disparities, including improving income transfers through the social security reforms.

The fifth policy recommendation is to address, control and manage the property market risks. These include the fiscal revenue sharing reforms that are currently being considered.

Last but not least is the need to deleverage the non-financial corporate sector and the local governments. China's household sector and central government still have the room to maneuver, as their leverage remains low. Based on this structure, one feasible policy direction is to adjust and transfer the leverage risk from the highly leveraged sectors to the ones with less leverage. The local debt–equity swap that is being carried out is an example of such a policy.

In summary, a structural and holistic analysis of the Chinese economy using the NBS approach helps to give a more comprehensive, integrated and more nuanced analysis of structural trends and interrelationships within an economy and between the different sectors.

Having a holistic picture and better quality information for analytical and policy formulation means that shadow banking must be examined in terms of its relationship with not only the formal financial sector, but also its interactivity with the real sector and subsectors.

These issues will be addressed in the following chapters.

REFERENCES

CBRC (China Banking Regulatory Commission). 2013. *Annual Report 2013*. Beijing: China CITIC Press. http://www.cbrc.gov.cn/chinese/home/docView/ 3C28C92AC84242D188E2064D9098CFD2.html.

FSB (Financial Stability Board). 2012. A Global Legal Entity Identifier for Financial Markets. http://www.financialstabilityboard.org/publications/r_ 120608.pdf.

IMF (International Monetary Fund). 2015. *Global Financial Stability Report*. April.

Li, Yang, Zhang Xiaojing, and Chang Xin. 2013. *China's National Balance Sheet 2013*. Beijing: China Social Sciences Press.

Li, Yang, Zhang Xiaojing, and Chang Xin. 2015. *China's National Balance Sheet 2015*. Beijing: China Social Sciences Press.

Mann, David, Chidambarathanu Narayanan, John Caparusso, and Prabhat Chandra. 2013. Asia Leverage Uncovered. Standard Chartered Scout Global Research, 1 July.

NAO, (National Audit Office of People's Republic of China). 2013. Audit Findings on China's Local Governmental Debts. http://www.audit.gov.cn/n1992130/n1992150/n1992500/n3432077.files/n3432112.pdf.

Natixis. 2015. China: The Struggle Between "Long-Termist" Economists and "Short-Termist" Policies. Flash Economics, Economic Research, 733, October 1.

PBOC (The People's Bank of China). 2014. Balance Sheet of Other Depository Corporations, July. http://www.pbc.gov.cn/publish/html/kuangjia.htm?id=2013s06.htm.

Rothman, Andy. 2014. China's Property Is Slowing, Not Crashing. *Financial Times,* 1 October. http://blogs.ft.com/beyond-brics/2014/10/01/guest-post-chinas-property-is-slowing-not-crashing/?hubRefSrc=permalink.

Sheng, Andrew, and Xiao Geng. 2014. China's Subprime Risks. *Project Syndicate,* 28 July. http://www.project-syndicate.org/commentary/andrew-sheng-and-geng-xiao-are-less-worried-about-the-volume-of-chinese-debt-than-they-are-about-the-allocation-of-credit.

Turner, Adair. 2011. Debt and Deleveraging: Long Term and Short Term Challenges. Presidential lecture, Centre for Financial Studies, Frankfurt, Financial Services Authority, 21 November.

U.S. Treasury. 2015. Foreign Holdings of U.S. Treasury Securities. 14 January. http://www.treasury.gov/ticdata/Publish/mfh.txt.

Wignaraja, Ganeshan, and Yothin Jinjarak. 2015. Why Do SMEs Not Borrow More from Banks? Evidence from the People's Republic of China and Southeast Asia. ADBI Working Paper, 509, Asian Development Bank Institute. January 2015.

Xu, Richard, Jocelyn M Yang, and Simon Mou. 2013. China Deleveraging – Can Banks Ride Out a Financial Storm? Morgan Stanley Research.

Zhang, Zhiwei, and Audrey Shi. 2015. China's Unexpected Fiscal Side. Deutsche Bank Research Special Report. 5 January.

Zheng, Bingwen, ed., 2012. *China Pension Report 2012.* Beijing: Economy & Management Publishing House.

CHAPTER 4

Shadow Banking with Chinese Characteristics

Wang Yao

4.1 INTRODUCTION

The earlier chapters in this book reviewed the international and national balance sheet within the context of the emergence of China's shadow banking. This chapter examines the definition of shadow banking in China, estimates its size, and looks at the implications for systemic stability.

There were essentially two major forces that created the conditions for the emergence of shadow banking in China.

The first was a genuine market demand for credit amid the stringent regulatory regime in the formal banking sector that inadvertently restricted access to bank credit, particularly for small and medium enterprises (SMEs). This arose under circumstances that were unique to China.

The second factor was the formal caps on bank deposit rates that motivated savers/investors to "search for yield," enabling non-bank financial intermediaries (NBFIs) to meet that demand through wealth management products (WMPs) and other innovations.

Because the definition of shadow banking in China is still under dispute, the size and estimation of the sector risks remain somewhat controversial.

There exists a wide range of estimations of the size of China's shadow banking industry, due to differences in definitions, classifications and methodologies (see Table 4.1).

Based on the People's Bank of China's (PBOC) definition and criteria by Yan and Li (2014),[1] the Fung Global Institute (FGI) estimates China's shadow banking at RMB 22.5 trillion (US$3.6 trillion) or 43.3 percent of GDP at the end of 2012. Our calculations show that shadow banks continued to expand to RMB 30.1 trillion (US$4.8 trillion) or 53 percent of GDP in 2013 and reached around RMB 32.2 trillion (US$5.2 trillion) or about 51 percent of GDP by the end of 2014.[2]

Our estimate encompasses trusts, banks' WMPs, entrusted loans, undiscounted banker's acceptance, trust products/loans, securities firms' asset management products (AMPs), microcredit companies, pawnshops, peer-to-peer (P2P) lending, financial guarantees, financial leasing, and private/informal lending, as shadow banking activities. It should be noted that the simple addition of different products and assets of shadow banking activities with specific characteristics inevitably introduces the element of double counting.

For example, WMPs of banks are often counted as "shadow banking" even though they are, strictly speaking, quasi-deposits that belong to the liability side of the balance sheet. They are linked with shadow banks because their underlying assets include assets packaged by shadow banks. Hence, the source of shadow banking funding is closely interlinked to the official banking sector.

It is the bundling of assets and risks that creates the lack of transparency and clarity of property rights arising from the shadow banks' activities. This chapter attempts to clarify these issues in order to assess the quality of shadow banks' underlying assets and its impact on the broader banking and financial system in China.

We must, however, put the problem in its proper context. By international standards, shadow banking in China is still relatively small and is essentially a domestic debt problem, as relatively few foreigners own Chinese WMPs. However, its rapid growth, lack of transparency and bundling of risks across shadow and commercial banks may lead to

---

[1]This is the most authoritative book on shadow banking in China as both authors were staff of the China Banking Regulatory Commission. Mr. Yan Qingmin was CBRC Vice Chairman. The book, available only in Chinese, was published in 2014.

[2]This latest estimate is based on PBOC's recently released data on stock of total social financing. Our earlier estimate – done in collaboration with OW – was RMB 31.2 trillion at the end of 2013.

liquidity and solvency issues for enterprises and financial institutions, which warrant closer policy attention.

The second point to remember is that the Chinese financial system is still largely state-owned with most credit exposure to state-owned enterprises and local government financing platforms. Essentially, shadow banking in China can best be understood as a moral hazard problem. To what extent should investors in the WMPs packaged by shadow banks be able to claim protection from risks of failure of the underlying assets from the implicit deposit insurance coverage of the banking system?

If WMPs, which are best understood as deposit substitutes, are covered under the implicit deposit insurance, then losses are borne by the state. If not, then underlying asset losses are borne by the investors. In the first instance, the question will be fiscal sustainability, as the state would cover the losses to the banking system. In the second case, the market will bear losses with little implications on the state.

In other words, it is not the growth of liabilities of the banks/shadow banks that matter so much as the quality of the assets of the banks/shadow banks. The system will suffer systemic risk if the quality of the assets deteriorates more than the capital of the financial system as a whole.

The third point to remember is that Chinese shadow banking is still fairly "plain vanilla" and not as sophisticated or highly leveraged as its counterparts in the advanced countries. Shadow banking in China has a geographical dimension, since certain cities and provinces have a higher degree of private enterprises that rely more on funding from shadow banking.

Are the shadow banking system risks so large and out of control that they pose the risk of crisis for the financial system as a whole?

Our bottom line is that the Chinese regulatory authorities understand these issues and have already initiated a number of policy measures to strengthen supervision to manage such risks.

Nevertheless, closer monitoring and management of shadow banking risks is urgently needed to preempt the build-up of shadow banking non-performing loans (NPLs) and contagion. To maintain economic and financial stability, providing the right level of liquidity and interest rate pricing would require a delicate balance between keeping aggregate demand at the appropriate level, without triggering off sharp asset price adjustments.

The recommendations for changes in policy, regulations and structure are discussed in Chapter 7.

4.2 NATURE AND SCALE OF SHADOW BANKING IN CHINA

The People's Bank of China (PBOC, 2013) officially defines shadow banking as credit intermediation involving entities and activities outside the regular banking system, with the functions of liquidity and credit transformation, which could potentially cause systemic risks or regulatory arbitrage.

A more comprehensive definition of shadow banking, issued by the State Council, classifies China's shadow banking into three categories (Sina Finance, 2014):[3]

1. Credit intermediaries that do not have financial licenses and are not subject to any regulations. Such credit intermediaries include the innovative internet financial companies, and the third-party financial institutions.
2. Credit intermediaries that do not have financial licenses and are subject to insufficient regulations. Such credit intermediaries include financing guarantee companies, and microcredit companies.
3. Credit intermediaries that hold financial licenses but are subject to insufficient regulation or regulatory arbitrage. Such credit intermediaries include money market funds, asset securitization and WMPs.

Based on PBOC's definition and Document 107's classification, Yan and Li (2014) summarized the common features of China's shadow banks and shadow banking activities as follows:

1. They involve liquidity transformation, or credit transformation, or high leverage. Shadow banks make use of low-interest, short-term funds, usually borrowed from the wholesale money market, and invest in long-term assets or projects to get higher returns.
2. They are subject to insufficient or no regulation and do not have access to the central bank's lender of last resort facility. Shadow banks are not subject to capital requirements, loan to deposit ratios or loan loss provisions.

---

[3]The document, "The Notice of Strengthening the Supervision of Shadow Banking" (Document 107) was only released to PBOC, CBRC, CSRC and CIRC, and is not publically available.

3. They have complicated structures/interlinkages with other financial institutions and commercial banks, and have the potential to cause systemic risks.

As most shadow banking activities are not subject to disclosure requirements, despite the official definition, there exist differences in assumptions, methodologies and classifications of shadow banking activities. So, it is not surprising that there are divergent estimates of the scale of shadow banking in China.

At the global level, the Financial Stability Board (FSB) estimated that Chinese shadow banking assets comprised US$2.1 trillion in 2012 or 3 percent of global shadow banking assets (FSB, 2013). In contrast, total global shadow banking assets in 2012 amounted to US$71 trillion, with the U.S. accounting for US$26 trillion (37 percent share), the eurozone for US$22 trillion (30 percent), and the United Kingdom for US$9 trillion (13 percent).

The IMF noted that shadow banks have become an important source of financing in China as a natural outcome of a reform process to diversify a bank-dominated financial system. Estimates of the size of non-bank credit outstanding (excluding bonds) vary, reflecting difficulties in measurement, a lack of disclosure and a large informal sector. Unofficial conservative estimates that cover only the formal sector range between 30–40 per cent of GDP, double the level in 2010 (IMF, 2014).

The China Banking Regulatory Commission (CBRC) reported that growth in shadow banking accelerated rapidly from RMB 800 billion (US$130 billion) in 2008 to RMB 7.6 trillion (US$1.2 trillion) or 14.6 percent of GDP in 2012 (Sheng and Xiao, 2013).

Total off-balance sheet banking activity in China – comprising credits to property developers (30–40 per cent), local-government entities (20–30 per cent), and small- and medium-size enterprises (SMEs), individuals, and bridge-loan borrowers – was estimated to be as high as RMB 17 trillion (US$2.7 trillion) in 2012, roughly one-third of GDP (Sheng and Xiao, 2013).

The Chinese Academy of Social Sciences (CASS), a premier government think tank, put the size of the sector – which covered all shadow-lending activities from WMPs and trusts to interbank business, finance leasing and private lending – at RMB 20.5 trillion (US$3.3 trillion) or 40 percent of GDP and one-fifth of the banking industry's total assets as at the end of 2012 (Aegon Industrial Fund Management, 2013).

TABLE 4.1 Shadow banking size in China – range of estimates at end-2012.

Institution	US$ trillion	% of GDP
FSB	2.1	25.6
IMF	2.5–3.3	30–40
CBRC	1.2	14.6
CASS	3.3	39.5
FGI	3.6	43.3
ANZ	3.7	45.1
Moody's	4.6	56.1
J.P. Morgan	5.8	70.1
RBS	4.7	57.3
S&P	4–5	48–61
Range	1.2–5.8	14–70

Note: # based on IMF's data of China's GDP of US$8.2 trillion in 2012.
Source: Official, media, and market sources.

Private sector estimates reveal a wider range, from ANZ's estimate of RMB 23 trillion (US$3.7 trillion or 45 percent of GDP) to JPMorgan's estimate of RMB 36 trillion (US$5.8 trillion or 70 percent of GDP) (Kawai, 2014; Bloomberg, 2013).

The different estimates of China's shadow banking size at the end of 2012 are listed in Table 4.1.

For 2013, UBS estimated that the size of China's shadow banking expanded to 50–70 percent of GDP, while RBS had a lower figure of 65 percent of GDP (Business Insider, 2014; Kawai, 2014).

To address the problem of different classifications and definitions, Yan and Li (2014) suggested three criteria for defining shadow banking activities:

1. It is a credit intermediary, or engaged in the business of credit intermediaries, but subject to insufficient or no regulation.
2. It has the characteristic of liquidity transformation, or high leverage ratio, or credit risk transformation.
3. It has the potential to cause systemic risk.

All three criteria need to be fulfilled for any financial institution or activity to be categorized as a shadow bank or shadow banking activity.

At the broadest level, definitions of shadow banking could include all the NBFIs' assets and activities, which covers trust companies, securities companies, insurance companies, leasing companies, guarantee companies, pawnshops, microcredit companies, Internet financing platforms, money market funds, WMPs, interbank assets, asset securitization, private lending and so on. However, not all of these activities satisfy all the three criteria proposed by Yan and Li (2014).

FGI has adopted the PBOC's definition of China's shadow banking activities, supplemented by the three criteria set out by Yan and Li (2014) to arrive at a more realistic estimate (as our focus is on systemic risks). Specifically, our estimate of the size of China's shadow banking sector encompasses the scale of trust companies, microcredit companies, pawnshops, private/informal lending, P2P Internet lending and guarantors, banks' WMPs and two kinds of interbank assets (entrusted loans and undiscounted banker's acceptances) (see Table 4.2).

The largest components of the shadow banking system comprise trust companies and banks' WMPs, both with the highest growth rates and highly correlated with each other. Trust companies rely mainly on commercial banks' distribution channels for fund raising and also package trust loans for funding in the interbank market. China's shadow banking activities are closely interlinked with commercial banks, which draw funds from banks (the major source of savings in the economy) to shadow banks to seek higher yields.

The high interrelationship between bank WMPs and trust companies means that there is an element of double counting in simply adding the two (bank WMPs and trust loans) together to arrive at the shadow banking exposure.

Although banks' off-balance sheet WMPs are a liability side item, risks arise from its underlying assets, most of which are de facto loans (issued by banks as well as other financial institutions (OFIs)) packaged by trust companies for banks.[4] By packaging such assets and keeping them off-balance sheet, banks can avoid capital requirements imposed on traditional bank loans. As we do not have detailed information on bank WMPs' underlying assets, the size of off-balance sheet WMPs is used as a proxy for shadow banking risk. Also, although the China Banking Regulatory Commission (CBRC) has imposed regulations on banks'

---

[4]Banks in China put their guaranteed WMP assets and liabilities fully on-balance sheet. Those that are not fully guaranteed are booked off-balance sheet. These are then counted as shadow banking risks.

TABLE 4.2 Rationale for FGI's shadow banking categorization.

Non-Bank Financial Institutions/ Business	Belongs to Shadow Banking?	Reasons
Credit assets of trust Companies	Yes	Subject to regulatory arbitrage, high leverage ratio, credit risk transformation, potential of systemic risks.
Financial Leasing	Yes	Business includes liquidity and term transformation. Regulatory arbitrage exists.
Financial Guarantee	Yes	Most of the guarantors are involved in the lending activities of shadow banks, such as trust, microcredit companies and P2P platforms. Have the potential of expanding credit and spreading risks.
Pawnshops	Yes	Non-bank credit intermediary, connected with banks. Although subject to approval of the Ministry of Commerce, effective supervision is limited.
Microcredit Companies	Yes	Non-bank credit intermediary, connected with banks. Regulatory arbitrage exists.
P2P Lending Platform	Yes	Non-bank credit intermediary, currently subject to little direct regulation. Have complicated lending structure and risks.
Money Market Funds	No	Low leverage, or liquidity transformation, and are subject to strict supervision.
Entrusted Loans	Yes	Loans removed from financial institutions' balance sheet and traded as interbank assets.
Undiscounted Bankers' Acceptances	Yes	Similar to banks' short term loans, but removed from banks' balance sheet and traded in interbank market.

TABLE 4.2 *Continued*

Non-Bank Financial Institutions/ Business	Belongs to Shadow Banking?	Reasons
Trust Loans	Yes	Loans made through bank-trust channel, kept off-balance sheet and traded in the interbank market.
Off-balance sheet Banks' WMPs	Yes	Involves loan assets, packaged, and sold to investors. Different from the above asset side measures, banks' WMP is a liability side measure, which may cause double counting with trust loans, and interbank assets.
Securities Companies' AMPs	Yes	Targeted asset management. Includes channel businesses.
Insurance Companies' AMPs	No	Do not involve liquidity transformation or high leverage; and are subject to CIRC supervision.
Asset Securitization	No	Restarted since 2012, still very small in scale.
Private Lending	Yes	The high interest rate portion is subject to high risk. Private lending can also transfer risks to commercial banks through a number of channels, such as credit card lending, commercial papers, and guarantee companies, etc.

Source: Yan and Li (2014), FGI analysis.

WMPs since March 2013, banks are always innovative in avoiding such regulations, as they did when CBRC regulated the bank–trust cooperation in 2010 (see discussion on bank–trust cooperation in section 4.3).

However, adding banks' WMPs to other shadow banking assets held by OFIs will certainly lead to double counting when banks package OFIs' assets, for example trust loans, as their off-balance sheet WMPs. If the trust company still reports the loan as a trust loan on their balance sheet, adding the two counts the same asset twice. On the other hand, if both treat the loan off-balance sheet, the loan does not appear anywhere (except as collateral for WMP owned by investors) and there is undercounting. Furthermore, undercounting will occur if the officially reported data had underestimated the scale of exposures.[5]

Unfortunately, there is no single authoritative data source on shadow banking activities, so our estimates are collected from different statistical reports, sources and agencies, some of which are also estimates. For example, PBOC's 2013 *Financial Stability Report* presented the most up-to-date overview on shadow banking in China, which included trust companies, banks' WMPs, microloan firms, P2P Internet lending platforms, guarantors, pawnshops, and informal/private lending. However, the PBOC report did not provide data on the size of all shadow banking sectors, as it focused on the size of microloan firms (RMB592.1 billion), and pawnshops (RMB 70.6 billion) at the end of 2012.

In January 2015, the PBOC published for the first time the stock numbers of total social financing (TSF), which included some of the balance sheet data of shadow bank assets. Previous data provided were only monthly or yearly flows. The official data implied that the total size of shadow banks was around RMB 33.2 trillion at the end of 2014. The estimates published by Oliver Wyman in January 2015 amounted to RMB 31.2 trillion at the end of 2013, based on earlier flow data of TSF released by PBOC (see Table 4.3) and including other shadow banking institutions described in Table 4.2. Using our methodology and assumptions (see below), which included assets of other shadow banking institutions on top of the PBOC-listed assets (described in Table 4.2) and excluding double counted assets, our estimates of the size of the shadow banking institutions at the end of 2012, 2013 and 2014 are RMB 22.5 trillion, RMB 30.1 trillion and RMB 32.2 trillion respectively (see Table 4.3).

The differences in estimates are mostly due to different accounting and disclosure treatment by different entities, which create some uncertainty and errors in the measurement of the true size of risks. Without direct examination of the books of each shadow banking institution, it would not be possible to eliminate all the double counting and under-counting, especially in the absence of the use of a national standard such as the Legal Entity Identifier (LEI). Nevertheless, the differences with the

---

[5]Chinese experts maintain that official data always have some estimation errors and omissions.

TABLE 4.3 Comparison of shadow banking size estimates – PBOC, FGI and Oliver Wyman.

In RMB trillion				
	End 2012	End 2013	End 2014	Source
Entrusted loans (new data)	5.8 (4.7)	8.9 (7.2)	10.1 (9.3)	PBOC
Banker's acceptance (new data)	6.7 (6.1)	8.9 (6.9)	9.7 (6.8)	PBOC
PBOC Implied Shadow Banking Size	21.8	28.2	33.2	PBOC Total Social Financing
FGI Estimation	22.5	30.1	32.2	FGI estimation
OW Published Estimates, Jan. 2015	23.0	31.2	n.a.	OW estimation

Source: PBOC, Oliver Wyman, FGI estimates.

official numbers are not significant, which suggest that our methodology of elimination of undercounting and overcounting is at least consistent with the official data methodology. To minimize the double counting/undercounting issue, we make the following assumptions:

1. Bank–trust cooperation refers to activities where banks buy trust companies' products (mainly trust loans) and record them as WMPs. Following the CBRC's regulation, the officially reported bank–trust cooperation products (around 20 percent of trusts' AUM[6] (assets under management)) are on both banks' and trust companies' balance sheets. These products are subject to adequate supervision, which are outside the scope of our definition of shadow banking assets.
2. To circumvent regulations, a new form of bank–trust cooperation was created by banks and trust companies. Assets under this new bank–trust cooperation appear on trust companies' balance sheets but are not reported as bank–trust cooperation products. Banks, however, report such products as non-guaranteed WMPs (off-balance sheet). The estimated size of the new form of bank–trust cooperation products was about 50 percent of trusts' AUM (Green and Li

[6]Data available at: http://www.xtxh.net/xtxh/statistics/index.htm

et al. 2014) (see section 4.3 for more information). Trust loans and non-discretionary businesses, which are the main credit assets of trust companies, are included under our definition of shadow banking. We assume that the new form of bank–trust cooperation also comprises 50 percent of trust loans and non-discretionary businesses.

3. Data on banks' WMPs include both on-balance sheet and off-balance sheet WMPs. However, banks' guaranteed WMPs are kept on-balance sheet, while non-guaranteed WMPs are kept off-balance sheet. So, before CBRC's regulation on WMP information disclosure, statistics of off-balance sheet WMPs may be subject to under counting. We assume that in 2012, 30 percent of such off-balance sheet WMPs were missed out, improving to 20 percent and 10 percent in 2013 and 2014 respectively.

4. To eliminate the double counting, as stated in assumption 2, and undercounting, as stated in assumption 3, for 2012 figures, we subtracted 70 percent of the new form of bank–trust cooperation (50 percent of trusts' AUM), from banks' WMPs as part of shadow banking. For 2013 figures, we again assume an improvement in data and subtracted 80 percent of the new form of bank–trust cooperation; and for 2014, we subtracted 90 percent of the new form of bank–trust cooperation from banks' WMPs.

5. Securities companies' AMPs' investment in corporate bonds, trust products, banks' WMPs and other funds are subject to double counting.

Financial leasing companies can issue loans, which are often packaged or securitized and sold to trust companies and banks in the form of WMPs. So, including financial leasing companies' asset as a shadow banking asset is subject to double counting.

Financial guarantees help to expand credit, but the guaranteed amount is already reported in other financial institutions' lending or assets; hence, including guaranteed loans would also be subject to double counting.

As there are few indicators of the extent of double counting for securities companies' AMPs, financial leasing and financial guarantees, we make a relatively conservative assumption to deduct 60 percent of securities companies' AMPs, financial leasing and financial guarantees from the total size of our shadow banking estimation.

Based on both PBOC's definition (PBOC, 2013) and the criteria of Yan and Li (2014), as well as the above assumptions, we list the shadow

TABLE 4.4 Estimation of the scale of shadow banking, 2012–2014.

Business/products	Scale in RMB bn.			Source
	End 2012	End 2013	End 2014[5]	
Entrusted loans	4,674	7,221	9,330	PBOC
Banker's acceptance	6,109	6,884	6,760	PBOC
Security firm AMP	144	587	n.a.	Wind
Corporate bond LGFV	1,161	1,268	n.a.	Audit Office of the People's Republic of China
Trust products/ loans[1]	4,141	7,007	9,835	China Trustee Association
Leasing	1,550	2,100	n.a.	Barclay
Financial guarantee	2,170	2,532	n.a.	Barclay
Pawnshop products	71	87	101.3	Ministry of Commerce
Microfinance loans	592	819	942	PBOC
Internet funds, P2P	6	12		PBOC
Private lending[2]	690	750	782	CreditEase, FGI estimation
Off-balance sheet Bank WMP[3]	4,970	6,617	8,382	CBRC
Less: overlaps trust loans & WMPs[4]	1,449	2,628	3,934	Standard Chartered estimation, FGI calculation
Less: overlaps SecuAMP/leasing/ guarantee	2,318	3,131	n.a.	FGI calculation
Total sizing	22,510	30,125	32,198	FGI calculation

Notes: [1]Trust products/lendings include trust loans and non-discretionary businesses, which are the main credit assets of trust companies.
[2]Although the size of private lending reached RMB 3.38 trillion in June 2011 (PBOC survey), and rose to RMB 5.28 trillion at the end of 2013 (CreditEase data), most of the credit did not incur interest charges and were actually family or related party loans. CreditEase data suggested that only 15% of these loans incurred interest charges and therefore only 15% of such private lending should be included as shadow banking assets. We used the compound growth rate to

(continued)

TABLE 4.4   *Continued*

extrapolate the estimated shadow bank numbers for private lending with interest at the end of 2012 and the end of 2014.

[3]There was no data available for bank WMP size as of December 2014, only the data as of end 2014: RMB 13.97 trillion. Using the historical data on a proportion of non-guaranteed WMPs (70% in 2012, 64.8% in 2013, CBRC annual report), we estimated that for the first half of 2014, 60% of bank WMPs were non-guaranteed WMPs (off-balance sheet).

[4]Based on assumption 2 and assumption 3, we subtract 35% of trust products/loans from off-balance sheet banks WMPs in 2012, 40% of trust products/loans in 2013 and 45% of trust products/loans in 2014.

[5]"n.a." stands for data not available.

banking assets in Table 4.4 (but exclude trust loans to avoid double counting of trust companies' assets and trust loans). The total shadow banking size is then estimated from 2012 to 2014.

The result (Table 4.4) showed that China's shadow banking was RMB 22.5 trillion (US$ 3.6 trillion) or 43 percent of GDP at the end of 2012, roughly in the middle of the range of most market estimates (Table 4.1). We estimated that it grew to around RMB 30.1 trillion (US$ 4.8 trillion) or 53 percent of GDP, at the end of 2013; and reached RMB 32.2 trillion (US$ 5.2 trillion), about 51 percent of GDP,[7] in 2014.

Between 2012 and 2013, the growth rate of shadow banking spiked to around 34 percent per annum, when the economy went through a patch of tighter liquidity, partly as a result of the economic slowdown and also tighter monetary policy stance. However, its growth slowed down to less than 10 percent year over year (YOY) in 2014, due mainly to closer supervision by the regulators. There were more disclosure requirements on shadow banks' products, and regulators directed the banks to shift the shadow banking assets back onto their balance sheets.

To compare China's shadow banking size globally, the FSB estimates of the Chinese shadow banking system of US$ 2.1 trillion or 26 percent of GDP in 2012 appeared small, relative to the U.S. shadow system assets of US$26 trillion or 167 percent of GDP. Using FGI's estimation of US$3.6 trillion, China's shadow banking would account for

---

[7]GDP in 2014 is calculated using the predicted GDP growth of 7.5 percent YOY (RMB 56.9 trillion * 1.0375 = RMB 59 trillion).

TABLE 4.5 Comparisons of shadow banking assets, 2012.

	China		U.S.		World	
	US$ Trn	% GDP	US$ Trn	% GDP	US$ Trn	% GDP
FSB	2.1	26	26	167	71	117
FGI	3.6	43				
JP Morgan	5.8	70				

Source: FSB, JPMorgan, FGI estimates.

43 percent of GDP in 2012 (Table 4.5), still less than one-third the size of the U.S. equivalent and half the size of the world average.

Table 4.5 showed that the highest market estimate (by JPMorgan) of US$5.8 trillion, at 70 percent of GDP was still smaller than the U.S. (167 percent) and global ratios (117 percent).

Comparing shadow banking assets with bank assets globally, at the end of 2012, global shadow banking assets represented 50 percent of global banking assets. The equivalent ratio for the U.S. was 175 percent (FSB, 2013). In contrast, Chinese shadow banking assets only account for about 10 percent of commercial banks' assets[8] (or 17 percent based on FGI's estimation).

What distinguishes China from the U.S. is that its financial system is skewed towards the banking system, with total bank assets comprising more than 200 percent of GDP, in the same league as Italy, Japan, Spain and Germany. In contrast, U.S. banking system assets represent less than 100 percent of GDP, reflecting a more diversified financial system (Figure 4.1).

Although China's shadow banking sector remained relatively small compared with the global average, its rapid expansion since 2008 (annual growth of 42 percent in 2012) was the highest reported in the FSB survey (FSB, 2013). Such rapid growth in shadow bank credit raised legitimate concerns on the quality of such credit and its possible adverse implications for the stability of the financial system in China.

---

[8]China's total bank assets were RMB 133.7 trillion at the end of 2012 (PBOC statistics). http://www.pbc.gov.cn/publish/html/kuangjia.htm?id=2012s06.htm

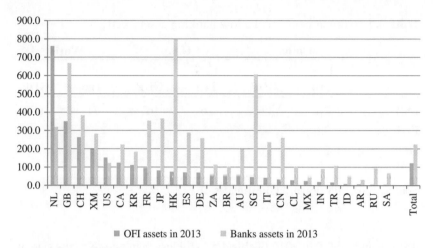

FIGURE 4.1   Shadow banking assets vs. banking assets, at end-2013 (%).
Note: Shadow banking is defined as a non-bank financial intermediary. AR = Argentina; AU = Australia; BR = Brazil; CA = Canada; CH = Switzerland; CN = China; CL = Chile; DE = Germany; ES = Spain; FR = France; GB = United Kingdom; HK = Hong Kong; ID = Indonesia; IN = India; IT = Italy; JP = Japan; KR = Korea; MX = Mexico; NL = Netherlands; RU = Russia; SA = Saudi Arabia; SG = Singapore; TR = Turkey; US = United States; XM = Euro Area; ZA = South Africa.
Source: Financial Stability Board, UBS estimates.

4.3 FACTORS SPURRING THE GROWTH OF SHADOW BANKS IN CHINA

As noted earlier, shadow banking in China arose to meet genuine market needs. The state-owned banks preferred to lend to large corporations, SOEs and local governments, which they considered more credit worthy with good collateral. In Chapter 2, we noted that around 30 percent of China's financial assets were held in the form of foreign exchange reserves. Around 60 percent of the remaining 70 percent of assets went in the form of credit to the government or SOEs/large firms. This meant that only approximately 25 percent of total financial assets went into credit to the private sector, which comprised largely of SMEs.

Moreover, because prudential regulations restricted the amount of credit for lending to real estate, real estate developers were willing to pay higher interest rates to shadow banks as their profit margins were higher during the rise in asset prices. Because these borrowers (SMEs and real estate developers) were willing to pay higher interest rates, the shadow bank intermediaries emerged to fill the financing "gap." To attract funding, the shadow banks were able to satisfy a concurrent demand for higher interest-yielding products by households and corporations as bank deposit rates were capped by regulation.

The explosion in China's shadow banking activities began following the government's RMB 4 trillion fiscal stimulus package in 2008. Indeed, the total credit to GDP ratio rose significantly from below 130 percent in 2008 to above 160 percent in 2009. The initial credit loosening benefited the real estate sector and local governments that used the opportunity to expand infrastructure investments using local government financing platforms (LGFPs). Some OFIs, such as trust companies, also took this opportunity to create products that packaged credit to infrastructure and real estate for sale to the banks as WMPs. As a result of easy credit, low interest rates and high demand, property prices surged.

In response, the Chinese authorities tightened monetary policy in 2010 to curb overcapacity in certain sectors and reduce domestic economic imbalances (such as high inflation expectations).[9] In 2012, broad money, M2, growth decelerated to less than 14 percent, down from more than 25 percent in 2009.[10] As China's GDP growth and exports also slowed down during the same period, many borrowers faced cash flow problems, and needed more credit. However, monetary tightening made it hard for these borrowers to obtain bank loans; so they turned to shadow banks for financing.

A further complication is the existing banking business model in China, which prefers to lend short-term loans rather than provide long-term loans, as these incur higher capital charges. The constant rollover of debts effectively lead to evergreening, especially indirectly through shadow banks, so that the loans either appear off-balance sheet or routed back to the books after being "parked" in packaged WMPs or with shadow banks. The evergreening issue is described in more detail in the box below.

---

[9]According to China Monetary Policy Report Quarter Four, 2010 and 2011, PBOC increased the required reserve ratios 6 times in 2010 (3 percent in total), increased the benchmark interest rates twice in the fourth quarter of 2010 and 3 times during the first three quarters of 2011.

[10]CEIC data, FGI calculations.

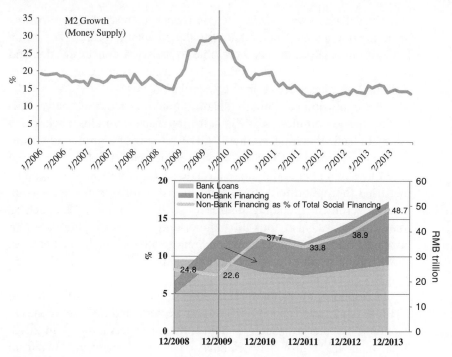

FIGURE 4.2 Monetary tightening and growth of China's shadow banking.
Source: CEIC.

Figure 4.2 shows that when M2 growth slowed down in 2010, growth in bank loans also decreased, but the scale of non-bank financing increased, with its share of total social financing rising from 25 percent to 49 percent.

This suggested that the credit squeeze actually shifted credit and monetary creation from the banking system into the shadow banking system and inter-enterprise lending. From 2007 to 2011, inter-enterprise liabilities increased significantly (see Chapter 3).

In 2007, total inter-enterprise liabilities of RMB 21 trillion were comparable in size with bank loans to enterprises (RMB 20.9 trillion[11]). However, by 2011, the inter-enterprise liabilities had grown to RMB 51 trillion, significantly larger than bank loans to enterprises (RMB 39 trillion).

---

[11]CEIC data.

Moreover, the inter-enterprise liabilities became much larger than inter-enterprise claims (Li et al., 2013), with the net difference increasing from RMB 8 trillion in 2007 to RMB 22 trillion in 2011. This suggested that enterprises may have shifted their claims to the financial sector (banking sector and shadow banking sector). This further suggested that enterprise liquidity had tightened, as they had to sell their assets to banks at a discounted rate; whereas the banks could package these assets into WMPs to sell to investors.

The monetary tightening in 2010 succeeded in constraining the credit expansion of the banking sector, but the total credit level remained high at more than 170 percent of GDP. Many foreign analysts consider that the Chinese credit-to-GDP ratio in excess of 200 percent had already reached an unsustainable level. Fitch Ratings suggested that 36 percent of all outstanding credit resides outside the loan portfolios of Chinese banks. Fitch subsequently downgraded China's sovereign credit rating from AA- to A+, citing rapid expansion of credit to 198 percent of GDP by the end of 2012, an increase of over 70 percentage points compared with 125 percent in 2008 (Reuters, 2013).

RISKS OF EVERGREENING

Evergreening involves the rollover of debt to ultimately the same borrower in different forms. This could be done via a direct rollover or indirectly through an intermediary such as a shadow bank, for example a trust company. The latter gives the appearance of a loan that is not impaired, whereas the interest and principal may have been rolled-over (evergreened) but credit risk has been increased without the necessary loan reclassification as a non-performing loan.

Evergreening or rollover of debt is not sustainable. Evergreening merely postpones the recognition of the NPL problem, which will increase fiscal difficulties in future (Walter, 2014). If evergreening is not stopped early, it appears as regulatory forbearance, which only delays resolution of credit and NPL problems.

Chinese trust companies repackage and sell loans as WMPs to corporates, but these loans do not appear to have NPL risks as WMPs are booked off-balance sheet and the loans rolled over upon maturity. However, when monetary conditions tighten, the loan underlying the WMP cannot be renewed, and the companies are forced to borrow from the shadow banks at high interest rates to avoid default. When the whole economy is slowing down, this problem can arise, with serious moral hazard issues because the ultimate risk will fall on the regulated banks.

Pettis (2014) has argued that the only viable debt solution lies in allocating the losses, either as soon as they are incurred or during a subsequent amortization period. There are three sectors where the hidden losses in the balance sheets of the banks and shadow banks could be allocated, namely, the banks and shareholders themselves, households, the private sector and the government. Losses could also be addressed through a combination of flows and stock adjustments, such as debt/equity swaps.

In terms of credit direction, Table 4.6 shows that between 2008 and 2012, the bulk (66 percent) of the credit expansion went to the manufacturing, wholesale and retail, local government financing platforms (LGFPs), real estate, mining sector, construction sector, and manufacturing and fixed asset investment (FAI)-related sectors. These sectors had higher credit risks due to excess capacity and other factors (Xu, Yang and Mou, 2013).

During the period 2007–2012, the Chinese banks' interest rates were not fully liberalized, which created the opportunity for the entry of shadow banks. As a result, there is a dual track interest rate system with policy rates and market rates co-existing within the financial system (Figure 4.3).

In terms of credit recipients, on average 60 percent of bank credit (bank loans) has gone to large enterprises and LGFPs since 2007 (Table 4.7). Although the amount of bank loans provided to small businesses has more than tripled from 2007 to 2012, it only accounted for about one-fourth of the total bank loans. The expansion in credit between 2008 and 2009 was mainly channeled to the SOEs/large firms. This left the private sector with little choice but to turn to non-bank channels for funding.

Officially, commercial banks take deposits at roughly 3 percent per annum for one-year fixed deposits (the prescribed policy rate), and lend at around 6 percent.[12] However, during the period of monetary tightening, the market was willing to pay higher than the policy rates for funds. In the

---

[12]The PBOC allowed banks to lend above their prescribed rate in October 2004 and fully liberalized lending rates in July 2013.

TABLE 4.6 Credit growth for different sectors, 2008–2012.

Total Credit	2012 (RMB Trn.)	2008–12 CAGR (%)	Exposure to Higher Risk Credit (%)
Manufacturing	20.5	27	16.9
Wholesale & Retail	17.0	32	11.6
LGFV	15.0	31	25.0
Real Estate	9.7	21	5.5
Mining	5.1	30	7.8
Construction	3.0	37	18.4
. . .			
Total Corporate Credit	92.2	25	12.1
Retail Credit	12.0	25	0.7
Central Government Credit	9.7	10	0.0
Total Credit	113.9	23	9.7

Note: Manufacturing & FAI-related sectors account for 66% of total credit.
Source: CEIC, WIND, Morgan Stanley Research Estimates.

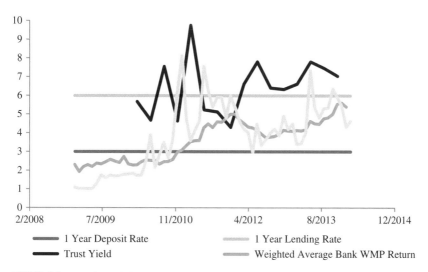

FIGURE 4.3 Dual track interest rates in China (%).
Source: CEIC.

TABLE 4.7 Loans to enterprises (RMB bn).

	2007	2008	2009	2010	2011	2012
Large and medium enterprises	15,339	17,521	21,159	22,643	24,722	30,269
Small business	5597	6,360	8484	12301	15489	17,274
LGFP	3563	4,400	7380	8468	9100	9,300
Consumers	3275	3,723	5,537	7511	8878	10,444
Total bank loans	27774	32,004	42560	50923	58189	67,287
Percentage of loans to large & mid-size, and small enterprises (%)						
Large and medium enterprises	55.2	55.0	49.7	44.5	42.5	45.0
Small enterprises	20.2	20.0	19.9	24.2	26.6	25.7
Total bonds	6,647	8,163	10,484	12,727	14,472	17,024
Total alternative financing	6,923	8,271	8,938	15,329	19,639	28,417
YOY growth of bank loans (%)		15.0	33.0	15.7	14.3	15.6
YOY growth of alternative financing (%)		20.0	8.1	71.5	28.1	44.7

Source: Morgan Stanley, FGI Calculation.

search for yield, depositors were anxious to receive higher deposit rates. Accordingly, banks issued WMPs by working with OFIs such as trust companies to invest/lend to projects that have higher yields than commercial bank loans. These WMPs could offer higher yields than official deposit rates and still be profitable.

Strictly speaking, the shadow banks helped the formal banking system to bypass official interest rates, and created deposit substitutes, whilst lending to higher risk enterprises and charging higher lending rates.

Moreover, the banks' non-guaranteed WMPs can move loans off-balance sheet and circumvent restrictions on their credit expansion. However, such practice generated higher leverage on an off-balance sheet basis. This is because the loans backing WMPs are moved off-balance sheet and not subject to capital requirements and loan-deposit ratio (LDR) restrictions, whilst fees earned from WMPs provide banks with a more diversified income structure.

Depositors were willing to invest in WMPs that offer higher returns than bank deposits, despite the lack of disclosure and perceived higher risks. This is because they treat WMPs as deposits with implicit bank guarantees. Seen from this perspective, the WMPs and OFIs' products functioned as a mechanism for investors and depositors to invest in the stock market, bonds, and infrastructure projects, with higher credit risks and less oversight in the system as a whole.

Different sectors of shadow banking have different funding channels, different operating models, different leverage ratios and different kinds of interactions with banks. In section 4.4 below, we elaborate on developments in each sector in greater detail.

4.4 DIFFERENT CHANNELS OF CHINA'S SHADOW BANKING

A key characteristic of China's shadow banking is that the shadow banking sectors are more or less financed by the banking sector. For example, the trust company sector (now the second largest financial sector in China after commercial banks) is estimated to have 70 percent of total funds sourced from banks. Microcredit companies source around 50 percent of their funding from the banks. Private money lenders also borrow funds at official rates from banks and lend out in the usury market. In other words, since shadow banks cannot fund directly from the public, they source funding from the banking system or sell WMPs to rich corporations and investors.

Such lending processes increase the length of the financing chain in the economy, and complicate the lending structure, with three kinds of risks. First, the prolonged financing chain made the ultimate use of funds unclear, with investors having difficulties in monitoring the quality of underlying assets (or collaterals). Second, the same assets, after securitization, packaging or tranching, could appear on more than one entity's balance sheet, which would inflate the size of the total assets in the financial sector, creating measurement problems. Third, because OFIs along the financing chain can fail, contagion can spread to banks with systemic impacts (Su, 2014).

4.4.1 The Trust Company Channel

Globally, trusts are legal entities for custody and fiduciary duties, often for regulatory or tax arbitrage. For example, private banking uses trusts to help clients manage their property inheritance and for charitable purposes. In China, however, trust companies have a special financial license that enables them to engage in the businesses that the traditional banking sector and capital market cannot fulfill; for example, private equity and asset securitization business in the name of financial intermediation.

The trust company license allows them to participate in money market businesses, capital market businesses and alternative investments. Thus, trust companies can help other financial institutions, including commercial banks, to carry on businesses that they are not allowed to do by themselves. Trust companies can lend to restricted or high-risk industries (for example real estate, LGFP). Because they act only in trust for their principals, there may be less due diligence on credit assets (trust lending) than bank lending, or capital market financing.

The trust company sector blossomed when the authorities imposed loan quotas on banks, prompting banks to restrict lending to property developers and local governments. Those that lost access to bank loans turned to trust companies for creative financing sources. AUM of trust companies have more than tripled since 2010, when the central bank tightened credit supply. They reached RMB 14.0 trillion by the end of 2014 (Figure 4.4); and had overtaken the insurance sector (with AUM of RMB 10.2 trillion) to become the second largest – after commercial banks – financial sector in China.

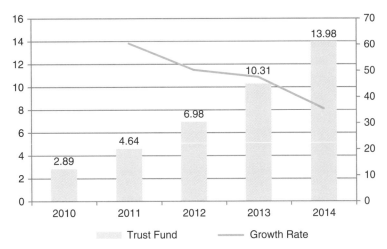

FIGURE 4.4 Trust fund scale (trillion RMB) and growth (%), 2010–2013.
Source: CEIC.

As shown in Figure 4.5, trust funds in 2014 were channeled mainly to the "fundamental industries" sector (manufacturing, energy, transportation and construction), industrial and commercial sector (mining, electricity, gas and water production and supply industry, wholesale and

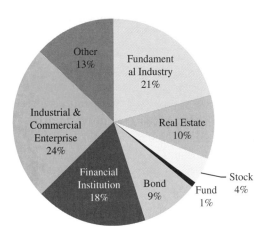

FIGURE 4.5 Trust investment distribution, 2013 (percentage).
Source: CEIC.

retail, accommodation and catering services, information transmission, and software and IT services) and the real estate sector.

Technically speaking, trust companies act as trustees and hold assets on behalf of the beneficiaries. So, according to trust company contracts, the risks of trusts' AUM belong to the investor and the investee. This explains why the trust sector is relatively thinly capitalized.

However, as shown in Figure 4.5, trust companies' AUM is concentrated in high-risk or policy restricted sectors. In times of economic slowdown or policy adjustments, such assets will be the first to be impacted, which is why the trust sector has experienced a number of near default events since 2013. Since trust companies have a thin capital base, even a small 3 percent default rate of underlying assets could wipe out their equity and put trust companies into bankruptcy (Cui et al., 2014).

Moreover, trust companies are closely related to the banking sector: 70 percent of trust funds are sourced from banks; and approximately 70 percent of trust funds are used to make loans through the bank–trust cooperation (Green et al., 2014). Consequently, any risks or crisis in the trust sector would spread to the banking sector.

BANK-TRUST COOPERATION

Bank-trust cooperation refers to activities where banks buy trust companies' products (either loans or investments) and record them as WMPs. Before 2010, when there was no regulation on bank-trust cooperation, trust companies did not report the scale of bank-trust cooperation, but only needed to set up 1.5 percent capital for such assets (same rate as the capital requirement on their non-bank-trust products). Such cooperation enabled the banks to use this bank-trust channel to avoid regulations on capital requirement, loan loss provisions and loan-to-deposit ratio.

However, in August 2010, to improve transparency, CBRC required banks and trust companies to disclose data of bank-trust cooperation products. Banks were required to bring all such WMPs (through the bank-trust channel) back onto their balance sheet. Furthermore, for those products that were not brought back on balance sheet by banks, trust companies need to set aside 10.5 percent capital for the AUM (higher than the previous 1.5 percent). After the regulation, the "benefits" of bank-trust cooperation disappeared, and the reported bank-trust cooperation decreased from 64 percent of trust AUM (September 2010) to 54 percent (December 2010), and further to 22 percent (December 2014) (China Trustee Association Statistics).

According to Green et al. (2014), a new form of bank-trust cooperation has evolved to avoid new regulations; a passive bridging entity between banks and trust companies is established to make it appear as if the money is not from the bank but from the bridging entity. Green et al. (2014) estimated that the actual size of bank-trust cooperation should be around 70 percent of trusts' AUM, instead of the officially reported 20 percent.

Moreover, risks also lie in the increasingly complicated lending structure and packaging/tranching processes of trust companies and trust WMPs. Trust companies get funds from various sources, including wealthy individual investors, banks' own investment portfolios, or small investors who participate by buying WMPs through banks. These funds are used for investments in assets such as LGFVs, real estate, bankers' acceptance bills, and SME loans, which, in turn, constitute the asset pool for the trust beneficial rights that the trust companies sell to the investors.

Some of the potential risks in the trust channel include the following:

1. Trust beneficial rights purchased by banks are kept under their investment book (not loan book) and therefore require less capital to hold. They are not subject to the LDR cap and may not be subject to loan loss provisioning.
2. The banks or investors may or may not have detailed information on the underlying asset quality in the asset pool managed by trust companies.
3. In the effort to market their products, trust companies usually offer guaranteed returns. In the short run, such products do not appear to have credit risks and can be rolled over (evergreened) in periods of high liquidity. Since trust companies have a thin capital base, this "guarantee" element would put their capital at risk (Cui et al., 2012).
4. Property in the form of land and real estate underlies many of the trusts. Even if the actual investment of the trust is not a property project, property or land could be provided as collateral or as equity in

the project. Land is frequently used as equity contribution by local governments or government-funded entities, or used as underlying collateral for the loan provided by the trust. Any decline in the value of land will reduce the value of collateral or equity in the trust and will hurt both the investment and the lenders.

There is a market misperception that Chinese trust companies or state-owned financing vehicles will never run into insolvency. During the Asian financial crisis in 1998, many Chinese local government trust companies and local government non-bank financial corporates could not meet their repayment obligations, amid rising bad debt and cash flow problems. The failure of GITIC (Guangdong International Trust and Investment Corporation) in 1998 revealed that the amount of outstanding debt from various local government trust companies and agriculture financing platforms was around RMB 100–200 billion (11–22 per cent of Guangdong's GDP). GITIC was liquidated with banks absorbing the credit risks, but the PBOC and Guangdong government provided funding to facilitate the debt resolution mechanism (Cui et al., 2012). There is therefore precedent that local government debt obligations do have credit risks.

The majority of the 68 trust companies in China are owned by SOEs, local governments and banks, which have strong incentives to ensure that the trust companies do not fail.[13] Nevertheless, the true credit risk within the trust company sector is an issue that needs clarification to reduce risk uncertainty in the system as a whole. The CBRC has requested that the banks should bring their off-balance sheet and trust-type risks back onto their balance sheets, so that the true exposures are more transparent and more manageable.

Central/local governments or SOEs own 64 percent of trusts (by asset size) in China. This includes 30 percent owned by local government/ SOEs (including cities and provinces), and another 34 percent by central government or central SOEs. Another 30 percent are owned by financial institutions, many of which are also state-owned. Specifically, banks own 20 percent of trust assets. Only 6 percent of trust companies' assets are owned by private entities or foreign investors (Figure 4.6).

These state linked operations of trust companies are important franchises, which have been profitable in recent years. Because trust licenses are valuable, it is likely that the shareholders of trust companies

---

[13]Source: China Trustee Association.

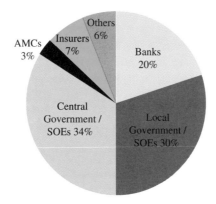

FIGURE 4.6 Share holders of trust companies.
Notes: AMC=Asset Management Companies. Others
include domestic private investors and foreign investors.

will try to avoid defaults of trust products, which will delay resolution of
the moral hazard risks.

4.4.2 Bank WMP

Banks' WMPs are actually "quasi-deposits," as their underlying assets
are mostly loans from banks or OFIs and their accounting treatment
moves the corresponding deposit and related assets off the banks' loan
books.

WMPs are effectively securitized bank asset products sold to customers. There are three sources of underlying assets. The first is the
securitization of bank loans that are already on banks' books, where the
securitization process, often through a trust company, removes the loan
from a bank's loan book. The second is the securitization of loans given
by another bank or shadow bank institution, such as a moneylender. The
third is the sourcing of new loans from the corporate sector, which
are then bought by banks and packaged into their WMPs. This means that
the underlying assets of bank WMPs could include bank assets (loans),
interbank assets (OFIs' loans/investments), and inter-enterprise assets
(inter-enterprise loans).

The structure of the WMP packaging process can be very convoluted
with more than one bank or OFI involved. Figure 4.7 illustrates the

- Bank A underwrites discounted bills to companies;

Bank A	
Discounted bills	Deposits

- Bank A sells the discounted bills to Bank B with buyback agreements;

Bank A		Bank B	
Discounted bills	Deposits	Reverse repo	Deposits

- Bank B sells discounted bills to Bank C, who then structures the assets as WMPs.

Bank A		Bank B		Bank C	
Discounted bills	Deposits	Reverse repo	Deposits		
					Off-balance sheet WMPs

FIGURE 4.7   How banks shift discounted bills into WMPs.
Source: FGI analysis.

process of how banks package their own (or others') discounted bills (de facto short-term bank loans) into off-balance sheet WMPs, using reverse repos. The final issuer of the WMP will disclose only the reverse repo (as part of its underlying asset) as an interbank asset. Strictly speaking, the underlying asset is actually a bank loan to enterprises. In short, a high-risk bank loan ends up disguised as a low-risk interbank asset, since the counterparty is another bank.

To further complicate matters, many banks engage in a fund/asset pool operation model to issue WMPs. They pool together various money market instruments, interbank notes, bonds, credit assets, etc., into an asset pool, and issue WMPs based on this asset pool to raise funds from different customers. Some issuing banks may offer to buy back these WMPs from other banks to enhance their liquidity. Such fund/asset pool models face problems of liquidity and maturity mismatches, as well as insufficient information disclosure on risk characteristics of the underlying assets. This business model was active in the interbank market until the CBRC issued Document 8 to ban such business.

The underlying risk of WMPs collateralized into interbank assets is that it hides the potential credit risks within the banking system. Assets in the WMPs are not subject to the same degree of scrutiny and monitoring, since banks treat other banks as high quality counterparties. Since these "interbank assets" are disguised bank loans, the risks are higher and should be subject to closer monitoring. For these reasons, foreign banks in China are reluctant to use such repos in the interbank market, because of the inherent risks involved in the repo collateral.

The size of bank WMPs increased rapidly since 2010, reaching RMB 14 trillion (US$2.25 trillion) at the end of May 2014; approximately

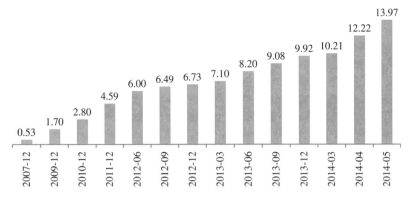

FIGURE 4.8 Scale of bank WMPs (trillion RMB).
Source: JPMorgan, based on CBRC statistics.

10 percent of banks' total assets (Figure 4.8). The weighted average yield of these products was 4.13 percent, compared to China's bank deposit rate of up to 3.3 percent for one-year deposits (CBRC, 2014).

We should therefore look at the true size of riskiness of the shadow banking assets, rather than just looking at the size of the liability side of bank WMPs. Banks' WMPs are kept both on-balance sheet and off-balance sheet. The on-balance sheet WMPs are guaranteed with principal payment, with most underlying assets being deposits, treasury bonds and interbank loan assets.

Off-balance sheet WMPs are not guaranteed, with most underlying assets being WMPs from OFIs (such as trust companies, microcredit companies, etc.). Only off-balance sheet WMPs should be treated as shadow banking assets, since on-balance sheet WMPs are already subject to NPL provisioning. Off-balance sheet WMPs have more convoluted packaging structures and do not necessarily have provisions for bad debt. The 2013 CBRC annual report indicated that 66 percent of WMPs are off-balance sheet. If such off-balance sheet WMPs include off-balance sheet loan assets, or credit assets packaged by shadow banks, the quality of such underlying assets is uncertain (CBRC, 2013).

The fundamental problem with shadow banking is the lack of clarity of property rights in the system and discipline that the financial system must bring to the functioning of credit. If the credit risks are unclear as to financial institution or the investor/public, then the financial system becomes an endogenous "opaque box" of inherent risks. This was the fundamental problem of the subprime fiasco in the U.S. and the debt problem in Europe. It took the de facto nationalization of bank losses to stem the "silent bank-run" in the 2008 crisis, through TARP (Troubled Asset Relief Progam), a state guarantee of various non-bank financial institutions (e.g. AIG and Fannie Mae, etc.), as well as liquidity provision on the basis that the authorities will take all necessary actions to avoid a crisis.

Moreover, the underlying moral hazard is that Chinese investors still view WMPs as "quasi" bank fixed deposits with the banks carrying all the risks of default. Since a number of WMPs have gone into default, there is an ongoing debate on how these losses will ultimately be shared.

Another principal issue is that the banks may simply "evergreen" the credit losses, by issuing new WMPs to cover the losses of old ones. This is clearly not sustainable, but the heart of the problem lies in the accumulation of unreported NPLs and credit losses in the banking system as a whole.

4.4.3 Interbank Assets: Entrusted Loans and Undiscounted Bankers' Acceptances (BAs)

Entrusted loans and undiscounted bankers' acceptances (BAs) are two major interbank assets. Entrusted loans are issued by principal owners specifying the counter party and details of loan to obtain funding through a bank. They are actually inter-enterprise credit, sold to banks for funding. An undiscounted BA is based on trading credits between enterprises. Once banks discount the bills, it becomes a trading instrument, rather than a loan, which is then treated as off-balance sheet (Tao and Deng, 2013).

The reason these interbank assets are categorized as "shadow banking" assets is that such interbank assets are actually loans between non-bank entities (governments, corporate, or individuals), with commercial banks as guarantors or custodians. However, they are traded as interbank assets between banks under repurchase agreements (repo), and categorized as interbank assets rather than on their loan book. Moreover, such interbank assets can be packaged into WMPs of banks, brokers and Targeted Asset Management Companies (TAMCs).[14] Wu and Li (2014) reported that when CBRC tightened the regulations on the trust market,

---

[14]TAMCs refers to subsidiaries of fund management companies established in accordance with Chinese company law by engaging in specific clients' asset managements, fund sales and other businesses approved by CSRC. http://www .csrc.gov.cn/pub/newsite/flb/flfg/bmgf/jj/gszl/201310/t20131021_236631.html

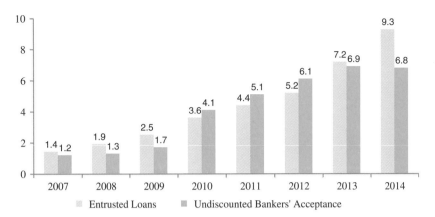

FIGURE 4.9 Annual flow of entrusted loan and undiscounted BA (trillion RMB). Source: PBOC Statistics 2007–2014.

TAMCs emerged as subsidiaries of fund managers to actively originate WMPs and manage asset pools. The size of TAMCs escalated from almost zero to RMB 1 trillion in 2013 alone (around 12 percent of total entrusted loans).

The annual flow of entrusted loans and undiscounted BAs is shown below in Figure 4.9. The flow amount of entrusted loans has continuously increased since 2007, while undiscounted BAs and other interbank assets have decelerated notably since mid-2012.

The inclusion of inter-enterprise assets in interbank assets resulted in the contamination of the interbank market's high credit standing. This was one reason why a senior Chinese banker labeled WMPs as Ponzi schemes, which are subject to evergreening and fraud. Bank of America Merrill Lynch's research suggested that if credit risk is properly acknowledged in the entrusted loans and trust loans, the increase in banks' risk-weighted assets (RWA) could be around 9 percent; and the potential NPL ratio would rise to 5 to 6 percent of RWA. This suggests that there should be more monitoring and cleaning up of the interbank asset quality (Wu, 2014).

4.4.4 Microcredit Companies

Microcredit companies were legalized as late as 2008, when the government decided to grant a license to some underground banks to help SME financing (Cui, Tian and Wei, 2012) (Zhang, 2014). However, the scale

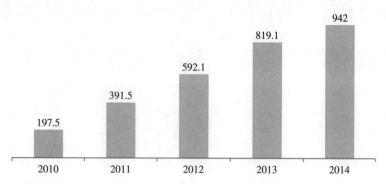

FIGURE 4.10 Microcredit loans (billion RMB), 2010–2014.
Source: PBOC Statistics 2010–2014.

of microcredit loans has increased significantly during recent years due to the high profitability from higher lending rates (Figure 4.10).

The main customers of microcredit companies are small businesses, which have been neglected by banks, and the microcredit companies are often their only source of credit. They offer convenience in lending, with good judgment of credit risks, as these companies are truly private sector lenders with their own money at stake.

Current regulations applicable to microcredit companies are highly restrictive. For example, they are subject to a strict amount of debt related to the size of their paid-in capital, and are not allowed to take deposits or borrow from the interbank market, or other sources.

Generally speaking, microcredit companies are permitted to charge customers as much as 4 times the official bank prime lending rate, meaning 24 percent per annum (at current levels), and the maturities of microcredit loans are mainly short-term of less than one-year tenure. Given such a high interest rate charge, microcredit companies can be very profitable. The profit distribution behind this business is shown in Figure 4.11.

4.4.5 Pawnshops

The total assets of pawnshops reached RMB 101.3 billion at the end of 2014.[15] Pawnshops are not regulated by CBRC, but by the Ministry of Commerce. Originally, the main customers of pawnshops were

---

[15]Ministry of Commerce. http://ltfzs.mofcom.gov.cn/article/date/201404/20140400557958.shtml

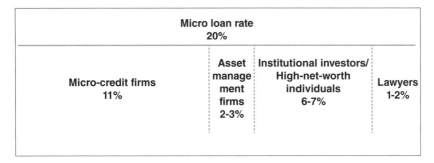

FIGURE 4.11 Microcredit companies – profit distribution.
Source: Zhang, (2014); FGI Analysis.

individual residents borrowing for social purposes and immediate cash flow requirements; but pawnshops today serve mainly China's SMEs. Pawnshops are mostly self-financed with only a small portion of bank loans. The major risk for pawnshops is the quality of their loans. Pawnshops are mostly small in scale with little debt, but even one default of their loans may cause the pawnshop to face bankruptcy. Anecdotal discussions with market experts suggest that pawnshops may not have systemic risks, given their relatively small scale; however, if they have engaged in illegal deposit taking, a failure of one pawnshop could have contagion implications at the local level.

4.4.6 Private/Informal Lending

Private lending (between individuals) is not subject to any kind of supervision, and the size of private lending is hard to estimate. The PBOC and CBRC conducted one survey in 2011 to estimate the size of the private lending market. According to the survey, private lending was around RMB 3.38 trillion or roughly 8 percent of total bank loans at the end of May 2011. Press reports suggest that the size of private lending increased rapidly after the global financial crisis,[16] and was estimated to reach RMB 5.28 trillion at the end of 2012.[17]

One reason for the rise of the informal lending market is the development of China's private economy. Private enterprises have

---

[16]For example, see news report: http://www.ce.cn/xwzx/gnsz/gdxw/201409/22/t20140922_3571132.shtml

[17]Based on CreditEase's report: Report on Development and Risk of China's Private Lending.

become the pillar of China's economic growth, with more and more SMEs entering the fast-growing track before the global financial crisis. Since the private lending market occurs without state intervention, the market is particularly active in provinces with dominant private economy such as Zhejiang, Guangdong and Fujian. The other reason is the imbalance of China's industrial structure. Most SMEs are concentrated in the manufacturing and light industrial sectors.

According to PBOC (2004), there are four types of private lending based on different fund use and interest rates:

1. Mutual financing among individuals with low interest rates
2. Credit lending with relatively higher interest rates between private enterprises
3. Informal lending, including underground banking and illegal fund raising
4. Internal financing of enterprises.

However, not all of the private lending activities are subject to high credit risk. According to the CreditEase (2013) report, private lending without interest charges could be seen as individual lending between family members or friends, with equity-like characteristics which do not carry high credit risk or spillover effect. Only the portion of private lending with high interest rates should be counted as shadow banking risky assets. The estimated portion of private lending with interest was around 15 percent in 2013 (CreditEase, 2013). If this is indeed the case, the estimated size of risky assets in China's private lending market is relatively small compared to other shadow banking assets.

There is, of course, an underlying risk with private lending, if such lending were based on Ponzi schemes, with high interest rates used to raise new funds and create the illusion of profits (Yan and Li, 2014). In 2009, when the PBOC tightened monetary policy, it became extremely hard for private lending entities to obtain credit from banks or OFIs. Consequently, a large number of funding chains broke up. There was, however, no systemic contagion effect.

4.4.7 P2P Internet Lending Platforms

There is considerable debate whether peer-to-peer (P2P) lending constitutes financial innovation. Such lending uses the online credit platform to facilitate credit information gathering for lenders and borrowers.

China's P2P lending has grown rapidly since 2006. Unfortunately, there are no official data for the size of this market. Without specific supervision for P2P lending, some new P2P platforms may not have the requisite capacity to control their risks. Default events or fraud in this market are also very frequent. However, successful platforms, such as RenRenDai and CreditEase have established specific and successful business models, which appear to be able to control their risks and facilitate SME financing (P2P and Internet finance are discussed in more detail in Chapter 6).

4.5 INTERCONNECTIVITY BETWEEN SHADOW BANKING AND THE OFFICIAL BANKING SYSTEM

As in other countries, there is a close nexus between the shadow banking entities described above – trust companies, banks' WMPs and the interbank market – and the official banking system. These financial institutions interconnect through holding each other's shares, investing in each other's products and using each other's distribution channels (mainly bank channels). Other entities, such as pawnshops, microcredit companies and P2P lending have grown in parallel, but may be less closely connected. Table 4.8 illustrates the connections between shadow banking and the official banking system in China.

To sum up, the risks embedded in China's shadow banking system include:

1. The borrowers are generally riskier, and the underlying asset quality is often hard to measure.
2. In the case of default, it is unclear who will assume the loss, because of the complicated product distribution channels and the cross-holdings in each other's products, as the ultimate holder of the assets may not be the originator.
3. Moral hazard from central and local governments' ownership in both banks and shadow banks. Contagion could spread from weaker financial institutions, as the stronger institutions with implicit deposit insurance may be asked to help resolve the weaker ones.
4. Retail investors assume that the WMPs and shadow bank assets that they hold or bought from a selling bank (not necessarily the originator) is responsible for default risk, as they (rightly or wrongly) believed in an implicit bank guarantee.

TABLE 4.8 The Chinese shadow banking–banking nexus (RMB).

	Size	Comments
Official banking system		
Banks/financing companies/leasing firms	Assets: 131 TN Loans: 67 TN	
Shadow banking		
Bank WMPs	Assets: 7.1 TN Credits: 1.8 TN	▪ Shift deposits back and forth ▪ Securitize loans as a channel to banks ▪ Generate fee income for banks
Entrusted loans	Credits: 5.7 TN	▪ Not counted as part of credit quota ▪ Act as bridge loans of corporates to repay or rollover existing bank loans
Trust companies	AUM: 7 TN Credits: 5.3 TN	▪ Banks distribute trusts and earn fee income ▪ Securitize loans as a channel to banks
Brokers' asset management	Credits: 1 TN	▪ Securitize loans as a new channel to banks
Informal loans	Credits: 4.5 TN	▪ Act as bridge loans of SMEs or property firms to repay or roll over bank loans
Corporate bonds	Size: 7 TN	▪ About 52% of bonds bought by banks and their WMPs ▪ A significant part underwritten by banks

Source: GacHua Securities Research (2012).

5. These non-standard credit assets are not subject to the same standards of oversight, supervision and transparency as commercial banks, and this leads to inadequate monitoring of asset quality, moral hazard and no accountability for ultimate credit losses.

6. In the end, funding costs may rise, triggering a possible vicious circle of higher lending rates, higher defaults and rising systemic risks.

4.6 SHADOW BANKING'S IMPACT AND REGULATORY IMPLICATIONS

While Chapter 7 provides a more detailed discussion of policy recommendations to deal with China's shadow banking problem, this section summarizes some of the key macroeconomic and financial implications.

4.6.1 Shadow Banking's Impact on the Macroeconomy and Financial System

The regulatory authorities understand that in fulfilling gaps in the formal financial system, the shadow banking industry brings benefits to the Chinese economy but there are also risks that need to be managed (Yan and Li, 2014).

4.6.1.1 Impact on Fiscal Policy

As a supplement of credit to the formal credit system, shadow banking has helped to relieve the funding pressure on local governments. Currently, more than 50 percent of total tax revenue accrues to the central government, but central government spending comprises only 10 percent of total government spending. Because the bulk of the fiscal spending is incurred by local governments, and tax revenues are inadequate, their funding pressure is enormous. Under these circumstances, local governments used their local government financing platforms (LGFPs) as vehicles in providing the necessary funding to promote economic development in their jurisdiction, particularly during the Asian and the global financial crises in 1997 and 2008 respectively.

LGFPs have played an active role in improving people's livelihood and protecting the environment. At the end of 2010, RMB 1.4 trillion of the local government debt was used to fund education, public health and other livelihood-related areas while RMB 401.6 billion funded energy conservation projects.

However, these financing platforms also pose risks to local government fiscal sustainability. A number of local governments have accumulated debts, including from shadow banking, that are beyond the levels permitted under the existing rules or regulations. Also, some local governments were willing to pay interest rates higher than their sovereign debt status would imply, thus worsening their risks of debt default. Moreover, LGFPs are not subject to prudential management or disclosure standards that ensure fiscal prudence.

A safe and sound financial system would clearly need measures to strengthen the fiscal sustainability of local governments, including higher transparency of local public finances, so that an efficient and stable municipal bond market can be built.

4.6.1.2 Impact on Regulatory Policy

In exploiting regulatory gaps and arbitrage, shadow banking can blunt regulatory policy and tools. For example, the credit provided to the real estate sector through shadow banking can offset the effects of macro prudential controls on bank lending to prevent a real estate bubble. On the other hand, by providing higher deposit rates to savers and returns to investors, shadow banking can reduce financial repression and inequality and alleviate the unintended consequences of official policies on controlled interest rates.

Furthermore, an unintended consequence of regulatory policy is the considerable difference in financing costs between SOEs and private firms, especially SMEs. Shadow banking can arbitrage out these differences, but at the same time blur the risks between the shadow and formal banking sectors by binding these risks through cross-holdings of WMPs.

4.6.1.3 Impact on Financial Stability

The rapid growth in shadow banking and lack of transparency has increased the potential risks to systemic stability.

Shadow banking credit activities have not necessarily added credit risks to sectors that already suffer from overcapacity, operating losses or are essentially non-viable. But being less transparent, and having bundled these risks into WMPs, the risks are now transmitted to the formal banking system. Resolution of these risks will, therefore, involve sorting out the economic viability, liquidity and solvency of the underlying borrowers, and clarifying the embedded maturity transformation, liquidity transformation, credit transformation and leverage within the entire financial system.

4.6.1.4 Impact on Mainstream Banking System

Shadow banking has challenged the traditional deposit-taking business model of commercial banks. Such challenge, however, has promoted the banking reform process and interest rate liberalization. Banks are now reconsidering their business model in the face of the challenges of both technology (e-finance) and market competition from shadow banking institutions.

As indicated above, the close interconnectivity between shadow banking activities and traditional banking business implies that shocks in any sector could be transmitted rapidly to other sectors. However, there are fundamental issues like the high level of inter-enterprise credit and lack of access by SMEs to equity capital, working capital and long-term funding, that must also be addressed.

4.6.1.5 Impact on Capital Market

On the positive side, shadow banking has promoted the deepening of the capital market by widening the tools and instruments of both indirect financing and direct financing. Privately led informal lenders often play the role of "merchant banks," by taking over inefficient borrowers and improving their asset utilization and efficiency. New forms of microcredit lending, P2P lending and private/informal lending give SMEs alternative choices of funding.

On the negative side, because shadow banking still relies on the official banking sector for funding, it has not improved significantly a major deficiency of the capital market, which is its limited capacity in raising equity capital for SMEs, for innovation and higher-risk higher-return ventures. A fundamental problem of the Chinese financial sector is its overreliance on the banking system, which is short-term in outlook, and based on debt financing. If leverage continues to increase, the system is inherently fragile. If the capital market does not evolve new forms of equity fund raising for SMEs and for innovation and growth, the system will continue to be short-term biased and become vulnerable to maturity mismatches.

4.6.2 Current Regulatory Reforms For Shadow Banking

In addressing the emerging shadow banking problem, China's financial regulators were aware of the need to maintain a fine balance between the need to maintain financial stability and the need to promote financial innovation, encourage positive interactions between financial markets and real economy, and maintain the sustainability of such interactions. Some of the inherent problems lie in the difficulties of coordinating the multiple regulators involved in supervising shadow banking activities.

There are about nine different regulatory entities overseeing China's shadow banking sector.[18] For example, guarantors are regulated by 7 entities: PBOC, CBRC, NDRC, Ministry of Finance, Ministry of Commerce, Ministry of Information and Information Technology, and State Administration for Industry and Commerce (Yan and Li, 2014).

At the beginning of 2014, the State Council issued Document 107 as a high-level supervision guide that proposes a general framework for supervision of shadow banking activities, with detailed rules or regulations by individual regulators that would follow the principles laid down by Document 107.

Specifically, the Directive aims to:

1. Make clear arrangements for shadow banking supervision powers and responsibilities, which will facilitate future implementation of specific policies.
2. Improve the production of shadow banking statistics, which should include data on business volume and the number and risk profile of shadow banking institutions.
3. Propose specific regulatory initiatives, including:
   a. Clearly define the scope of business (i.e., activities not allowed):
      i. Banks' wealth management funds should be separated from their own funds and should not be used to purchase their own loans or conduct wealth management fund pooling.
      ii. Trust companies should not conduct non-standard wealth management fund pooling; banks should not guarantee bonds and notes.
      iii. Small-loan companies should not take deposits.
   b. Impose stricter capital and provisioning requirements.

Document 107 is a framework guideline issued by the State Council, while specific regulations will be introduced by PBOC, CBRC and other related agencies to give effect to the guideline. The current regulations are shown in Table 4.9.

---

[18]The nine entities include PBOC, CBRC, CSRC, CIRC, NDRC, Ministry of Finance, Ministry of Commerce, Ministry of Information and Information Technology, and State Administration for Industry and Commerce.

TABLE 4.9 Regulations on the shadow banking system.

WMP	■ CBRC requires banks to limit the investment of WMP proceeds in credit-related assets at any time to below 35 percent of WMP fund balance or 4 percent of banks' total assets, whichever is the lower. ■ CBRC: Banks are also prohibited from providing explicit or implicit guarantee to these non-standardized credit assets (which include loans, trust loans, entrusted loans, bank acceptances, letter of credit, receivables, equity investments with repo clause, etc.). ■ CBRC: Separate accounting is required for each product. Any change of asset quality needs to be disclosed to investors within 5 days. ■ CBRC: Banks' on-sale of other institutions' products need to be approved by their headquarters. ■ PBOC bans bond trading between banks' proprietary books and WMP accounts and requires banks to have separate accounts for every WMP.
Bank off-balance sheet assets	■ CBRC requires global systemically important banks and banks with total assets (on- and off-balance sheet) of over RMB1.6 trn to disclose 12 indicators by end-July every year. These indicators include on- and off-balance sheet assets, interbank assets and liabilities, financial instruments issued, trade payments, entrusted assets, underwriting business, derivatives, trading and available for sale (AFS) securities, tier-3 assets, and cross-border assets and liabilities.
Trust	■ CBRC requires trust products to discontinue the asset/fund pool business model. ■ CBRC plans to launch a registry system for trust products, and make trust company staff (including project managers, project companies, department heads and shareholders) liable for trust projects for life.
LGFV	■ CBRC requires banks to 1. not increase bank loan exposure to LGFVs; 2. incorporate bonds, trust products and wealth management products into the calculation of total LGFV exposure;

(*continued*)

TABLE 4.9   *(Continued)*

	3. centralize the approval to their headquarters regarding LGFV bond purchase; 4. stop providing guarantees to LGFV bonds. In addition, banks need to contain the share of LGFV loans which have less than 100 percent cash flow cover or debt/asset ratio of over 80 percent. ■ New LGFV loans should be extended mainly to provincial-level LGFVs, social housing projects and central government projects. ■ For LGFV loans maturing in 2013, banks need to work with borrowers and local governments and submit detailed loan collection plans by end May.
Shadow banking	■ The State Council's guidelines call for tighter regulation of banks' off-balance sheet lending and specify that trust companies should return to their original purpose as asset managers and not engage in "credit-type" business.

Source: PBOC, CBRC, Thomson Reuters DataStream, Caixin, Business Daily, Trust Daily, HSBC.

Implications of new shadow banking regulations on the economy and financial markets are summarized below (Yan and Li, 2014).

1. Monitor and manage the impact on financial institutions and price of money.

    The tightening of regulations on shadow banking activities will initially tighten financing conditions in relation to the private sector. In the short term, increased regulation of shadow banking in terms of business scope, capital and liquidity will constrain shadow banks' credit expansion and lead to relatively higher lending rates.

    Given the fact that the demands for funding from the private sector are unlikely to change in the short term, it is likely that the overall financing costs of the non-financial sector will increase. Specifically,

    a. Bank lending rates could rise, as reduced financing from shadow banks will give traditional lenders more bargaining power.

    b. Capital requirements on financial institutions will increase as a result of these regulations. Financial institutions will need to either increase capital or reduce risk assets. The risk premium demanded by financial institutions in raising capital will increase their financing costs, which will prompt banks to charge higher lending rates.

c. The cost of informal financing may also increase. As total financing to the private sector is restrained due to strengthened shadow banking regulation, some enterprises might have to borrow through other informal financing channels.

d. Impact on bond yield will be unclear. Supply of bonds may increase, as companies rely more on bond financing due to restrictions on financing through non-standard (shadow banking) channels. But demand may also increase, as the strengthened regulations would force banks to cut their allocation to non-standard assets and increase banks' investment in bonds. But before aggregate domestic demand is restrained, corporate bond yields are unlikely to decline, given the tighter credit conditions and strong funding demand.

In the short-term, banks' interest spreads could widen, as a result of strengthened shadow banking regulation. The current regulations essentially require banks to move away from shadow banking business and return to the traditional deposit-taking and lending business. In other words, banks will rely more on deposits rather than interbank borrowing for funding.

With deposit rates still subject to government control, banks will have stronger bargaining power over the household sector and other fund providers. So, before the deposit rate liberalization, banks' interest spreads could expand. But, as their asset expansion is under stricter regulatory control, and will be slower, banks' profit growth would not necessarily accelerate.

2. Heightened regulation may be short-term negative to the economy, but long-term positive.

In the short term, reduced financing may dampen aggregate domestic demand, especially investment demand. But in the long run, stricter regulation of shadow banking will help reduce financial risk, improve the economic structure, enhance economic efficiency and promote more sustainable growth.

Specifically, in the short term, there will be three main negative impacts on the economy:

a. Slower growth in total financing and higher financing costs for the private sector will hold back investment; and put downward pressure on economic growth. To some extent, this is desirable, as the overall investment rate is already too high.

b. Credit default risk would increase in the short term. The tightened total financing may leave some companies cash-strapped in the short term. But this risk is already inherent in the system due to the transition from an energy inefficient, manufacturing-based economy to a green, more inclusive and service-based economy.

c. Risk premium might rise as the debt default risk in the economy increases, which would put pressure on the price of risky assets. The move of riskier shadow banking business back on to banks' balance sheets and a decline in total social financing will lower overall risk appetite, which will lead to higher risk premium. The emergence of higher risk premium is exactly what the market needs in working to differentiate between bad projects and viable projects.

However, in the long term, the strengthened shadow banking regulation will help reduce financial risks, improve the economic structure and make resource allocation more efficient. The strengthening of shadow banking regulation is intended to prompt financial institutions to deleverage and rein in the rapid expansion of their financing to the private sector. This will help slow the rise of total credit as a percentage of GDP. Note that since 2008, total credit is growing faster than GDP.

Specifically, control of credit expansion will help reduce speculation in the economy, especially in real estate. The current self-reinforcing cycle of real estate bubble and credit expansion needs to be broken. This is an appropriate time to do so, when the balance of supply and demand for real estate has reached approximate equilibrium and real estate prices are becoming more affordable.

One of the specific benefits of heightened prudential oversight on shadow banking is that it will generally strengthen the macro-prudential framework, which will help mitigate the pressure on the central bank to tighten monetary policy in the short term, and offer some scope for monetary easing. Currently, China's inflation is not too high, and economic growth is moderating, so there is room for some monetary easing. In the past, the fear of credit expansion through shadow banking business prompted the PBOC to increase the required reserve ratio (RRR) and use higher interbank market interest rates to prevent excessive growth in shadow banking. The PBOC is experimenting with different forms of liquidity easing to ensure that its control of overall credit is not undermined through shadow banking activities. One of the more innovative tools used is the direct lending of RMB 1 trillion to the China Development Bank for the funding of shanty town rejuvenation. This would generate direct funding of social infrastructure without sparking off excessive interbank liquidity that could be abused to fund speculative activities.

4.7 CONCLUSION

Given the high growth of China's shadow banking sector, its impact on the real economy, the banking system and China's financial reform, the assessment of the quality of shadow banking assets is critical to determine their potential implications on financial stability. Chapter 5 examines in greater detail the quality of the shadow banking assets in China.

REFERENCES

Aegon Industrial Fund Management. 2013. CASS: China's shadow banking sector valued at around RMB 20.5 trillion, about half of GDP, 9 October. http://www.xyfunds.com.cn/info.dohscontentid=101712.htm.

Bloomberg-Businessweek. 2013. China's Shadow Banking Sector Tops $5.8 trillion – Report Says, 8 May. http://www.businessweek.com/articles/2013-05-08/chinas-shadow-banking-sector-tops-5-dot-8-trillion-report-says.

Business Insider. 2014. UBS: China's Shadow Banking Sector is Small. 27 March. http://www.businessinsider.com/chinas-shadow-banking-sector-is-small-2014-3.

CBRC (China Banking Regulatory Commission). 2013. China Banking Regulatory Commission 2013 Annual Report. http://www.cbrc.gov.cn/chinese/home/docView/3C28C92AC84242D188E2064D9098CFD2.html.

CBRC (China Banking Regulatory Commission). 2014. Notice on Improving Banks' Organization and Management System on Financial Services. http://www.cbrc.gov.cn/chinese/home/docView/057AFF8CA028474FB5 4CD5B52537C3D9.html.

China Securities Times. 2014. CASS: China's Shadow Banking Scale is about RMB 27 Trillion. 21 May. http://www.stcn.com/2014/0512/11408092. shtml.

CreditEase. 2013. Report on Development and Risk of China's Private Lending.

Cui, David, Bin Gao, Ajay Singh Kapurand, Winnie Wu, Tracy Tian, and Katherine Tai. 2014. The Coming Trust Defaults. Bank of America Merrill Lynch.

Cui, David, Tracy Tian, and Zhen Wei. 2012. Shadow Banking: Risky Business. Bank of America Merrill Lynch.

FSB (Financial Stability Board). 2013. Global Shadow Banking Monitoring Report 2013. http://www.financialstabilityboard.org/publications/r_131114.htm.

Green, Stephen, Wei Li, Lan Shen, David Jinhua Yin, and Dorris Chen. 2014. China – A Primer on Banks' Wealth Management. Standard Chartered. https:// research.standardchartered.com/configuration/ROW%20Documents/China_ %E2%80%93_A_primer_on_banks%E2%80%99_wealth_management__07 _01_14_06_18.pdf.

IMF (International Monetary Fund). 2014. Global Financial Stability Report Moving from Liquidity- to Growth-Driven Markets. http://www.imf.org/ external/pubs/FT/GFSR/2014/01/pdf/text.pdf.

Kawai, Masahiro. 2014. Financial Reform and Stability in China. April 18. Paper presented at Joint Workshop on New Phase of Chinese Reform and Growth, Beijing. National School of Development, Peking University and ADBI.

Li, Yang, Xiaojing Zhang, and Xin Chang. 2013. *China's National Balance Sheet 2013*. Beijing: China Social Sciences Press.

Pettis, Michael. 2014. China's Bad Debts Can't Be Simply Socialized. EconoMonitor, 14 July. http://www.economonitor.com/blog/2014/07/chinas-bad-debts-cant-be-simply-socialized/.

PBOC (People's Bank of China). 2004. The Report of Operation of China's Regional Finance, 2004. http://www.pbc.gov.cn/publish/goutongjiaoliu/524/ 2014/20140624195602579944558/20140624195602579944558_.html.

PBOC (People's Bank of China). 2013. China Financial Stability Report 2013. http://www.pbc.gov.cn/publish/english/959/2013/2013081315143434965 6712/20130813151434349656712_.html.

Reuters. 2013. Fitch warns on risks from shadow banking in China, 10 June. http://www.reuters.com/article/2013/06/10/us-china-lending-idUSBRE95 90UN20130610.

Sina Finance. 2014. Document 107: Basic Regulatory Principals of China's Shadow Banking, 12 February. http://finance.sina.com.cn/money/bank/ bank_hydt/20140212/152618188013.shtml.

Sheng, Andrew, and Xiao Geng. 2013. Lending in the Dark. 22 April. Project Syndicate. http://www.project-syndicate.org/commentary/the-risk-profile-of-chinese-shadow-banking-by-andrew-sheng-and-geng-xiao.

Su, Xinming. 2014. Research of Mechanism of Bank Wealth Management Products. Chinese Academy of Social Sciences (CASS) Ph.D. Dissertation.

Tao, Dong, and Weishen Deng. 2013. China: Shadow Banking – Road to Heightened Risks. Credit Suisse Economics Research. https://doc.research-and-analytics.csfb.com/docView?language=ENG&format=PDF&document_ id=1010517251&source_id=emcmt&serialid=VLRQ4TgNxWzk%2fTvHi-nuua2HrCBNc0syIwcysInvEMe0%3d.

Walter. Carl E. 2014. China and its Financial Priorities (Presentation). Center for Financial Stability, Vulnerabilities Working Group, New York, 8 April.

Wu, Winnie. 2014. An Industry Overview Report. Bank of America Merrill Lynch Global Research.

Wu, Winnie, and Michael Li. 2014. Entrusted loans: the largest 'shadow banking' component. Bank of America Merrill Lynch Global Research.

Xu, Richard, Jocelyn M Yang, and Simon Mou. 2013. China Deleveraging – Can Banks Ride Out a Financial Storm? Morgan Stanley Research.

Yan, Qingmin, and Jianhua Li. 2014. *Research of China Shadow Banking Supervision*. China Renmin University Press.

Zhang, Joe. 2014. *Inside China's Shadow Banking: The Next Subprime Crisis?* Enrich Professional Publishing.

CHAPTER 5

Inherent Risks in Chinese Shadow Banking

Wang Yao and Jodie Hu

5.1 INTRODUCTION

The analysis so far suggests that we need a system-wide view of China's credit system in examining whether the shadow banking system, which is inextricably tied to the formal banking system, poses systemic risks.

China is a net lender to the world, and any emerging shadow banking debt problem will be a domestic one without direct global systemic implications. However, corporate defaults which include debt in foreign currency such as the default of a Chinese property developer's bonds in 2014 suggested that a domestic problem can spill over to foreign banks and investors, as China is increasingly integrated with the global financial system.

While there is no room for complacency, several factors suggest that at this point in time, the potential losses from credit defaults in the Chinese financial system are still manageable. These factors include the following:

1. China is still a fast-growing economy with GDP growth at around 6–7 percent per annum, which would allow it to grow out of rising NPL or credit losses.
2. China has a high level of domestic savings, which enables the household sector to absorb a significant amount of shocks.

3. Total government debt is still manageable, even taking into consideration potential losses from the shadow banking system.

Capacity to grow out of internal losses: Being a continent-sized economy helps to sustain the growth momentum and distributes risks geographically. The Chinese economy is still urbanizing rapidly, with roughly 20 million people moving into the cities every year, so that the demand for infrastructure investment and residential property continues to grow (Zhu et al., 2014). For example, even though the coastal regions may be slackening due to slowing export growth, the inland provinces are still growing steadily, reflecting internal consumption and investments. Consequently, GDP growth at around 6–7 percent per annum would allow new growth to deal with some of the legacy losses that have been built up.

High level of domestic savings enables sectors to absorb shocks: In the last decade, China has maintained a high gross savings rate ranging from 45 to 52 percent of GDP.[1] Household savings in the form of bank deposits on average account for 82 percent of GDP, whilst household debt remains low at 35 percent of GDP. The largest component of household assets remains residential homes, estimated at 245 percent of GDP, whilst residential mortgages and consumer credit amount to not more than 23 percent of GDP. Hence, Chinese households have significant capacity to absorb shocks.

The Chinese corporate sector also has high savings in the form of depreciation allowances and retained earnings. Part of this is due to higher levels of profitability in state-owned enterprises (SOEs) that took a monopoly position in earlier years. The corporate savings was nearly 20 percent of GDP, about the same level as in the U.S. One reason for the high corporate savings is that Chinese corporations tend not to pay out dividends (Geng and N'Diaye, 2012).

In assessing the credit risks of the Chinese banking system, one needs to appreciate a signal difference between Chinese banking practice and Western banks. Chinese banks lend by immediately crediting the borrower with an equivalent deposit, hence corporate deposits are high relative to loans, because of the implicit "collateral" of the borrowers with the banks.

For example, at the end of 2013, corporate deposits with the Chinese banking system amounted to RMB 51 trillion or 89 percent of GDP, compared with 7 percent of GDP in the U.S. (Table 5.1). Such deposits

---

[1] CEIC data.

TABLE 5.1 Non-financial corporate and household sectors credit.

		China						U.S.		
		2007			2013			2013		
		RMB TN	% GDP	% Loans	RMB TN	% GDP	% Loans	US$ TN	% GDP	% Loans
Non-financial corporate sector	**Deposits**	18	67	78	51	89	85	1	7	48
	Loans	23	85	100	60	105	100	2	14	100
	Net credit	5	19	22	9	16	15	1	7	52
Household sector	**Deposits**	17	63	340	47	82	235	9	51	64
	Loans	5	19	100	20	35	100	13	79	100
	Net credit	−12	−44	−240	−27	−47	−135	5	29	36

Data sources: PBOC 2013, FRB 2014.

amounted to 85 percent of total bank loans to the non-financial corporate sector. In the U.S., the equivalent amount was 48 percent. The simple reason is that the Chinese domestic savings rate also comprises high corporate savings. Many foreign analysts fail to appreciate that the high credit ratio in China has a counterparty in its high corporate deposit level. This does not mean that there is no credit exposure on individual loans, but it does mean that the banks' control over credit exposure to the corporate sector is better because there is a "deposit collateral." However, it is possible that some corporate deposits may have been drawn down quickly or used to guarantee third party loans and losses could be borne by the guarantor. Nevertheless, the exposure of the banks is limited to the extent that such collateral exists. The credit risks are complicated where inter-enterprise credit guarantees exist.

About 60 percent of bank loans are to SOEs, which also account for a large proportion of corporate deposits. As SOEs are ultimately backed by the Government, the credit exposure of the banks to SOEs is to quasi-sovereign risks. The same applies in the case of loans to local government financing platforms (LGFPs).

Total government debt is still manageable: Part of the concerns of many analysts is the growing level of debt of local governments. In 2013, the National Audit Office (NAO) undertook a comprehensive survey of the total debt of the government, focusing particularly on local government debt. As of June 30, 2013, the NAO estimated that gross government debt was RMB 30.3 trillion, of which central government debt was RMB 9.5 trillion and railway debt RMB 2.9 trillion. Local government debt was RMB 17.9 trillion, of which agency debt was RMB 7.8 trillion and LGFP debt was RMB 10.1 trillion. Since RMB 30.3 trillion represents 53.3 percent of GDP, China's total government debt is still manageable compared with an average of 111 percent for OECD (Organisation for Economic Co-operation and Development) countries in 2013.

The concerns over local government debt were mainly due to the inability of some local governments to pay interest and principal. This would vary from district to district, with the first-tier cities being in a much better debt servicing position. Furthermore, according to the Ministry of Finance, net assets of SOEs (excluding direct ownership of land by different levels of government) under the control of central and local governments amounted to RMB 16.5 trillion and RMB 15.2 trillion respectively at the end of 2013, sufficient to cover the total gross government debt of RMB 30.3 trillion (BBVA, 2014b).

5.2 GETTING TO THE HEART OF THE PROBLEM – THE UNDERLYING ASSET QUALITY

Research by Richard Xu of Morgan Stanley illustrated that the ultimate credit exposures of the Chinese banking system (including shadow banks) ultimately fall on four major categories of borrowers – large corporations (in the Chinese context, mostly SOEs), private sector SMEs, real estate companies, and LGFVs (Xu et al., 2013a). Assessment of the quality of these four different classes of banking assets will provide an indication of the potential risks of such assets becoming NPLs, as well as the likely impact on the formal banking and broader financial system.

Since 2008, the Chinese economy (being a net saver) has been investing its funds largely in fixed asset investment (FAI), either in the form of residential and commercial buildings and infrastructure.

Using simple flow calculations from China's national income accounts, the value of FAI from 2008–2013 amounted to RMB 168.7 trillion. Such FAI was largely funded through domestic savings, of which a large proportion was channeled through the financial system. For example, total social funding (TSF) for the period 2008–2013, based on the People's Bank of China (PBOC) estimates (a flow concept) was RMB 80.8 trillion, of which RMB 50.7 trillion or 63 percent came from the banking system via broad money (M2 or currency + deposits). According to PBOC data, the increase in loans by depositary institutions during the same period was only RMB 47 trillion, which meant that more than RMB 120 trillion (RMB 168.7 – 47 trillion) in funding for FAI came from non-bank sources.

The difference between FAI and TSF was RMB 87.9 trillion, or 52.1 percent of total FAI. This seems too large to be wholly financed from own (internal) resources. For example, even though local governments would finance their FAI using fiscal resources, at least 80 percent of their total funding came from bank loans, build-transfer schemes (BT) and the bond market. The best of the real estate developers would fund at most 30 percent of their projects through equity. Assuming that self-funding through equity was 30 percent of total FAI, the unexplained funding element would be roughly RMB 37 trillion or 72 percent of 2012 GDP.

This figure roughly corresponds to the size of the shadow banking system.

This crude estimation is important because if the self-funding was mostly equity and retained earnings, then the impact of losses from lending to FAI on the financial system would be small. If most of the funding was derived from the shadow banks and banking system, then losses would have an impact on the financial system as a whole.

In February 2015, the PBOC released the TSF stock data for the first time (Table 5.2), providing an official estimation of the stock size of four major categories of shadow banking, namely, entrusted loans, trust loans, bankers' acceptances and microloans. These products grew rapidly from RMB 3.9 trillion or 10 percent of TSF in 2008 to RMB 22.5 trillion or 18 percent of TSF at the end of 2014.

From 2003 to 2012, the NPL of China's banking system had been declining steadily; however, it reversed trend and rose gradually to above 1 percent in the first quarter of 2014. Although this level of NPL is still low by international standards, the regulators have required the banks to provide higher provisioning against such NPLs, equivalent to an average of 280 percent. The banks' capital adequacy ratio (CAR) at the end of 2012 was 13 percent. An estimate by a leading bank economist for the China Development Reform Forum suggested that the rising pressure of NPLs can be offset by economic growth of more than 7 percent, containing bank NPLs at a level below 1.5 percent. In a pessimistic scenario where GDP growth slows down to less than 6 percent, banks' NPLs could rise to 5 percent and trigger a credit problem (Table 5.3).

In the shadow banking system, where regulatory oversight is less intensive, there is insufficient official data on the status of NPLs, provisioning and CAR, but they are likely to be worse than those of the banks. Shadow banks borrow mostly from the banking system, with a relatively small amount of self-financing. If shadow banks went into financial difficulties, their NPLs could spread to the banking system, impairing its asset quality. This means that the NPLs of the whole banking system could be higher than the 1 percent disclosed in the banks' books, but a more realistic estimate would have to examine the potential credit losses in the shadow banking sector.

There is no authoritative assessment of the NPLs of China's shadow banks. It is important to recognize that shadow banking adds an extra "layer" to the financial intermediation process of the formal banking system. In doing so, the shadow banks offer alternative channels of

TABLE 5.2 Stock of total social financing in China, 2007–2014 (RMB trillion).

	TSF	RMB loans	Foreign currency-denominated loans	Entrusted loans	Trust loans	Bankers' acceptances	Corporate bonds	Equity financing	Other*
2007	32.1	25.2	1.1	1.4	0.4	1.2	0.8	1.4	0.7
2008	38.0	29.9	1.2	1.9	0.7	1.3	1.4	1.6	0.1
2009	51.2	39.2	1.9	2.5	1.1	1.7	2.7	1.9	0.2
2010	65.0	47.0	2.2	3.6	1.5	4.1	3.8	2.5	0.3
2011	76.7	54.6	2.4	4.4	1.7	5.1	5.2	2.9	0.4
2012	91.4	62.8	3.1	5.2	3.0	6.1	7.5	3.2	0.6
2013	107.5	71.7	3.3	7.2	4.8	6.9	9.3	3.4	0.8
2014	122.9	81.4	3.5	9.3	5.4	6.8	11.7	3.8	1.0

Note: includes real estate for investment and loans by microloan companies.
Data sources: PBOC 2015; author's calculations.

TABLE 5.3 Estimates of GDP growth and NPLs.

	GDP Growth Rate	Range of Bank NPLs
Optimistic scenario	Higher than 8%	Under 1%
Stable scenario	7.5–8.0%	1–1.2%
Pessimistic scenario	7–7.5%	1.2–1.5%
Stress scenario	Lower than 6%	More than 5%

Source: CDRF (2014).

funding to the real sector, but they have also complicated the identification of credit risks.

As such, we need to evaluate the non-performing loans (NPLs) of shadow banks via an assessment of the quality of their underlying assets. If the underlying assets turned bad, the high leverage of the intermediaries would spread contagion throughout the whole financial system.

Since shadow banking institutions are mainly exposed to their non-financial clients, namely, the corporate sector (SOEs and SMEs), real estate companies and LGFPs, this section examines these four sectors in more depth in terms of their exposures as well as the implications for the NPL ratio of the formal and shadow banking system.

5.3 NON-FINANCIAL CORPORATE SECTOR (EXCLUDING REAL ESTATE COMPANIES)

SOEs and non-SOE enterprises (large private sector corporates and SMEs) are major users of banking and shadow banking credit. As China's GDP growth moderates, concerns have been raised about their debt servicing capacity. Slower growth will affect their operating performance, notably productivity and profitability, which in turn determines debt-servicing capacity. Thus, it is the productivity and profitability of the enterprises in the real economy that ultimately determines the underlying asset quality in the banking as well as shadow banking system, and hence, the potential risk of NPLs.

5.3.1 The Surge in Credit to Enterprises

Since 2008, total credit provided to enterprises has increased significantly, especially for small businesses. As shown in Table 4.7 in

Chapter 4, bank loans to large and mid-sized enterprises almost doubled from 2007 to 2012. At the same time, bank loans to SMEs tripled, in line with strong government support and the rapid growth of guarantee companies (that can share SME credit risks with banks). At the end of 2013, the size of loans to small and microenterprises is estimated to have risen to as much as 29.4 percent of total bank lending (PBOC, 2013). In addition, the proportion of loans offered to small businesses increased from 20.2 percent in 2007 to 25.7 percent in 2012; while the proportion of loans to large and mid-sized corporations fell from 55.2 percent in 2007 to 45 percent in 2012.

It is also noteworthy that the annual growth of alternative financing (generally referred to as shadow banking activities)[2] had exceeded growth in bank loans since 2010. As SMEs often face constraints in accessing bank credit relative to SOEs and large corporations, it is therefore likely that a larger part of credit offered through alternative financing channels is for small businesses. Concomitantly, the increase of total credit to small businesses could be larger than that indicated by the growth in bank loans.

5.3.2 Increase in Enterprise Leverage amid Lower Profitability

Along with the increase in credit, enterprises' leverage also increased (as suggested by the high debt to GDP ratio of enterprises), with the leverage concentrated in SOEs and large corporations (Figure 5.1).[3]

However, while enterprises have increased their leverage, China's GDP growth has slowed down since 2010, reducing the level of new business opportunities. Thus, part of the rising leverage was due to

---

[2]Morgan Stanley research (Xu et al., 2013a/b), defines alternative financing as Trust loans, Entrusted loans, Securities firms' assets management products, Interbank entrusted payment, Undiscounted bank acceptance, Asset cross sale via financial asset exchange, Pawnshop loans, Financial leasing, Microlending and Underground lending.

[3]According to Ministry of Industry and Information Technology of China, large enterprises refer to enterprises with more than 1,000 employees and more than RMB 400 million in annual revenue. Mid-size enterprises refer to enterprises with 300 to 1,000 employees and RMB 20–400 million in revenue. Small businesses refer to enterprises with less than 300 employees and less than RMB 20 million in revenue.

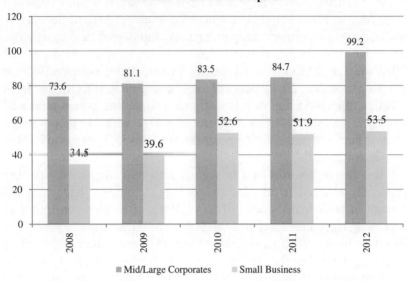

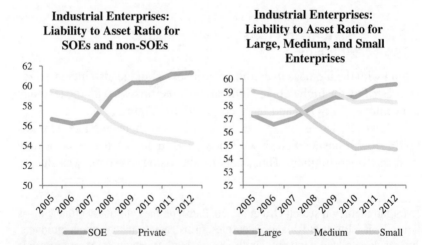

FIGURE 5.1 SOEs vs. non-SOEs: Selected financial indicators.
Source: Xu et al. (2013a), CEIC.

continued commitments to long-term FAI, lower cash flow, higher interest payments, rollover of existing debt or sustained losses from operations. Figure 5.2 shows that the debt-servicing ability of enterprises (as indicated by the interest coverage ratio: Earnings Before

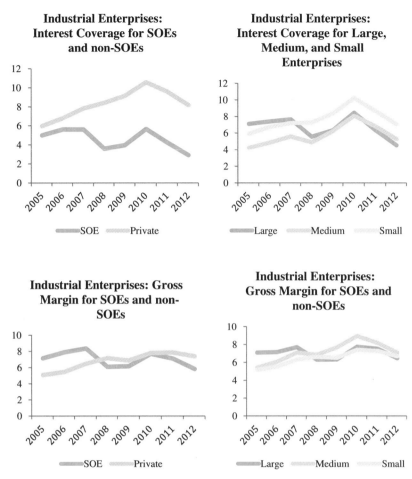

FIGURE 5.2 Interest coverage and gross margin for industrial enterprises.
Source: CEIC.

Interest and Taxes (EBIT)/interest payment) has declined significantly since 2010. Moreover, SOEs have lower interest coverage than private enterprises, while large/mid-sized enterprises have lower interest coverage than small enterprises. Gross margins (EBIT/total revenue) also decreased significantly for SOEs, which is an indicator of excess capacity.

The increase in leverage with declining interest coverage ratios and gross margins suggests that the productivity growth of enterprises is not keeping pace with credit growth.

5.3.3 State-Owned Enterprises (SOEs)

SOEs have lower productivity compared to non-SOE "large enterprises."[4] In the past, the Chinese government relied on massive investments to drive economic growth, often implemented through SOEs with preferential policy incentives. Policy-led investment drives often do not take into consideration the commercial implications of industrial capacity or market demand.

As market demand has shrunk in recent years, many large SOEs are facing the problems of over capacity and low profitability. To avoid mass unemployment and the social impact of bankruptcy among underperforming large SOEs, government subsidies have been used to keep such SOEs afloat. The decline in SOEs' productivity in industries experiencing overcapacity is a major risk to their debt repayment ability. Figure 5.3 shows that SOEs are more vulnerable to over-capacity problems in the mining, manufacturing, and construction sectors (with return on assets (ROA) much smaller than non-SOE large enterprises).

5.3.4 Small and Medium Enterprises (SMEs)

Although the official data shows that small businesses and larger non-SOEs are more efficient than SOEs; such data is subject to survivorship bias. The official data on the proportion of small enterprises that suffered losses is lower than mid-sized and large enterprises, which does not seem plausible or realistic. In fact, anecdotal evidence suggests that many SMEs simply "disappear" without bothering to file for bankruptcy. Some caution is therefore called for when interpreting the official statistics about small businesses being the best performers among private enterprises.

The problem with the entire SME sector, however, lies in the lack of a level playing field in terms of access to funds, markets and other resources. However, unlike the large SOEs, SMEs have fewer problems of overcapacity and inefficiency.

Although the proportion of bank lending to small businesses has significantly increased, the large state-owned commercial banks (SOCBs) are still lending mainly to big SOEs; the majority of the bank loans to SMEs are generated through smaller, rural and city commercial banks. Also, the majority of small enterprises still fund

---

[4]"Large" refers to enterprises with more than RMB 5 million revenue before 2007 and above RMB 20 million revenue after 2007.

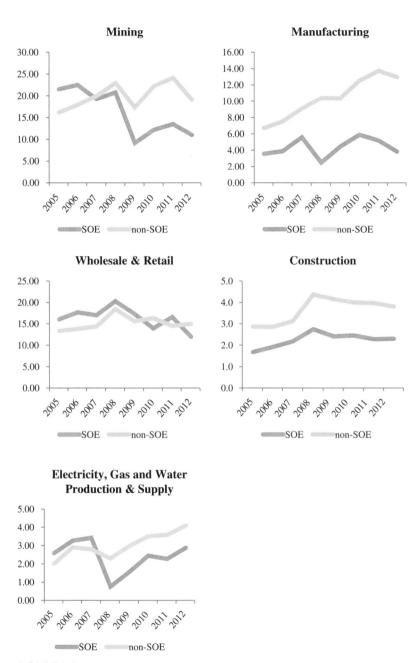

FIGURE 5.3 ROA for SOEs and non-SOEs in different sectors.
Source: National Bureau of Statistics.

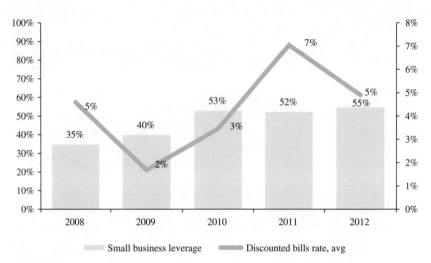

FIGURE 5.4 The rapidly increasing leverage of SMEs since 2010.
Source: CEIC; Morgan Stanley Research.

themselves through non-bank financing, which accounts for the rapid growth of shadow banking. For example, private lending of RMB 4.8 trillion (sometimes called underground lending) arose to meet the credit needs of individuals and SMEs (KPMG, 2013).

SMEs with an accelerated increase in leverage are a potential source of NPLs for the shadow banks in China (Figure 5.4). The increased risk of SME business is often attributed to the decline in export demand and the volatility in China's financial markets since 2011. With less capital and smaller scale, small businesses are more vulnerable to any economic slowdown. As shown earlier in Figures 5.2 and 5.3, although small businesses showed better performance than large enterprises, their interest coverage and gross margin have decreased since 2010.

Shadow banks' lending activities to SMEs are riskier than bank lending, because:

1. Shadow banks are subject to less prudential regulations and more willing to assume higher risks while providing less capital buffer.
2. Shadow banks may not exercise the same level of due diligence as formal banks or have access to nationwide data on credit quality, which may lead to higher NPLs.

Recent reports of fraud in SME lending add to these concerns. Regulatory support and innovations enabled banks to offer short-term discounted bill loans to SMEs at below 2 percent per annum in 2010. When the CBRC scrutinized discounted bill-related interbank innovation after the 2011 financial turmoil, some trade finance bills were found to have been used for speculative purposes and unsound projects (KPMG, 2013).

Moody's suggested that the SME NPL ratios are already three times higher than the overall average NPL ratio of the formal banking system (KPMG, 2013). Other factors that contribute to the risks of loans to SOEs and SMEs include the potential loss in real estate loans due to property market price corrections.

MUTUAL AND CROSS GUARANTEES IN CHINA

In China, a mutual guarantee operates on the basis of two borrowers each taking individual bank loans but simultaneously guaranteeing to the bank(s) the liability on each other's loan in case of default. Cross guarantees operate on a similar basis for a group (three or more) of borrowers who promise to settle the outstanding loans in any member's default.

Cross guaranteed loans are estimated to account for 0.5 percent of the total loans in China (Liang, 2014) or 5 percent of the loans of small and microenterprises (Lian and Xu, 2014), with a high growth rate in recent years. About half of the 2500 listed companies are involved in mutual or cross guarantee schemes (Lian and Xu, 2014).

Since 2011, the risks of cross guaranteed loans have surfaced across the guarantee network. In Zhejiang, some SMEs encountered financial difficulties and "contaminated" other firms in the same guarantee group, resulting in a shutdown of the whole circle of firms. A sample from People's Court in Longwan, Wenzhou showed that 97 per cent of the disputes between banks and enterprises in 2012 involved cross guarantee arrangements (Wen, 2014).

Cross guarantee schemes can help alleviate the problem of information asymmetry for the lending bank. However, in China's case, the interaction between government, banks and enterprises makes the cross guarantee process dysfunctional, with high risk and potential for contagion.

The cross guarantee program enabled SMEs to bind their risks with SOEs by entering into the same guarantee network. It revealed

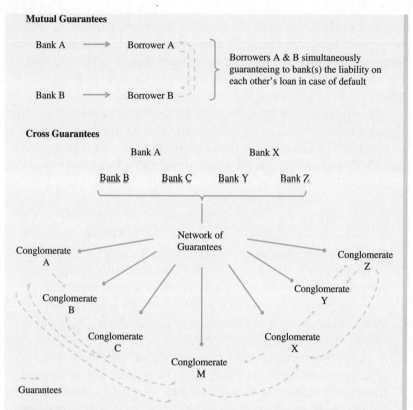

FIGURE 5.5 Network of guarantees of conglomerates heightens chain reaction of defaults.
Source: FGI Analysis.

a fundamental problem in the SOEs' corporate governance. SOEs engage in cross guarantees in order to help their suppliers or customers along their supply chain. However, normally companies that provide credit guarantees to another should have sound reasons to persuade their board of directors to approve the issuance of the guarantee. Since Chinese corporate authority lies somewhere in between the CEO alone or with the consensus of the board, such ambiguity has led to cases where guarantees have been provided based on non-business-related interests, which reflects a failure in corporate governance.

Banks are supposed to take the central role in credit assessment by reviewing the credit rationale for guarantees and recent financial statements and qualifications of the borrowers. However, as the cross guarantee program is encouraged by local governments who sometimes intervene in the process, banks perceive less responsibility to fulfill the due diligence check.

The guarantee practice itself creates another layer of information asymmetry on top of the absence of credit records, because individual banks may not be aware of the cross guarantees that their borrowers may have made with other banks. For example, the six subsidiaries of Wantong Group and Yatai Group in Shandong made guarantees to each other and also involved seven other companies, making a very complex guarantee network (see Figure 5.5). Companies that participate in such multiple guarantee programs may not be aware of the full implications of all their guarantees.

There is increasing awareness that such cross guarantees weaken the credit due diligence process.

Fixed assets of small businesses increased from RMB 1.6 trillion in 2001 to RMB 7.5 trillion in 2012; while that of mid-sized/large enterprises increased from RMB 4.8 trillion to RMB 21 trillion during the same period (CEIC). A large portion of those fixed assets are real estate, and are highly likely to be used as collateral to obtain loans from banks or shadow banks. Thus, if real estate prices fell significantly, the declining value of collaterals would, in turn, impact the RMB 30.3 trillion and RMB 17.3 trillion of bank loans to mid-sized/large enterprises and small businesses respectively.

Furthermore, enterprises' other financial assets (particularly wealth management products (WMPs)) have increased dramatically from RMB 1.4 trillion in 2004 to around RMB 30 trillion in 2012 (Ma et al., 2012), or more than 16 percent of total assets. If the investments in WMPs turn bad, it will reduce enterprises' cash flows and liquidity ratios.

5.4 REAL ESTATE COMPANIES

Real estate companies warrant special attention in terms of risk analysis because of their special role in the economy. The construction sector is one of the largest sectors in the economy and its performance has direct and indirect effects on the profitability of many other industries along the

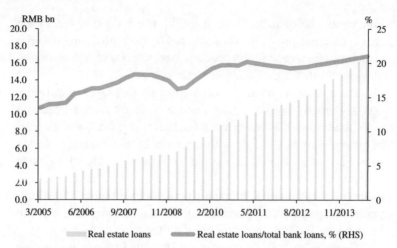

FIGURE 5.6 Real estate loans account for one-fifth of bank credit.
Source: BBVA (2014a).

supply chain. Market estimates suggest that real estate is commonly used as collateral for about 20–25 percent of bank loans (Zhu et al., 2014). Hence, a property price correction can affect NPLs as well as government revenue (value of land sales and property tax). As the largest assets of the households, real estate values have a strong wealth effect on consumption. All these interconnections can amplify the impact of developments in the real estate sector on the overall economy.

5.4.1 The Financial Sector's Exposure to Real Estate Companies

Real estate loans, namely mortgage loans and loans to real estate developers, account for an increasing share of total bank loans (Figure 5.6). The percentage of real estate loans reached 20 percent of total loans in 2010 and has remained high ever since. On the shadow banking side, the real estate sector accounted for over 30 percent of the total new issuance of combined unit trust products in 2010 and 2011 (KPMG, 2012) and for almost 10 percent of existing trust products by the end of 2013.[5]

---

[5]China Trust Association publishes the trust statistics on a quarterly basis. The data is available from http://www.xtxh.net/xtxh/statisticsEN/19913.htm

As discussed earlier, the real estate sector plays a critical role in China due to its strong linkages to other sectors through both the economic and financial channels. One well-recognized channel is the use of real estate as collateral in securing bank credit. The IMF estimated that 30 to 45 percent of loans extended by the five largest banks have been backed by collateral, the majority of which is real estate (IMF, 2011). CBRC staff estimated that around 50 percent of bank loans are directly or indirectly connected with the real estate sector. Any property price correction will impact asset quality by not only rendering property projects less profitable, but also by reducing the value of property offered as collateral by SOEs, LGFPs and SMEs.

The real estate sector is at the heart of the problem because of its wide-ranging and complex interconnections with other sectors (Figure 5.7). Any slowdown in the real estate sector would adversely affect construction-related industries along its entire supply chain, including steel, cement, and other construction materials (Zhang et al., 2014). The quality of the loans extended to those related industries will also be affected, leading to higher NPLs.

Shocks to the real estate sector could have an even wider impact on banks' asset quality. Chinese households have more than 40 percent of their total wealth in the form of housing (Borst, 2014). Lower property prices impose a negative wealth effect on households and will reduce

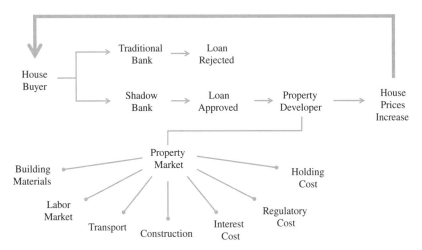

FIGURE 5.7 How property market and shadow banks affect the real economy.
Source: FGI Analysis.

consumption demand. This will feed back into lower corporate sales and profits and ultimately, slower GDP growth. Weaker corporate profits and negative household wealth effects will reduce debt-servicing capacity. Consequently, avoidance of any sharp fluctuations in real estate prices will be important to prevent systemic shocks to the whole economy and the financial system.

5.4.2 Risks of the Financial Sector from the Real Estate Industry

Whilst the critical role and size of the real estate sector is directly relevant to the health of the financial sector, in China as elsewhere, there are several factors which mitigate the downside risks.

First, the growth rate of aggregate investment in real estate has decelerated from 35 percent in 1998 to 11 percent in 2012, the lowest in the past 15 years (CDRF, 2014). As China is turning into a mature market where the overall economy will grow at a more moderate rate, it is natural for the real estate sector to slow down to a more normal path of moderate growth.

Second, the size of mortgage loans from banks is more than twice that of the loans to real estate developers. Residential mortgage loans in China are not likely to be a source of systemic stress at current levels. The household sector has large savings relative to their low level of debt. Most households should be able to sustain a drop of 15–20 percent in property prices, although a larger price plunge of 30–50 per cent could be problematic.

Although there could be short-term swings in the property market, over the long term, China is still far from being fully invested in real estate and infrastructure. China's capital stock remains below US$10,000 per capita; the equivalent figure is above US$90,000 in the U.S. and more than US$200,000 in Japan at 2011 prices (Ogus, 2012).

China's mega cities such as Beijing and Shanghai have seen huge demand for residential properties, resulting in prices comparable to global cities. However, in the second- and third-tier cities, property prices remain reasonable. Most Chinese cities have not reached the level of real estate stock that exists in the middle-income countries, holding potential for further growth in China's property market for both residential and commercial development (Rothman, 2014).

On the other hand, credit extended to property developers is at higher risk because they are more highly leveraged, and face downward pressure

TABLE 5.4 NPL ratios of banks under varying real estate price assumptions (in %).

Drop in real estate prices	Incremental NPL ratio of real estate loans	Incremental NPL ratio of mortgages	Total increase in NPL ratio
<30	negligible	Negligible	0.1–0.2
30–40	1.4–2.8	0.6–1.3	1.9–3.8
40–50	2.8–4.2	1.3–1.9	3.8–5.6
>50	>5	>2	>7

Source: CDRF (2014).

of property prices without sufficient capital buffers. Home sales and new home starts both fell, and the inventory of homes in the ten largest cities increased from 10 months' sales at the beginning of the year to 17.7 months in April 2014 (Zhu et al., 2014). As a result of the recent property price inflation, chances of default by the real estate sector are as high as in any other Chinese industry experiencing overcapacity.

How much would banks' NPLs rise in face of a sharp correction of property prices? Research by Bank of Communications Financial Research Center suggested that the effect would be negligible if the drop in real estate prices is less than 30 percent (CDRF, 2014). If the real estate market were to fall by 50 percent, the NPL ratio of commercial banks could rise by 7 percent or more (Table 5.4).

Over the long term, the real estate market will see a huge, genuine demand, as the housing sector still needs to be upgraded. Chinese families living in the older apartments often need to share common toilet and kitchen facilities. Moreover, the living space per capita in China is 215 sq. ft., whereas the U.S. equivalent is 916 sq. ft. (Rothman, 2014). These factors are continuously creating the desire for new housing to enhance the standard of living, making the real estate market driven more by owners and occupiers rather than speculators. Despite the short-term uncertainty, the property market in China is unlikely to collapse because of the strong fundamental demand from the real sector.

However, the risks in the property market should not be under-estimated. Early signs of oversupply in the tier-three and tier-four cities have led to questions about the sustainability of the housing market. Since

2011, the home supply indicator[6] rose and remained above 4, which means it would take more than four years to sell all the properties currently under construction (Zhu et al., 2014). This is driven by the accumulation of property inventory in tier-three and tier-four cities, where real estate prices are mostly likely to drop if the oversupply continues. This situation could worsen if the PBOC were to tighten monetary policy and or impose more restrictive credit controls on the property sector.

5.5 LOCAL GOVERNMENT FINANCING PLATFORMS (LGFPs)

LGFPs are the largest borrowers on behalf of local governments, with a debt burden of RMB 7 trillion or 39 percent of the total local government debts by June 2013. LGFP indebtedness is manageable because the scale is no more than 12.3 percent of GDP or 9.4 percent of total bank loans and is backed by a substantial amount of municipality-owned assets, including land. However, from a cash flow point of view, some LGFPs could get into trouble if their local governments do not have sufficient revenue to maintain interest payments.

More than half of the local government debts are borrowed from banks (Table 5.5). Typical shadow bank borrowing, including trusts, individual loans, leases, collective funds, and other financial institution financing, accounted for RMB 1.7 trillion or 16 percent of the total local government debts. Meanwhile, the contingent liabilities of local governments to shadow banks are as high as RMB 1.2 trillion in total (Table 5.6).

A precise assessment of the LGFPs' shadow banking risks is difficult due to the lack of timely data on local governments' fiscal position, particularly for the revenue and expenditure items outside the budget. An alternative approach to risk assessment would be to consider the possible scenarios that could trigger losses and affect the LGFPs' debt servicing capacity. Fundamentally, losses can rise if (1) the productivity of the LGFP projects declines to the point where the rate of return is lower than the cost of debt servicing; (2) there is fraud/mismanagement/cheating in the LGFPs; and (3) the real estate market collapses, impairing the debt servicing ability of land finance. These three scenarios are considered below.

---

[6]Home supply indicator equals total residential floor space under construction divided by annual home sales.

TABLE 5.5   Channels of local government debt balance (RMB billion).

Entity	Debt for which govt. has repayment responsibility	Debt guaranteed by govt.	Other relevant debt (govt. may rescue)
LGFPs	4,076	883	2,012
Govt. departments and institutions	3,091	968	0
Institutions with govt. subsidies	1,776	103	516
Govt.-owned/controlled corporations	1,156	575	1,404
Independent institutions	346	38	219
Public institutions	124	83	0
Others	316	14	190
Total	10,886	2,666	4,339

Source: NAO (2013).

5.5.1 Productivity

Local governments have accumulated a large amount of quality assets, including transportation infrastructure, water and electricity facilities, railways, highways and airports. The completed projects in these sectors are generating sufficient operating income to repay the debts incurred for their development, especially in the first- and second-tier cities. For example, low-cost housing projects are generating stable sales or rental income upon completion of construction. (Table 5.7)

However, there are also well-documented concerns that some infrastructure projects are unable to generate sufficient cash flows for debt servicing. This is particularly true for the ring roads and highways that are toll free. The local government debts outstanding for highways are RMB 1,942 billion, while those for secondary roads are RMB 443 billion. These represent two of the largest infrastructure sub-sectors that have raised local government debts but are least productive in terms of return on investment (at least in the immediate term) and may therefore face debt servicing problems.

TABLE 5.6 Sources of funds of local governments (RMB billion).

Sources	Debt for which govt. has repayment responsibility	Debt guaranteed by govt.	Other relevant debt (govt. may rescue)
Bank loans	5,525	1,909	2,685
BT*	1,215	47	215
Bonds	1,166	167	513
Local government bonds	615	49	0
Corporate bonds	459	81	343
Mid term notes	58	35	1,020
Short term bills	12	1	22
Payables	778	9	70
Trust	762	253	411
Other institution and individual loans	668	55	116
Accrued expenses	327	1	48
Securities, insurance, and OFI financing	200	31	106
Treasury/foreign bonds	133	171	0
Lease	75	19	138
Collective funds	37	4	39
Total	10,886	2,666	4,339

Note: BT: Build-Transfer, financing by leveraging on non-fiscal funds to build up non-operating infrastructure.
Source: NAO (2013).

Since many LGFPs are involved in large infrastructure projects, their loans are of longer maturities. The increase in long-term loans could create a maturity mismatch and have adverse implications for banks' asset quality.

The central government has already announced a "no-bailout" policy for local government debt, which means that the local governments would be forced to restructure existing debt or engage in asset sales to bring debt to more manageable levels. In individual cases, there will be

TABLE 5.7 Uses of funds of local governments (RMB billion).

Uses	Debt for which govt. has repayment responsibility	%	Debt guaranteed by govt.	Other relevant debt (govt. may rescue)
Municipal construction	3,794	37	527	1,483
Land overhaul and preservation	1,689	17	108	82
Transportation infrastructure	1,394	14	1,319	1,380
Low income housing	685	7	142	268
Education, science, culture, and public health	488	5	75	409
Water-conservancy in agriculture and forestry	409	4	58	77
Eco-conservation and environmental protection	322	3	44	89
Industry and energy	123	1	81	26
Other	1,216	12	211	255
Total	10,119	100	2,564	4,068

Source: NAO (2013).

situations when banks would have to share some of the losses with local governments, but the scale of such losses is difficult to estimate at the present moment, although it is unlikely to be systemic in scale.

5.5.2 Fraud and Cheating

During its audit in 2013, the NAO uncovered 51 illegal cases in local government borrowing, involving RMB 246 billion of inappropriate Build-Transfer (BT) schemes and borrowing from non-financial institutions and individuals; RMB 336 billion of debts that should not have been guaranteed by local governments; and RMB 42.4 billion of bonds improperly issued by LGFPs.

Some LGFPs borrow in the name of government projects but invest the funds in capital markets, real estate markets or the construction of luxury buildings. The NAO reported that the misdirected funding in these three categories amounted to RMB 2.3 billion, RMB 7.1 billion and RMB 4.1 billion, respectively. In 2010, the central government prohibited LGFPs that only implement public projects with no expected profits from undertaking new borrowing, but 533 of them still incurred additional debts.

Such lack of discipline in local government debt management must be addressed in a timely manner. The central government would have to use a combination of "carrots and sticks" to ensure the effectiveness of any measures to improve the debt servicing ability of LGFPs.

5.5.3 Interconnection with Real Estate Markets

LGFP loans are vulnerable to fluctuations in the real estate market because land is used as the main form of collateral for such loans. The NAO report estimated that 37 percent of the local government debt repayment relied totally on the proceeds of land sales. Hence, the recent downward adjustment of land and real estate prices could hurt the debt servicing ability of local governments and impair shadow banks' asset quality (Deutsche Bank, 2014).

China still has a large amount of land available for construction. During its 2013 audit, the NAO reported that 34 big cities (including 4 municipalities, 5 cities specifically designated in the state plan, and 25 capital cities) have accumulated 160,000 hectares of land reserves. In recent years, local governments have been more concerned about improvements in land quality, putting RMB 1.7 trillion of the funds raised through local government debts into land rehabilitation and preservation projects. However, if the heavy reliance on land sales revenue continues, the receipts from the sale of land lease rights may come to an end in ten years. The end of the land capitalization process would imply rising NPL ratios in both the banks and shadow banks.

5.5.4 How Losses will be Allocated between Government and Banks Remains Unclear

The NAO revealed that more than 80 percent of the local government debts would mature before the end of 2017. Since roughly 40 percent are

TABLE 5.8   LGFP repayment projection.

Year	Debt for which govt. has repayment responsibility		Debt guaranteed by govt.		Other relevant debt (govt. may rescue)	
	RMB bn	%	RMB bn	%	RMB bn	%
Jul–Dec 2013	2,495	23	247	9	552	13
2014	2,383	22	437	16	748	17
2015	1,858	17	320	12	600	14
2016	1,261	11	261	10	421	10
2017	848	8	230	9	352	8
2018 and beyond	2,042	19	1,171	44	1,667	38
Total	10,886	100	2,666	100	4,340	100

Source: NAO (2013).

already falling due, this puts pressure on debt being rolled over or restructured. Restructuring of municipal debt could become an important area of fiscal reform in the coming years (Table 5.8).

BBVA research has estimated the incremental NPL in the extreme scenario in which the central government declines to bail out any of the LGFPs and requires the banks to absorb the cost of impaired debts, carrying them as NPLs for an extended period, rather than writing them off as they become due. Based on the assumptions that the central government would only assume responsibility for the direct debt of local government agencies (RMB 7.8 trillion) and that 50 percent of LGFV debt will go bad over the next five years, BBVA estimates that the bad loans would increase the banking sector's NPL ratio by 3.6 percentage points to 7.3 percent by end-2018 (BBVA, 2014b).

Shadow banks that invest extensively in LGFPs are mainly asset management and finance companies and other financial institutions (RMB 3.5 trillion), transfer of credit assets on the financial asset exchanges (RMB 1.5 trillion), asset management plans of securities companies (RMB 2 trillion) and trust loans (RMB 5 trillion). The rest of these shadow banks' investments are concentrated in SOEs and real estate companies. In total, 86 percent of the investments are funded through banks in the form of interbank assets and wealth management products, implying that banks will absorb most of the shadow banks' losses from LGFPs (Xu et al., 2013a). Assuming that their investments are equally divided between SOEs, LGFPs and real estate companies, the shadow banks' total investment in LGFPs is roughly RMB 4.3 trillion. Under the BBVA scenario, shadow banks may need to transfer RMB 2.2 trillion NPLs to the banking system, thereby pushing the NPL level to 4.5 percent.

The key issue is whether LGFP debt counts as quasi-sovereign debt. China's case is different from other countries, because the lenders (the formal banking system) are largely state-owned and the borrowers (local governments and LGFPs) are also state-related entities. Since local governments have high net assets in the form of land and SOE equity, the issue is more of a liquidity rather than a solvency issue. Local governments can sell assets in order to settle their LGFP debt, or rely on their revenue to settle such debt, though their willingness to do so is not clear.

The current calculation of local government debt already covers the government-owned or controlled corporations. However, there is some ambiguity about the extent of the government's responsibility (if any) in the event of bankruptcy of such companies. As the market expects the government to intervene and resolve the debt problems of SOEs, the liability numbers here are deliberately conservative by incorporating the potential or contingent obligations. It is important that this issue of quasi-fiscal liability should be clarified in the reform of SOEs.

We consider that it is unlikely that the LGFP NPLs will be fully shifted to the banking system and, in individual cases, some losses will be borne by the lenders. In fact, total LGFP debts that are overdue amounted to RMB 1.1 trillion by June 2013. There is no doubt that the banking sector would have to refinance LGFP loans if the projects are completed but not generating income (based on the expectation that their future cash flows can cover payments). This would require case-by-case debt negotiations with the local governments.

However, the shadow banks are less well-equipped to deal with debt restructuring because of their own reliance on short-term funds. With a larger maturity mismatch, shadow banks would face greater difficulties in dealing with LGFP debt problems.

On October 1, 2014, the State Council issued Directive No. 43 to tighten controls on local government debt. The *Opinions on Strengthening Local Government Debt Management* seeks to improve management of local government borrowings, their use and repayment:

1. Local governments cannot use corporations, such as LGFPs, to borrow and LGFVs will not be allowed to pass on their debt to local governments.
2. All local government debt, including guarantees, should be incorporated into government budgets and approved by the State Council and the National People's Congress.
3. In principle, the central government will not bail out local government debt and local governments will have to control their investments, cut expenditure and dispose assets to repay debt where necessary.
4. Local governments will not be allowed to intervene in financial institutions, and the staff of financial institutions will be held responsible for any lending to local governments that contravenes regulations.
5. Local governments are strictly forbidden to use unapproved land sales to raise funds.
6. The debt level will become a Key Performance Index in assessing whether local officials will be promoted or sanctioned.

We remain of the view that since LGFP debts are quasi-sovereign debt, these will be managed to ensure that they will not lead to a systemic crisis.

5.6 NON-PERFORMING ASSETS IN THE SHADOW BANKING SYSTEM

The analysis of asset quality of SOEs and SMEs shows that most of the increase in bank credits was flowing into SOEs and large enterprises, which has led to an increase in their leverage ratios. However, the productivity and debt servicing ability of SOEs and large firms are lower than private firms and small businesses, especially in sectors experiencing excess capacity. Even though small businesses should have lower credit risks because they are more efficient, privately owned and managed, they are perceived to be high-risk and continue to face difficulties in accessing bank loans and have to borrow more heavily from shadow banks. The high interest that they have to pay for shadow bank loans has affected their debt repayment ability, even though they have higher productivity. Thus, credits provided to SMEs are also exposed to high risk. Ultimately, however, the bulk of the exposure of the shadow banks will be to the corporate sector. We need to estimate the scale of such exposure and the impact it has on the banks' NPLs.

5.6.1 Estimation of NPLs for Shadow Banks

The estimation methodology of NPLs for shadow banks used primarily the experience of the international management consulting firm, Oliver Wyman, in dealing with NPL estimations based on credit ratings differentials in other markets. A proper analysis can only be achieved through on-site examination of the credit books of individual shadow bank institutions.

We estimate the NPL ratio for the shadow banking sector by estimating the NPL ratio of the funding obtained from shadow banking for each industry and computing the average NPL ratio across the industries, weighted by the size of funding they get from shadow banking.

We start from the NPL ratios for the bank loans to each industry provided by CBRC statistics (Table 5.9, Column 3) and match the bank NPL ratios to corresponding credit ratings (Table 5.9, Column 4).

The next step was to downgrade the credit rating for bank loans to a lower quality level for shadow bank loans. We benchmark shadow banking exposures in China against those of other Asian countries. In particular, we find that Korea had the most similarities with China since interest rate differences between bank and non-bank financing are largely the same. The credit ratings for shadow banking exposures in Korea are on average at least three notches lower than banking-related exposures. We therefore assume for our Optimistic Scenario that shadow banking exposures should be downgraded by three notches compared to the related banking exposures. In the other three scenarios, namely, a Base Scenario, a Pessimistic Scenario and a Disaster Scenario, we apply the credit ratings for shadow banks by downgrading their ratings by 4 notches, 4–5 notches and 5 notches, respectively. The distinction of downgrading reflects different severity of the asset quality problem of the shadow banking sector across different scenarios. By mapping the resultant credit rating for shadow banks to the corresponding NPL ratios, we get a proxy for the NPL ratios for the shadow bank for each industry (Table 5.9, columns 6–9).

The shadow banking asset distribution across industries (Table 5.9, column 5) is based on estimates from Morgan Stanley research (Xu et al., 2013b). Using the asset size as weights, we calculate the weighted average of shadow banking NPL ratios across the industries and get

TABLE 5.9 Estimation of the NPL ratio for the shadow banking sector, 2013.

Loan by industry	Banking NPL (RMB BN)	Banking NPL ratio %	Banking loan credit rating	Shadow bank asset weight %	Shadow bank sensitivity (credit rating/PD%)			
					Optimistic 3 notches	Base 4 notches	Pessimistic 4–5 notches	Disaster 5 notches
Manufacturing	215	1.8	BB	20.0	B/8.0%	B–/19.6%	CCC–C/48.4%	CCC–C/48.4%
Wholesale & retail	170	2.2	BB	25.0	B/8.0%	B–/19.6%	B–/19.6%	CCC–C/48.4%
LGFV	1	0.3	BBB+	12.0	BB+/1.1%	BB/1.5%	BB/2.3%	BB–/2.3%
Real estate	21	0.5	BBB+	18.0	BB+/1.1%	BB/1.5%	BB/2.3%	BB–/2.3%
Mining	5	0.3	BBB+	7.0	BB+/1.1%	BB/1.5%	BB/2.3%	BB–/2.3%
Transport/storage/post	32	0.7	BBB	2.0	BB/1.5%	BB–/2.3%	BB–/2.3%	B+/3.9%
Electricity/gas/water	14	0.5	BBB	2.0	BB/1.5%	BB–/2.3%	BB–/2.3%	B+/3.9%
Construction	13	0.5	BBB	3.0	BB/1.5%	BB–/2.3%	BB–/2.3%	B+/3.9%
Leasing & commercial	8	0.3	A–	0.0	BBB–/0.8%	BB+/1.1%	BB+/1.1%	BB/1.5%
Public utility	2	0.1	A–	0.0	BBB/0.5%	BBB–/0.8%	BBB–/0.8%	BB+/1.1%
Farming, forestry, animal & fishery	26	2.3	BB	0.3	B/8.0%	B–/19.6%	B–/19.6%	CCC–C/48.4%
Others	2	0.9	BBB–	10.0	BB–/2.3%	B+/3.9%	B+/3.9%	B/8.0%
Total					4.4%	10.0%	16.1%	23.9%

Source: CBRC data, FGI and Oliver Wyman analysis.

an estimation of the NPL ratio for the whole shadow banking sector. The results show that the NPL ratio for the shadow banking sector is 4.4 percent in the Optimistic Scenario, 10 percent for the Base Scenario, 16.1 percent for the Pessimistic Scenario and 23.9 percent for the Disaster Scenario.

It should be noted that during the early 2000s, Chinese banks' NPL ratios rose to about 30 percent. However, the Chinese authorities managed the problem and prevented China's banking system from going into crisis. A similar restructuring exercise will have to be conducted for the shadow banking system, but this has to be achieved on a case-by-case basis. As shadow banks' NPLs can have significant impact on banks (as discussed in the following section), an exit mechanism is urgently needed for both banks and non-bank financial institutions that are no longer viable, as well as enterprises that have failed.

5.6.2 The Impact of Shadow Banking NPLs on Banks' NPLs

Based on the risk profiles, we divide the shadow banking activities into three segments. The first layer is the banks' off-balance sheet funding (bank OBSF), including WMPs, banker's acceptance, securities firms' AMPs, and bank–trust cooperations. The linkage between the OBSF layer and the banks is tight as many of these can switch from contingent liability to realized liability for banks given that the implicit guarantees for investors persist in the market. The second layer is the non-bank credit enhancement to facilitate lending, including guarantees. Banks are subject to risk when credit enhancers fail to repay for defaulted corporate loans. The last layer is the non-banking lending, for example, P2P (peer-to-peer) and microfinancing.

Each of the three risk layers comes with a different level of transferability into the banking system. Hence, we calculate which share of NPLs is likely to be transferred from the shadow banking to the formal banking system (Table 5.10).

It should be noted that the "transferability" analysis is based on discussions with market professionals. If the level increases, then the impact on the banking system would be larger. Furthermore, we have not estimated what would happen if the stress scenarios also affect the banks' NPLs adversely.

We estimate the impact of shadow banking non-performing assets on banks' NPLs in two tracks. One is to load the shadow banking NPLs on

TABLE 5.10 "Transferability" analysis for shadow banking NPLs on formal banking.

	Asset size	Percentage range of damage transferable to formal banking		Range of damage transferable to formal banking	
	RMB TN	Lowest %	Highest %	RMB TN	RMB TN
Bank OBSF layer	10.7	60	100	6.4	0.7
Credit enhancement layer	1.9	20	60	0.4	1.1
Non-bank lending layer	18.6	0	10	0.0	1.9
Total	31.2			6.8	13.7
		Weighted average		22%	44%

Source: Expert interviews, Oliver Wyman analysis, FGI analysis.

the base of banks' current NPL ratio (Table 5.11, Columns 3–5). Under the Base Scenario with 33 percent of shadow bank NPLs transferred to banks, the banks' NPL ratio will rise from the current level of 1.5 percent to 2.5 percent, which is still within the banking system's current provisioned levels of 4.6 percent of risk-weighted assets. In the Disastrous Scenario, banks' NPL ratio will rise to 4.8 percent, slightly higher than the banking system's current provisions on risk-weighted assets.

The other track is to sum up banks' current NPL ratio and the additional provision first, and take it as the base of banks' NPL (Table 5.11, columns 6–8). This is to cover the concern that the NPL ratios reported by banks underestimate the actual problem. Under the Base Scenario, the banks' NPL ratio remains under 5 percent, while in the Disaster Scenario, it can go up to 7.1 percent.

The above analyses suggest that the Chinese banking system remains resilient, due to high interest rate margins, high domestic savings and continued growth. Shadow banking risks can have contagion impact on the financial system and the "new normal" of slower growth and continued reforms, but the risks are manageable.

Nevertheless, there is very little room for complacency. The underlying credit risks are vulnerable to major changes in the external

TABLE 5.11 Scenario analysis – shadow banking NPLs' impact on banks' NPLs, 2013.

	Shadow Banking NPL	Estimated Banks' NPL					
		Banks' current NPL (1.5%) + Shadow banking NPL's impact on banks			Banks' existing provision (2.8*1.5%=4.2%) + Shadow banking NPL's impact on banks		
		22%	33%	44%	22%	33%	44%
Optimistic Scenario	4.4%	1.7%	1.8%	1.9%	4.2%	4.2%	4.2%
Base Scenario	10.0%	2.2%	2.5%	2.7%	4.7%	4.9%	5.0%
Pessimistic Scenario	16.1%	2.7%	3.2%	3.6%	5.1%	5.6%	5.9%
Disastrous Scenario	23.9%	3.3%	4.1%	4.8%	5.8%	6.4%	7.1%

Data sources: CEIC, Oliver Wyman and FGI estimation.

environment and a sharp decline in real estate prices. As the international experience has shown, sharp drops in real estate prices could trigger a banking crisis. Hence, reforms in addressing the industries with excess capacity and evergreening in the credit sector cannot be delayed.

Thus far, the corporate sector in China runs on the twin engines of the SOEs, which enjoy monopoly power in a number of industries such as telecommunications, electricity and aviation. But there are also a number that suffer from inefficiencies, overcapacity and reliance on cheap credit. On the other hand, the private sector and small businesses have become quite competitive and productive, but they suffer from financial repression, as they lack access to formal bank credit. They are also vulnerable to a slowdown in external and domestic demand, because higher real interest rates could lead to a vicious circle of tighter liquidity, declining asset prices and credit failure.

Taken from a global perspective, the Chinese banking system is adequately provisioned with an NPL ratio of 1.6 percent and 2.9 times provisioning coverage, giving an average of 4.6 percent coverage of their risk-weighted loans. Barring any serious erosion of its capital, it will take the Chinese banking industry 10–15 years to exhaust its provisions, based on its current level of profitability. The historical average of the U.S. and European experience in NPLs was around 3 percent, increasing at times of high levels of economic stress (see Appendix on International Financial Crises: Lessons for China).

Since Chinese banks still have a high net interest margin, the industry has the time to restructure the risky assets before they become NPLs. The estimates that we have made are not forecasts, but judgments of what may happen if no further action is taken, or if the risky credits are allowed to roll over or if regulatory forbearance is given. Time is therefore of the essence. Action must be taken quickly to deal with the fundamental issues that give rise to NPLs in China's banking and shadow banking system. From the regulatory point of view, the transferability of NPLs from shadow banks to the banking system suggests that the share of shadow banking NPLs that are closely interrelated with banks should be incorporated in the banks' balance sheets. The problem is not totally the fault of the banking system, but lies at the structure of how the real sector is funded. This involves real sector structural issues that are industry-specific and context-specific. These policy issues are discussed in greater detail in Chapter 7.

REFERENCES

BBVA (Banco Bilbao Vizcaya Argentaria). 2014a. China Real Estate Outlook.

BBVA (Banco Bilbao Vizcaya Argentaria). 2014b. Is China Ready for Asset Sales to Address Its Local Government Debt?

Borst, Nicholas. 2014. How Vulnerable are Chinese Banks to a Real Estate Downturn? Peterson Institute for International Economics, China Economic Watch. 24 April. http://blogs.piie.com/china/?p=3868.

Deutsche Bank, China's Unexpected Fiscal Slide, December 2014.

CDRF (China Development Research Foundation). 2014. China: To Comprehensively Deepen Reform. Background Report for China Development Forum, Diaoyutai State Guesthouse, Beijing, March.

Geng, Nan, and Papa N'Diaye. 2012. Determinants of Corporate Investment in China: Evidence from Cross-Country Firm Level Data. IMF Working Paper No. 12/80.

IMF (International Monetary Fund). 2011. People's Republic of China: Financial System Stability Assessment. IMF Country Report No. 11/321. http://www.imf.org/external/pubs/ft/scr/2011/cr11321.pdf.

KPMG. 2013. Global Debt Sales: China.

KPMG. 2012. Mainland China Trust Survey.

Lian, Ping, and Xu Wenbing. 2014. How to Prevent and Resolve Cross-guarantee Risks. In CF40. 2014. Risks of mutual and cross guarantee. Special topic series, Issue 254, China Finance 40 Forum. 16 June.

Liang, Hong. 2014. Mutual- and Cross-Guarantee: From Regional to Systemic Risks? Roundtable discussion, CF40 Forum, June 10.

Ma, Jun, Zhang Xiaorong, and Li Zhiguo. 2012. *A Study of China's National Balance Sheet*. Beijing: Social Sciences Academic Press.

NAO (National Audit Office of People's Republic of China). 2013. Audit Findings on China's Local Governmental Debts. http://www.audit.gov.cn/n1992130/n1992150/n1992500/n3432077.files/n3432112.pdf.

Ogus, Simon. 2012. Retaking Stock of China's Capital. DSG Asia.

PBOC (The People's Bank of China). 2013. Annual Credit Survey. http://www.pbc.gov.cn/publish/diaochatongjisi/133/index.html.

Rothman, Andy. 2014. China's Property Is Slowing, Not Crashing. *Financial Times,* 1 October. http://blogs.ft.com/beyond-brics/2014/10/01/guest-post-chinas-property-is-slowing-not-crashing/?hubRefSrc=permalink.

Sheng, Andrew, Christian Edelmann, Cliff Sheng, Jodie Hu. 2015. Bringing Light upon the Shadow – A review of the Chinese shadow banking system. Oliver Wyman and Fung Global Institute Report.

Wen, Xinxiang. 2014. The Key to Resolving Regional Mutual- and Cross-guarantee Risks. Special topic series, issue 254, China Finance 40 Forum, June 16.

Xu, Richard, Jocelyn M Yang, and Simon Mou. 2013a. China Banks Asia Insight: The New Financial Channels – What Will Be Scrutinized, How, and When? Morgan Stanley Research, Asia Pacific.

Xu, Richard, Jocelyn M Yang, and Simon Mou. 2013b. China Deleveraging – Can Banks Ride Out a Financial Storm? Morgan Stanley Research.

Zhang, Wenlang, Han Gaofeng, and Steven Chan. 2014. How Strong Are the Linkages between Real Estate and Other Sectors in China? HKIMR Working Paper No. 11/2014.

Zhu, Haibin, Grace Ng, and Lu Jiang. 2014. China's Property Market: a Major Macro Risk. J.P. Morgan, Asia Pacific Economic Research.

CHAPTER 6

Impact of Technology on China's Financial System

Li Sai Yau and Cathleen Yi Tin

6.1 INTRODUCTION

China is at the critical point of transforming its development model, where technological innovations will play a central role in ensuring that transformation. This chapter considers the rapid rise of e-commerce and e-finance in China and their impact on the financial system in China. It also examines how such developments have facilitated the growth of online shadow banking activities.

E-commerce creates new value and markets, while being able to generate productivity and efficiency gains. The rise of e-commerce was accompanied by rapid growth of e-finance[1] in China. Using new technology, e-commerce and Internet companies have entered into the payments, lending and wealth management businesses of the banking sector. These innovations dramatically helped small and medium-sized enterprises (SMEs) by granting them improved and faster access to financial services in a financial sector where large state-owned banks preferred to serve state-owned enterprises (SOEs) and larger clients. Leveraging on technology, shadow banking activities in China have increasingly become digitized, enabling them to scale up at low costs with wider geographical and market reach.

---

[1]The focus of this chapter is on the payment, lending, and e-wallet wealth management businesses of e-finance.

Technological innovations simultaneously create and destroy value, because the conventional business models of brick-and-mortar businesses ("bricks") that rely on expensive branches and distribution hubs are challenged by Internet platforms that reach customers through technology and smart phones via "clicks." E-commerce has a wider footprint in customer coverage, low transaction costs and are much more user-friendly. Consequently, their adoption in China has been rapid, transforming the incumbent logistics and even finance business models. China is experiencing a major competition between "clicks" versus "bricks," with each sector rapidly buying into the other in order to meet the competition head on.

The publicly listed e-commerce companies have an advantage over traditional "brick" retailers and logistics companies, because their higher market valuation and market capitalization enable them to buy into the latter companies and then compete on cost, market reach and scale.

The challenge for policy makers lies in harnessing disruptive technology as a catalyst for growth. The increased competition between e-finance and the conventional banking sector has changed China's financial landscape. The rise of e-finance showcases how the financial industry can leverage web technologies to obtain better credit information and best meet fast-changing consumer preferences. The increased competition between e-finance and banks can spur innovation and productivity, as well as set the scene for liberalization in the financial industry.

This chapter uses the rise of Alibaba as an example to illustrate recent developments in e-commerce and e-finance in China. It shows how China is becoming increasingly innovative in the new mobile Internet business space, aiding the transformation of China's development model. To fully capture the rapid advances of technological innovation requires China to rethink its regulatory and policy development with the new sets of opportunities and risks created by e-commerce and e-finance.

Whilst mobile technology is changing consumer and investor behavior, as well as production, distribution and marketing business models, the role of government is important in facilitating institutional, process and product innovation. Internet business operations carry with them concerns regarding cybersecurity, identity theft, cheating and fraud, as well as contagion and moral hazard risks. Because e-finance and e-commerce cuts across the jurisdictional lines of traditional regulators, the lack of disclosure, capital and provisioning standards as well as the absence of a level playing field make regulation and enforcement problematic. Closer regulation is also warranted to curb usury, exploitation and fraud on less-sophisticated, retail customers who are not well-versed or equipped to deal with such abusive activities. The financial services industry will also need to adapt its business model and strategy to meet the challenges posed by mobile and Internet technology and the rise of e-finance.

E-finance innovations have clear implications, both for the incumbent Chinese banks and global financial institutions seeking to gain a foothold in the Chinese market. As e-finance platforms continue to encroach into the banking system's core businesses, domestic banks and non-bank financial intermediaries need to adapt, cooperate and move rapidly in this area, improving their mobile banking and cybersecurity capabilities to become the trusted partner in finance for retail and business customers. Global banks and financial institutions need to learn from China's breakthrough in e-commerce and e-finance and adopt reverse engineering to strengthen their own online strategies abroad using China's experience. At the same time, they can help improve the credit culture and offer innovative products in the growing China market in wealth management.

6.2 THE RISE OF E-COMMERCE IN CHINA AND ITS IMPLICATIONS

Over a decade ago, China's Internet usage was nascent, with few e-commerce applications. Fast-forward to 2013, China has attained over 600 million Internet users, with an Internet penetration rate of 44 percent and a smartphone penetration of over 70 percent (CNNIC, 2013; Nielson, 2013). Over the last decade, the Internet has grown rapidly in both scope and influence in China, with the rise of e-commerce being a world-changing development.

In 2013, the gross market value (GMV) of China's e-commerce sector, represented by the markets for Consumer to Consumer (C2C), Business to Customer (B2C) and Business to Business (B2B) transactions, was almost RMB 10 trillion (iResearch, 2014a). By 2013, the most active segment, SMEs' B2B transactions, accounted for 51.7 percent of total GMV in the e-commerce market (iResearch, 2014b). As China's consumer class continues to expand and the Internet continues to penetrate into different industries, the market is forecast to experience rapid annual growth of over 15 percent through 2017 (Figure 6.1).

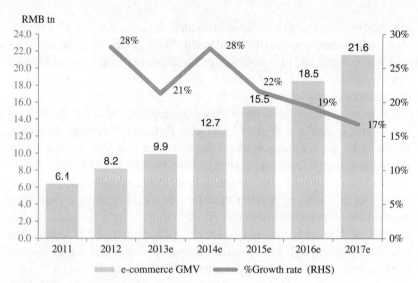

FIGURE 6.1 China's e-commerce revenue projection, 2011–2017.
Source: iResearch (2014a).

Another important driver of China's e-commerce is the growth of e-tailing, represented by the C2C and B2C markets. In 2012, the sales revenues for online retailers (RMB 1.3 trillion) surpassed that of department stores (RMB 974 billion) in China for the first time (Figure 6.2).

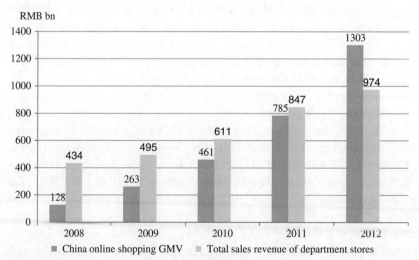

FIGURE 6.2 E-tailing sales surpassed department stores in China.
Source: iResearch (2014c), National Bureau of Statistics.

The online shopping market GMV has reached RMB 1.8 trillion in 2013 and is forecast to capture a growing share of sales of consumer goods in the coming years, from 2.9 percent in 2010 to 16 percent by 2017 (iResearch, 2014d).

Online shopping has been facilitated by rapid improvements in the logistics and transport industry. E-retailers are now able to deliver most online purchases door-to-door within 24 hours. This aspect of convenience has meant that consumers now tend to browse in retail shops or department stores, before buying on the Internet, creating a "showrooming" effect.

However, strong growth in online retailing (e-tailing) does not necessarily reduce demand in the offline (brick and mortar) retail industry. The growth in e-tailing is most obvious in the third- and fourth-tier-cities in China, where goods in retail stores are more expensive, with little product choice. Consequently, e-tailing penetration has been rapid and deep in these cities, creating demand where there was little supply or choice. On the other hand, the retail stores in the coastal and first- and second-tier cities have market incentives for innovation in technology, improving their service quality while allowing SMEs to sell directly in e-tailing marketplaces.

In the coming years, the rise of e-commerce will drive a rapid transformation in consumption, logistics and productivity. E-commerce marketplaces enable SMEs to scale up rapidly at low cost, as well as provide instant and direct access to consumers. While being a source of creative destruction to conventional business models, innovation has also created new value and allowed manufacturers to reach new markets that were previously constrained by the geographic and demographic limitations of old business models.

Nonetheless, for the economy as a whole to gain from the rise of e-commerce, value creation from the clicks (online businesses) has to be larger than the value losses from the bricks (offline businesses). Currently, the net benefits are unclear, but the trend of mobile e-commerce and e-finance is irreversible.

6.3 THE RISE OF E-FINANCE IN CHINA AND ITS IMPLICATIONS

The rise of the Internet and e-commerce parallels the growth of e-finance. By putting logistics and distribution and payments on the same platform, the e-commerce and e-finance model challenged the previous segmentation of the market in the logistics field, dominated by non-financial companies and the highly regulated financial industry. The existing financial sector has long been dominated by the formal banking sector, where large state-owned commercial banks (SOCBs) typically serve SOEs, leaving the SMEs underserved, although they account for a large share of GDP, employment and innovations. Moreover, banks also prefer to serve high-net worth customers, imposing stringent investment thresholds for wealth management-related financial services that preclude low and middle-income savers/investors.

Recognizing the large demand for financial services from SMEs and savers/investors, e-commerce and other Internet companies have progressively entered into the financial sector, with their footprints in the payment, lending and wealth management businesses. The rise of e-finance brings clear benefits in terms of greater convenience, efficiency, and market access, and at lower costs. However, it also poses new risks and challenges, which requires rethinking the approach of regulatory and policy development. With proper management and safeguards, e-finance can play a valuable role by channeling funds to capital-starved sectors and promoting financial inclusion in areas that are underserved by the formal banking sector.

6.3.1 Third-Party Online Payment System

Online third-party payment transactions grew more than five times to RMB 5.37 trillion between 2010 and 2013, and are forecast to reach over RMB 18 trillion by 2017 (iResearch, 2014e) (Figure 6.3). As of July 2014, there were 269 licensed third-party payment operators in China (PBOC, 2014c). Between 2008 and 2013, Alibaba's third-party Internet payment service, Alipay, had an almost 50 percent market share (iResearch, 2014e).

The rise of third-party online payments has transformed the business model of SMEs in e-commerce. Initially, the e-tailing businesses ran on a cash-on-delivery business model but currently the third-party online payment systems provide escrow facilities for e-tailers' online transactions. This reduces transaction costs as there are little or no or installation and transaction fees, and escrow facilities have become an essential element in e-commerce, allowing firms to speed up transactions at lower cost.

RMB tn

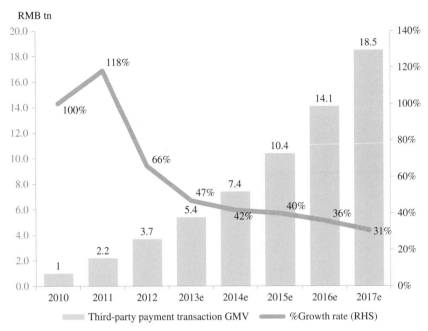

FIGURE 6.3 China online third-party payment transaction projection, 2010–2017.
Source: iResearch (2014e).

6.3.2 Lending Businesses of e-commerce and Internet Companies

Recognizing the business opportunity where SMEs often face difficulties in obtaining bank loans, e-commerce and Internet companies such as Alibaba, JD.com and Suning have set up microlending businesses to offer credit to SMEs.

Leveraging the credit and behavioral data of their customers through transactions and credit performance on their e-tailing platforms, e-commerce companies are able to develop proprietary credit assessment models to evaluate their borrowers' creditworthiness using big data analytical techniques. Through this operation model, e-commerce companies are able to provide an easy and convenient source of alternative finance to SMEs without the need for collateral.

Operating in an increasingly digitalized environment, access to borrower credit information has become a key to competitiveness in the financial industry. The lending businesses of e-commerce companies showcase how the financial industry can leverage the big data analytics in their credit risk assessments in enhancing loan quality (Xie, 2012).

Furthermore, big data analytics help identify customer preferences enabling service providers to better meet fast-changing customer demands and to suggest new product choices. Banks, such as China Construction Bank and Bank of Communications, have opened their own e-commerce platforms (for example buy.ccb.com and jiaobohui.com) to access more transaction data from their commercial banking customers and compete with e-commerce companies.

While serving the financing needs of SMEs, there are some potential risks involved in the microlending businesses of e-commerce and Internet companies. The lack of expertise and experience in financial services may affect the capacity of their credit assessment models to accurately predict the creditworthiness of their borrowers, which could lead to a rise in NPLs.

Strategic partnerships between Internet finance companies and the formal banking sector can enhance mutual benefits and may become an alternative way of market evolution. The partnership established in September 2013 between Alibaba and China Minsheng Bank (CMB) is an example of a partnership that brings the expertise of both sectors together. Through the partnership, Alibaba is able to leverage CMB's expertise in financial services, whilst CMB can tap into Alibaba's credit data of borrowers to enhance loan quality and expand its customer base. Going forward, such developments will continue to transform the way that the formal banking sector and other financial institutions (including e-finance and shadow banks) operate.

Another important driver of the online shadow banking activities in China is the rise of peer-to-peer (P2P) lending platforms. P2P lending platforms match the demand of investors looking for high return options with small and micro businesses that need quick funding but lack access to formal bank loans due to restrictive lending practices and collateral requirements. By 2013, P2P had an accumulated transaction volume of over RMB 60 billion; and at end of June 2014, there were 1,263 P2P lending platforms, up from 50 in 2011 (PBOC, 2014a; Xinhua News Agency and Internet Society of China, 2014).

While serving as an alternative funding source to Chinese SMEs, P2P platforms do pose risks as they operate outside the purview of regulators. Since P2P lending platforms simply provide a space to match borrowers and lenders, they are not subject to the same rules as, say, financing guarantee companies. Moreover, P2P platforms such as CreditEase, are increasingly making deals under individual names, instead of the registered microcredit companies, in order to bypass regulations.

P2P lending platforms operate a high leverage model where their operating size is often much larger than their registered capital. Although the 2010 CBRC guidelines, *Interim Measures for the Administration of Financing Guarantee Companies,* stated that the minimum registered capital of financing guarantee companies shall not be less than RMB 5 million, a number of P2P platforms do not meet this requirement. For instance, the initial registration capital of renrendai.com, ppdai.com and p2peye.com was only RMB 1 million each, but their average lending size was RMB 80 million in 2013 (Social Credit Fund, 2014). It was only in response to the rapid growth in their lending size that renrendai.com increased its registration capital to RMB 100 million in March 2014 (Renrendai, 2014).

Since the maturities of P2P lending vary, a significant increase in the number of NPLs can cause a liquidity problem. This will result in insufficient capital flows in P2P platforms, where borrowers with good projects may not receive new credit even if they have repaid old loans (*The Economist*, 2014). In addition, the high leverage nature of P2P business can result in the collapse of platforms, especially those that have guaranteed principal for investors. This means that P2P platforms have to repay the bad loans themselves. The collapse of a P2P platform can lead to considerable losses for its investors. As their capital funding might originally have come from the traditional banks, this could impose stress on the formal banking sector.

Some P2P platforms operate like Ponzi schemes, where they attract new lenders by offering high interest rates and use the fresh investment funds to repay old debt. This risky business model is inherently fragile and unsustainable. Together with the lack of sufficient financial information and lending expertise, the business model of these P2P platforms creates a weak institutional structure that casts doubts on their operations. Since P2P platforms are not registered as microcredit companies, they are not subject to the same regulations. Hence, there is no clear guideline on collateral requirements and default procedure.

The potential risks of the P2P lending platforms were reflected by a wave of P2P runs that led to numerous bankruptcies in 2013. It was not clear how losses would be borne. In 2013, 74 P2P platforms were closed, with some under investigation for illegal fund-raising (*Wall Street Journal*, 2014a). This illustrates the importance of a regulatory framework that can accommodate the growth of new lending models such as

P2P platforms, while mitigating their risks and ensuring investor protection.

6.3.3 Wealth Management Business of e-commerce and Internet Companies

While wealth management products (WMPs) issued by the banks offer more attractive yields than regulated bank deposits, the minimum investment thresholds are typically high. This effectively precludes most low- to middle-income investors, leaving them with limited investment choices and wealth management options. Leveraging their established presence in the e-commerce market, e-commerce companies launched deposit-taking e-wallets offering online WMPs, such as Yu'E Bao by Alibaba and Licaitong by Tencent to fill this gap.

The e-wallet WMPs gained enormous popularity, as they typically have very low barriers to entry, where investors can invest as little as they want and withdraw their funds at any time. They also offer attractive annual yields of between 5–7 per cent, compared to the capped 3.3 percent rate on one-year bank deposits.

Although the scale of the e-wallet WMPs is not yet large enough to pose an immediate threat to banks, they are already affecting the banks' business model and debt structure. Since these e-wallet WMPs first raise and accumulate funds before depositing them back to the banks, this operation model increases banks' cost of debt and reduces their interest spreads (Ma, 2014).

Moreover, the financial landscape is shifting. Banks have long dominated China's financial system, where they earn substantial net interest margins from the 3.3 per cent interest rate cap on deposits whereas they can charge higher interest rates on loans. In an underdeveloped financial market, Chinese depositors have limited investment choices where there is little market competition. But increased competition from online WMPs offers depositors greater incentives to move their money away from banks to obtain higher returns for their savings.

While more competition in the financial market fosters innovation and diversity, the battle for higher yields to compete for deposits is both unsustainable and unprofitable for all. Due to the high-yield benchmark set by online WMPs, banks may be forced to offer similar high-yield money market products to compete. This will drive up the banks' funding costs, and eventually push up lending rates. Such a development may erode banks' credit discipline and expose them to additional risks. As

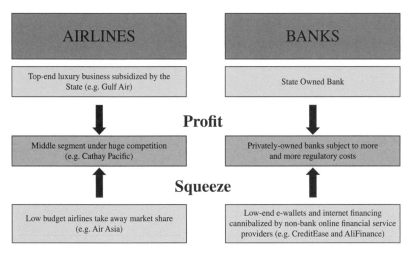

FIGURE 6.4 Network industries share similar challenges.
Source: FGI.

competition intensifies, any erosion in credit discipline could increase systemic instability.

As a network industry, China's banking sector faces challenges similar to those of the airline industry (Figure 6.4). At the top end of the market, the profit margins of commercial banks are being squeezed by competition from SOCBs, which enjoy strong government support. This is similar to the dilemma faced by private, full-service airlines, in competing against state-owned/highly-subsidized airlines. At the bottom end of the market, banks are being cannibalized by online financial service providers offering low-end payments and products, the same way that budget airlines are squeezing out full-service operators. In addition, banks are subject to increased regulatory requirements that add to costs, whereas the online shadow banks are not.

There is also a question of who should bear the losses in the event of defaults. Although e-wallet WMPs' returns are not explicitly guaranteed, investors may expect giant e-commerce companies to bear the losses in case of default to protect their reputation and positions as the largest brand names in China. This uncertainty carries considerable risk that is as yet untested.

It is likely that the way forward to a more stable environment is the promotion of strategic partnerships between Internet companies and banks. This may improve client service, offer better product choices, enhance transparency and governance, and eventually lead to even greater innovation in the financial sector.

THE RISE OF ALIBABA AND ITS IMPLICATIONS

The Alibaba Group consists of 25 business units, including Internet finance, supply chain management, cloud computing and online messaging services. By 2013, the Alibaba Group collectively controlled four-fifths of all China's e-commerce and is the largest online and mobile commerce company in the world in GMV terms. There are 279 million active buyers and 8.5 million active sellers using Alibaba's online services every year and 14.5 billion annual orders are made via Alibaba e-platforms (SEC, 2014).

The rise of Alibaba illustrates one of the most dramatic market shifts in China over the last decade – the explosion of e-commerce. The Alibaba Group continues to dominate the e-commerce sector in China, where it takes the market lead in the B2B sector with alibaba.com, the e-tailing sectors with Tmall (B2C sector) and TaoBao (C2C sector). Unlike e-commerce models such as eBay in the U.S., which is an e-commerce platform, Alibaba has evolved a market ecosystem through its range of services for SMEs and consumers (Figure 6.5).

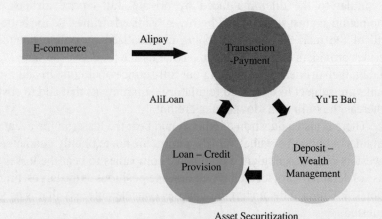

FIGURE 6.5   Alibaba's financial services businesses.
Source: Social Credit Fund (2014), FGI compilation.

Alibaba Group runs on a third-party platform business model, whereby they do not engage in direct sales, compete with their merchants or hold inventory. This business model enables Alibaba to act as a middleman, connecting buyers and sellers and facilitating the transactions between them. Alibaba does not charge listing fees and makes most of its revenue from the advertisement fees from merchants. This business model is not investment intensive and enables Alibaba to generate high profit margins.

Leveraging the influence of its e-commerce market presence, Alibaba Group has progressively entered the Chinese financial services sector via its footprint in areas such as payment, lending and wealth management businesses.

Although Alipay is not part of the Alibaba IPO listing, Alipay was the key to opening up the finance window for Alibaba. Alipay was established and registered as a third-party payment institution in China in 2004, providing e-payment services for Alibaba's e-tailing platforms including Taobao, Tmall and 1688.com. In fiscal year 2014, Alipay handled 78.3 percent of the GMV on Alibaba's e-tail marketplaces in China.

In June 2013, Yu'E Bao, an online money market fund investing in interbank loans, government and corporate bonds under Alipay was co-launched with Tianhong Asset Management. Initially a simple excess cash management tool for Alibaba's online shoppers, it became an e-wallet WMP that combines e-commerce and e-finance. Within its first year of launch, Yu'E Bao has garnered over 100 million investors, raising RMB 574 billion (US$ 92 billion), making it China's largest and the world's fourth biggest money market fund.

Yu'E Bao offers alternative private wealth management solutions at a much lower entry barrier (as little as RMB 1) with competitive yield (annual yield of 5–7 percent) compared to Chinese banks' one-year, capped deposit rate of 3.3 percent. In China, traditional banks' WMPs target high net worth customers with a minimum investment threshold of as much as RMB 500,000. Therefore, Yu'E Bao developed not only into a substitute to cash deposits at banks but also an e-finance solution for potential investors who are underserved by the traditional banks due to their high investment threshold.

Recognizing the business opportunity where SMEs often face difficulties in obtaining loans from the traditional banking channel, Alibaba entered the SME financing business with its launch of

AliFinance in 2007. By March 2014, AliLoan, AliFinance's lending vehicle, had total outstanding loans of RMB 13.2 billion (US$2.1 billion), provided to 342,000 SMEs (Alibaba IPO prospectus 2014).

AliLoan's mainstream customers are the sellers on Alibaba's e-tailing platforms and wholesale marketplaces. Leveraging its credit and behavioral database through customers' transaction history and credit performance on the e-tailing platforms, Alibaba was able to develop proprietary credit assessment models, which evaluate borrowers' creditworthiness using big data analytics. Through this operation model, Alibaba is able to provide easy and convenient alternative financing solutions (up to RMB 3 million) to SMEs without collateral.

THE ALIBABA FACTOR

The rise of Alibaba illustrates how hybrid platforms that link both the clicks (Internet platforms) and bricks (retail outlets) have emerged to dominate both the logistics and payments marketplace in a digitalized environment. Such development creates new value and markets with a range of new opportunities and risks.

At the core of the ecosystem of Alibaba is the network effect, where the operations of Alibaba spread across different industries and markets. Alibaba uses its network effect to acquire key players (both bricks and clicks) in different markets, networking their producers, distributors or customers into one large network with lower transaction costs and higher convenience.

The powerful network effects created by Alibaba, given its scale and operations in the Chinese economy, potentially pose a moral hazard risk in the event that Alibaba becomes either too big or too connected to fail. Any disruption in the Alibaba network may impose systemic risks in the economy, creating moral hazard risks that could prompt the state to intervene. Given the size and scale of operations, there are operational risks, issues of cybersecurity, personal data security and also questions of anti-money laundering, terrorist funding and other compliance measures that the licensed banks have to comply with. At some point or other, it would be important for China to consider whether there should be an effective exit mechanism for the stability of e-commerce platforms in large networks that are dominant in their field.

Having achieved a dominant market position in China, Alibaba has expanded to foreign markets with its IPO in the U.S. in September 2014. If its footprint in the financial services industry continues to gain significance, the key question is whether it would develop into a domestic systemically important financial institution (D-SIFI), or even a global systemically important financial institution (G-SIFI). Reaching that scale would mean that it could be subject to the global financial regulations that are applicable to G-SIFIs. Operating in foreign jurisdictions such as the U.S. will subject Alibaba to new regulatory scrutiny, including to the risks of class action suits. These questions inevitably will raise the need for more domestic regulatory scrutiny, which directly affect the future development of e-commerce and Internet finance. Yet, what is clearly missing is a level playing field between licensed banks and e-commerce and e-finance companies.

6.4 THE ROLE OF TECHNOLOGICAL INNOVATION IN CHINA'S TRANSFORMATION

China is on the cusp of transforming its old growth model, based on cheap labor, heavy capital investment and manufacturing exports, into one that is knowledge-based and consumption- and services-driven. In one sense, the Alibaba phenomenon combined technological innovation in production, logistics and consumer demand.

There is little doubt that technological innovation is a central driving force that will shape China's breakthrough out of the "middle-income trap" and emerge as a highly service-oriented and knowledge-based economy.

In the face of this transformation, many industries, including the financial sector, will enter a period of disruptive change where conventional business models will undergo creative destruction. Although this may result in some short-term displacement of the labor force and the brick-and-mortar markets, technological innovation will create new value and new markets and foster productivity and efficiency gains over the long term.

E-commerce firms, such as Alibaba, Baidu, JD.com and Tencent, have demonstrated that the clicks are able to leverage new technologies to play a central role in determining business competitiveness. With the rapid adoption of web technologies and cloud computing alongside the rise of e-commerce and e-finance, SMEs can overcome some of the disadvantages they face in competing with SOEs and entrenched incumbents, many of which are bricks.

Web technologies and e-commerce marketplaces provide a powerful platform for SMEs to develop production and distribution networks while reducing sunk and operational costs. They also enable SMEs to develop better supply chain management with support in payment, logistics and customer engagement. The overall effect of these developments will increase competitive intensity and accelerate the growth of the most innovative and efficient enterprises, fostering the development of market forces and eventually improving the performance of the broader economy.

However, the convergence of e-commerce and e-finance has also changed the funding game for large-scale investments in technology. The market capitalization of Alibaba, Tencent and Baidu today exceed US$100 billion each, larger than some of the biggest listed banks and conventional brick SOEs. These clicks have demonstrated that they are willing to use their funding power to change the investment game, by investing in innovative SMEs or buying up inefficient bricks to gain competitive advantage against incumbent players.

Structural change is therefore taking place within different industries, including the financial industry. The increased competition from the Internet and technology companies will put pressure on further liberalization in the Chinese capital and financial markets. In the face of an increasingly digitalized environment, competition between the click models and the brick models of financial services will rapidly converge. Such developments would change both the production, distribution and financial landscape in China, where the bricks will need to keep pace with technological advancements to stay competitive and best meet the fast-changing consumer preferences.

In the U.S., the emergence of Apple Pay, the iPhone payments platform, has forced the banks to cooperate with Apple to gain market share and enter new and previously unbanked markets. Even the U.S. banks have recognized that the rise of Internet and web technologies has created powerful tools to obtain large volume, real-time data from a wide range of sources, changing the pattern of consumption, for example, via the power of "recommended purchases" by Amazon.com. Big data analytics will improve banks' information on borrowers and depositors, helping them to reduce the risk of NPLs and provide better services to SMEs. The resultant increase in banks' capacity in SME lending will have an overall positive effect on the economy and job creation due to increased efficiency in capital allocation.

To enable technological innovation to play a central role in ensuring a smooth transformation in the Chinese development model, a rethink of China's regulatory and policy development in the financial sector will be necessary to accommodate the new sets of opportunities and address the emerging risks.

6.5 RETHINKING CONVENTIONAL FINANCIAL REGULATION AND DEVELOPMENT

In the development of regulations for the Internet finance sector, regulators need to strike a balance between controlling risks and encouraging financial innovation and healthy competition to ensure financial stability and consumer protection. There is a risk of over-regulation that can kill innovation, whilst under-regulation could lead to usury, fraud and even system disruption through unforeseen events, such as cyber-attacks or bank runs.

The orderly development of Internet finance requires an enabling environment for new ideas and innovations, with a clear set of standards to ensure compliance and competition (Wang, 2014). A level playing field must be set up to promote innovation and attract new investment (both domestic and foreign). A good example is Silicon Valley in the U.S., which accounted for 41 percent of total U.S. venture capital investment in 2013 (PWC, 2014).

Service delivery must be consistent and quality standards maintained between online and offline channels. With regards to P2P lending, standardized entry requirements and information management can minimize risk and filter out speculators and fraudsters. Other complementary factors to incentivize research and development in Internet finance include intellectual property right protection and tax incentives (*Wall Street Journal,* 2014b).

Regulators should see e-platforms as new opportunities for finance business, and facilitate their development and transition. As Jack Ma, chairman of Alibaba, once commented, Chinese banks cannot resist change, as they will be compelled to change. While regulatory oversight is important to prevent abuses and undesirable activities, overly stringent regulations can lead to unintended consequences, including higher costs and impeding innovation in e-finance.

There is willingness on the part of the authorities to experiment with a self-regulatory system, similar to the Chartered Financial Analyst (CFA) Institute, to govern the industry's development. At the early stages of fast development, it may be useful for the industry to establish its own ground rules and guidance in areas such as risk management, operations and technological innovations to uphold professionalism, entrepreneurship and social responsibility (Yan, 2014). In April 2014, the State Council approved the establishment of China's Internet Finance Association, under the leadership of the PBOC. On July 18, 2015, the PBOC issued new guidelines on promoting the healthy development of Internet finance[2].

Currently, there is little or no regulation on Internet finance in China. They are not subject to traditional banking regulations such as reserve requirements, capital adequacy ratios, and loan-deposit ratios. In March 2014, PBOC banned payments made by quick response (QR) codes and virtual credit cards, pending a review of regulatory concerns. (*China Daily*, 2014).

To address the potential risks emerging from the rise of online payment systems, the PBOC has drafted regulations relating to online and mobile payment services. They include a number of proposed provisions relating to account management and security measures, which would set transaction limits on individuals using funds in their online and mobile payment accounts with third-party payment providers (PBOC, 2014b). In April 2014, the PBOC and CBRC issued "Joint Circular 10," which requires banks and financial institutions to conduct additional customer verification procedures prior to setting up an automatic payment link between customers' banks accounts and their third-party payment providers (CBRC, 2014).

The PBOC and CBRC's view on Internet finance remains open and supportive. However, it is recognized that traditional banking should continue to be the mainstay of finance, whereas Internet finance

---

[2]*Wall Street Journal*. 2015. China Looks to Regulate Internet Finance. 20 July. http://www.wsj.com/articles/china-looks-to-regulate-Internet-finance-1437223179

should play a supportive role and should not change the nature of risk in finance. In addition, Internet finance and banks should not compete directly. Yan and Li (2014) recommended that specific rules should be put in place to enable parallel development between Internet finance and traditional finance to maintain overall financial stability; to ensure Internet finance serves the real sector; to train complex talents for Internet finance; and to reform the sub-sector's management system. Financial reforms in response to the rise of Internet finance would include:

1. **Prudential Supervision and Financial Consumer Protection**
   Prudential rules can curb illegal Internet financial activities in deposit-taking, financing and securities trading. Liquidity management is important to avoid maturity mismatches and liquidity problems. One option is to introduce differentiated licensing to manage different classes of risks and protect consumers.
2. **A Sound Information and Credit System**
   A generalized data system should be set up for e-finance companies to share information and to function as a transaction record, for tracking and investigative purposes (Yan, 2014). Mandatory credit ratings on SMEs can help improve loan quality and reduce e-financing NPLs.
3. **Cyber and Data Security**
   The Center for Strategic and International Studies, and McAfee, a computer security firm, estimated that cybercrime can cost as much as US$100 billion per annum in the U.S. (*Wall Street Journal,* 2013; Ponemon Institute, 2013). The costs include loss of intellectual property and customers' data, and upgrading of cyber defenses. In China, the September 2013 Trojan virus attack affected over 500,000 Internet payment users, resulting in loss of credits in wealth management funds. In the future development of Internet finance, China should introduce compulsory identity verification, a blacklist system and a reward and report system (Xie, 2014).
4. **Standardization and Joint Efforts with Regulatory Authorities**
   Such an initiative can help fight cybercrime and illegal financial activities by securing online identities. New cybersecurity technologies, such as biometric identification on personal mobile devices or desktops, could be a potential solution. The presence of a cooperative industry self-regulatory body enhances functional and behavioral regulations, and helps improve regulatory efficiency and transparency.

5. Education, Training and New Culture

Customers need to be better informed about the potential benefits and risks involved in online financial services and online shadow banking products. More importantly, investors need to understand the risks that they are taking and that their responsibility for any loss is the same as in the offline channel. For developers, a new culture of willingness to take risks, innovate and fail is important; for consumers, a new culture of willingness to understand, accept, and adopt Internet finance, holds the key to its further progress.

6.6 IMPLICATIONS FOR THE FINANCIAL SERVICES INDUSTRY

The Chinese market has one of the fastest technology adoption rates and the rise of e-finance and other innovations have clear implications, both for the incumbent Chinese financial services players and global entities seeking to gain a foothold in the Chinese market.

For the incumbents, efforts to strengthen industry capabilities will be decisive in determining the future winners in China's banking system, particularly in the following areas, by:

1. further strengthening the credit culture by leveraging on available data;
2. building strong deposit mobilization and pricing capabilities, particularly in view of further interest rate liberalization and the opening of the capital account;
3. strengthening asset/liability management capabilities, covering both on- and off-balance sheet components;
4. developing an integrated investor product perspective (across various layers of WMPs, mutual fund products, brokerage/asset trading offerings, deposits, and potentially insurance/pension solutions); and
5. innovating and expanding in terms of SME/retail investor financing products.

The agenda for global players needs to follow a different path, particularly as most of them have struggled to build a sustainable and profitable business in China in the wholesale banking segment, serving their global MNC clients, mergers and acquisitions (M&A) banking and trade finance. The rise of shadow banking offers new opportunities in the fast-growing retail/SME sector.

Global players need to look for new investment opportunities beyond the banking sector such as P2P platforms, financial asset trading platforms and so forth. This sector is also less regulated in terms of foreign ownership and hence creates an opportunity for a higher level of management influence.

Another window of opportunity is to leverage on the China (Shanghai) Pilot Free-Trade Zone (SHFTZ) to channel offshore RMB liquidity into higher yielding onshore investment opportunities for their global investor clients. In a global low-yield environment, this can become an attractive differentiator for institutions serving the investor segment.

The major transformations confronting China today require a reversing of the global players' mind-set. Instead of only looking for areas where their global capabilities can be important in China, successful banks must also look at the opposite: leveraging Chinese Internet finance capabilities in their home markets.

6.7 CONCLUSION

The explosive growth in e-finance and e-commerce reflects fundamental changes in China's supply chain production, distribution and consumption patterns. The boom in e-finance also represents a part of the market response to a genuine demand for financial services in an environment where the large state-owned banks typically prefer to lend to large SOEs, leaving the private sector and SMEs underserved.

While creating new value and markets, e-finance and e-commerce will continue to challenge the conventional brick-and-mortar retail stores and bank branches, leading to some value destruction and job losses.

The Internet provides a powerful platform for the development of e-finance. It provides easy and convenient access to financial services at low cost, offering vast potential to improve financial inclusion. This will have strategic implications, requiring changes in the business models of incumbent Chinese and global players seeking growth opportunities in China. The rise of e-finance also poses challenges that will require regulators to rethink their approach to regulatory policy. It is recognized that one of the primary roles of regulators is to reduce the risks of fraud and moral hazard concerns in e-finance by addressing prudential concerns, especially the lack of disclosure, capital and provisioning standards. The challenge lies in striking a fine balance between encouraging financial innovation, while mitigating the potential risks and upholding consumer protection. Regulators also need to level the playing field between Internet finance companies and conventional banks, and between domestic and foreign players, to maintain healthy competition that encourages innovation and ensures that finance serves the real sector.

In essence, the lessons of shadow banking and e-finance suggest that the line between finance and the real sector has blurred under technological and financial innovation. In such circumstances, financial regulation must recognize that partial solutions do not solve system-wide problems. A holistic solution requires a holistic mind-set, recognizing that the greater good of the system as a whole overrides the interests of different segments, including the financial sector.

REFERENCES

CBRC (China Banking Regulatory Commission). 2014. Joint Circular 10. 9 April. http://www.cbrc.gov.cn/govView_EA1CC481C843441FA93AE486 FD03B43D.html.

China Daily. 2014. Online Finance Needs More Checks. 31 March. http://www .chinadaily.com.cn/business/tech/2014-03/31/content_17391630.htm.

CNNIC (China Internet Network Information Center). 2013. Statistical Report on Internet Development in China. http://www1.cnnic.cn/IDR/ ReportDownloads/201310/P020131029430558704972.pdf.

Jack Ma commented that "If the banks don't change, we will change them." http://blogs.ft.com/beyond-brics/2013/07/01/alibaba-shaking-up-chinese-finance/.

iResearch. 2014a. iResearch Releases China E-commerce Forecast. 14 April. http://www.iresearchchina.com/views/5584.html.

iResearch. 2014b. China SMEs' Revenue from B2B E-commerce Sets a New Record. 19 February. http://www.iresearchchina.com/views/5466.html.

iResearch. 2014c. 2012–2013 China Online Shopping Report (Brief Edition). http://www.iresearchchina.com/samplereports/5152.html.

iResearch. 2014d. China Online Shopping Market Slows Down While Mobile Buying Outbursts. 26 March. http://www.iresearchchina.com/views/5548. html.

iResearch. 2014e. China Online Third-party Payment Market Structure Remains Stable. 9 April. http://www.iresearchchina.com/views/5575.html.

Ma Tianping. 2014. The impact of Online Finance and Internet Finance on Commercial Banks: Evidence. China Finance 40 Forum, August issue, pp. 4–8.

Nielson. 2013. Decoding the Asian Mobile Consumer. http://ddwgames.com/insea/insights/Decoding_the_Asian_Mobile_Consumer.pdf.

PBOC (People's Bank of China). 2014a. China Financial Stability Report 2014. http://www.pbc.gov.cn/publish/english/955/2014/20140701173013533443319/20140701173013533443319_.html.

PBOC (People's Bank of China). 2014b. Management of Internet Payment via Payment Service Providers (Draft for Comment). http://www.pbc.gov.cn:8080/image_public/UserFiles/goutongjiaoliu/upload/File/支付机构互联网支付业务管理办法(征求意见稿).doc.

PBOC (People's Bank of China). 2014c. List of Licensed Third-Party Payment Operators. http://www.pbc.gov.cn/publish/zhengwugongkai/3580/index_14.html.

Ponemon Institute. 2013. 2013 Cost of Cyber Crime Study: United States. Benchmark Study of U.S. Companies. http://media.scmagazine.com/documents/54/2013_us_ccc_report_final_6-1_13455.pdf.

PWC (PricewaterhouseCoopers). 2014. Money Tree Report: Q4 2013/Full Year 2013. http://www.pwc.com/en_US/us/technology/assets/pwc-moneytree-q4-and-full-year-2013-summary-report.pdf.

Renrendai. 2014. News Release: Renrendai Increased its Registered Capital to RMB 100 Million. 4 April. http://www.renrendai.com/about/detail.action?news_id=news_319.

SEC (Securities and Exchange Commission). 2014. Alibaba Group Holding Limited. Amendment No. 4 to Form F-1 Registration Statement (IPO Prospectus). Washington, D.C., 12 August. http://www.sec.gov/Archives/edgar/data/1577552/000119312514306647/d709111df1a.htm.

Social Credit Fund. 2014. China's Internet Finance Sectoral Advance Research Report. http://mat1.gtimg.com/tech/sunshi/hulianwangjinrong.pdf.

The Economist. 2014. Alibaba's Maturity Mismatch. 24 July. http://www.economist.com/blogs/freeexchange/2014/07/chinese-finance.

Wall Street Journal. 2013. Annual US Cybercrime Costs Estimated at $100 Billion. 22 July. http://online.wsj.com/news/articles/SB10001424127887324328904578621880966242990.

Wall Street Journal. 2014a. China Warns of Rising Risks from 'P2P' Lending, 21 April. http://online.wsj.com/news/articles/SB10001424052702304049904579514820323810610.

Wall Street Journal. 2014b. New Tax Bug Bites Tech Companies. http://online.wsj.com/news/articles/SB100014240527023046263045795095239711997320.

Wang Yanxiu. 2014. Banking Sector in Internet Finance: Opportunities and Challenges. Internet Finance: Regulatory Principles. Roundtable Discussion, China Finance 40 Forum, 260.

Xie Ping. 2012. A Research on Internet Finance Model. China Finance 40 Forum Expert Report, 4–7, 23–26.

Xie Ping. 2014. P2P Lending: Benefits and Regulations. China Finance 40 Forum, 261.

Xinhua News Agency and Internet Society of China. 2014. China's Internet Finance Report. http://www.thfr.com.cn/images/p2p2014.pdf.

Yan Qingmin. 2014. The Hot Wave of Internet Finance: Roots, Risks and Regulations. China Finance 40 Forum, vol. 260.

Yan Qingmin and Li Jianhua. 2014. *Supervision of China's Shadow Banking*. China Renmin University Press, pp. 300–303.

CHAPTER 7

Implications for Reform Agenda

Andrew Sheng

7.1 INTRODUCTION

The Global Financial Crisis (GFC) highlighted the risks of shadow banking in contributing to greater financial fragility in the advanced economies.[1] This book has concluded that, based on currently favorable conditions, a shadow banking crisis is unlikely in China as it is essentially a domestic debt problem where the authorities have the policy flexibility and resources to deal with any emerging risks.

This assessment is based on the national balance sheet analysis, which provides a top-down, snapshot view of the situation in China and a review of current conditions. It does not attempt to forecast dynamic changes in the Chinese economy and global conditions. Conditions could well change dramatically for the worse if growth falters or property prices collapse due to some unforeseen shock. Hence, the rapid growth in shadow banking credit warrants closer monitoring and management to preempt any escalation of risks and contagion effects. The priority is to address prudential concerns and the risks of rising shadow banking NPLs and potential failures. Closer cooperation and coordination among regulatory authorities and greater clarity of their respective roles will be important to reduce regulatory gaps and overlaps, and address the lack of transparency, consumer protection and moral hazard issues and the bundling of shadow banking risks with the formal banking sector.

---

[1]See Appendix on Evolution of International Financial Crises: Lessons for China.

However, reform measures also need to address the key structural issues of how China's real economy should be financed, as the shadow banks revealed several structural mismatches in the current financial system.

First, overreliance on bank lending has exacerbated the maturity mismatch, with the investment-driven economy increasingly reliant on short-term bank funding, rather than long-term funding from insurance and pension funds.

Second, although China has no foreign exchange mismatch due to its large foreign exchange reserves, there is an incentive to borrow in foreign currencies to fund domestic assets because of the belief that the RMB will appreciate in the long run and that U.S., Euro and Yen interest rates will remain low. Despite exchange controls, tightening domestic interest rates risk attracting capital inflows to meet domestic liquidity needs. RMB weakness could trigger outflows.

Thirdly, due to the implicit deposit insurance and high state-ownership in the financial system, the moral hazard risks are large for a bank-dominated financial system. The sharp rise in debt and leverage ratio implies that there is an inherent shortage of equity funding in the system, because private sector enterprises have difficulty accessing IPOs in the A-share market, and SOEs and LGFPs can raise funds cheaper through the banking system due to their superior credit rating.

There are four aspects revealed by the emergence of shadow banking (including internet finance).

1. First, despite the problems of underregulation or regulatory arbitrage, shadow banking activities represent a roundabout channel to fulfill real market needs of funding at higher interest rates. Unfortunately, certain shadow bank activities require closer regulatory oversight to protect consumers from financialization, usury, fraud and hidden risks.
2. Second, there are two types of shadow banking – one uses product packaging similar to asset securitization for attracting funds at higher interest rates and the other uses new technology to provide financial services at greater convenience and lower costs.
3. Third, both types provide services and credit in areas not previously tapped, but they manage risks in different ways. Private lenders perform stronger due diligence and take calculated risks, whereas Internet finance providers have detailed data on their customers' creditworthiness that enable them to lend without collateral.

Traditional banking is facing competition from both fronts, which should not be stamped out to protect banks, but encouraged to create space for fair competition.

4. Fourth, although shadow banks provide credit, they rarely provide long-term equity or credit, which is the role of pension, social security, insurance and private equity funds. As long as borrowers are highly leveraged, further credit creation from whatever source does not enhance system resilience.

In other words, reform of shadow banking must be undertaken within the wider context of a holistic review of China's funding model to meet the changing requirements of the real economy. The present financial system needs to reform to accommodate China's economic transformation from a state-owned production environment to one that is more market-led and closely integrated with the world economy. Successful reforms require innovations in the financial and real sectors, so that growth in income and value creation exceeds growth in expenditure and value destruction. Hence, the role of government is important in facilitating institutional, process and product innovation.

As discussed in Chapter 6, technology has blurred the lines between the real sector (production and distribution, including logistics) with finance. Hence, the emergence of e-commerce and e-finance means that regulation and policy need to look at creating a level playing field for both sectors, rather than looking at each from a sectoral or segmented basis.

The shadow banking problem therefore represents a golden opportunity for a holistic solution to address the structural imbalances in the Chinese economy and financial system. Piecemeal reforms and more regulations are not enough to maintain financial stability and ensure that finance serves the real sector.

First, the reforms must address the short-termism and fundamental mismatch in the Chinese financial system brought about by over-reliance on the banking system.

Second, institutional reforms must be directed towards injecting capital for the borrowers, either in the form of debt/equity swaps or in the form of greater access by SMEs to equity capital.

Third, the evergreening and inter-enterprise bundling of risks through shadow banking and cross-guarantees must be unwound and sorted out, in order to define debt accountability and build up proper credit culture. Unwinding of these risk-bundling activities will require close coordination among lenders and regulators to identify the ultimate bearers of risks. Ultimately, on-site examination and debt resolution/ restructuring cannot be avoided.

Fourth, reforms must build on the technological innovations brought by Internet finance platforms that improve on credit evaluation and provide funding and transactions at lower cost and greater convenience.

Fifth, there must be a more level playing field between regulated banks and less regulated shadow banks to facilitate healthy competition and greater efficiency in the allocation of capital to generate higher returns and more sustainable growth.

Sixth, reforms must enhance the corporate governance and credit culture, reduce fraud and market abuses, including predatory lending, and improve overall credit discipline.

7.2 ONGOING SHADOW BANKING REFORMS IN CHINA

The Chinese regulatory authorities have implemented pre-emptive policies to address emerging shadow banking concerns. These include measures to improve transparency and reduce information asymmetry, create firewalls between banks and shadow banks to block risk transmission channels, improve investor education and clarify the scope of lender of last resort facilities.

The China Banking Regulatory Commission (CBRC), for example, enhanced supervisory measures on bank–trust cooperation in credit asset transfer in 2011, based on three principles of truthfulness, completeness and clean transfer. Additional regulations on specific shadow banking activities include closer monitoring of banks' WMPs via an electronic information registry system; creation of a bankruptcy mechanism; and the transfer of trust activities back to traditional trust business and wealth management business. Guarantors will be prohibited from engaging in deposit-taking and making loans while specific regulations will be introduced to enable parallel development of Internet finance and traditional finance. The State Council's Directive No. 43 also introduced specific rules on local government borrowing and debt management. In particular, local governments are prohibited from using local government financing platforms (LGFVs) to borrow, and all local government debts, including guarantees, are subject to central government approval. Local governments must also reduce expenditure and dispose of assets to repay their debts but land sales to raise financing require approval.

Such pre-emptive measures are important in preventing the shadow banking industry from becoming a future source of stress. In this regard, it is important that regulations are fit for purpose and customized to local conditions. Indeed, the FSB Regional Consultative Group for Asia noted that shadow banks mean different things in different jurisdictions, and national discretion is key in identifying non-bank financial institutions (NBFIs) that require policy attention, based on the level of interlinkages in the financial system and their systemic risks, while minimizing any unintended effects on their role in financial inclusion and market development (FSB, 2014).

The U.S. experience in dealing with its shadow banks' money market funds showed that more regulation per se is no solution (Borst, 2013). As indicated above, there are contextual and infrastructure reasons why a credit culture is not prevalent in China. In the absence of a reliable rating and credit information industry that fully discloses the riskiness of borrowers, Chinese enterprises are able to borrow and issue short-term debt that can be easily rolled over and "evergreened." Any move towards requiring banks and shadow banks to invest in highly-rated securities will not be effective unless the rating system is reliable. Tightening regulation in this area will drive high-risk borrowers to game the ratings system in order to gain access to financing. Indications are that Chinese banks and shadow banks continue to game the regulations by introducing more complicated transactions and products.

Recent research by the Development Research Center of the State Council (Lei, 2014) suggests that China's recent shadow banking regulations have helped to improve transparency and risk mitigation but are not sufficient to promote the healthy development of shadow banks because of:

1. Lack of clear supervisory principles on shadow banks' WMPs (for example, treatment of the non-principal guaranteed WMPs of banks – either as traditional on-balance sheet business or as part of banks' collective investment program).
2. No explicit regulatory requirements on asset quality, maturity mismatch and liquidity of WMPs.
3. Different regulatory agencies have different supervisory policies, leading to regulatory arbitrage.
4. Existing regulations do not pay sufficient attention to systemic risks such as bank runs, liquidity and counterparty risks.

The GFC revealed that during periods of economic and financial insecurity, relatively small losses in short-term financing pools can quickly evolve into either a retail bank run or a wholesale bank run (banks cutting exposure to a weak bank). The short-term nature of most Chinese WMPs makes them vulnerable to similar risks. A high-profile default of a WMP could trigger large withdrawals of liquidity from the market as investors stop rolling over into new products and shift their funds back into traditional bank deposits. This would strain the entire Chinese economy as companies and banks that rely on short-term financing will be confronted with a credit crunch.

Hence, closer prudential supervision and monitoring of shadow banking and stronger progress in financial reforms are needed to ensure that shadow banking does not become a potential source of financial fragility in China. To avoid the dangers of overregulation based on a "one-size-fits-all" approach, such reforms should be tailored to China's domestic conditions, focusing on specific areas where systemic risks could arise.

In particular, the reform agenda needs to be differentiated across the three risk layers of shadow banking, addressing the respective root causes (Table 7.1).

TABLE 7.1 Root issues/opportunities and regulatory implications

Layers	Key issues/ opportunities	Regulatory implications
Bank OBSF* layer	■ "Hidden bomb" to the banking system, due to increasing opaqueness of funds channeling ■ Most risk mismatch concentrated in the bank OBSF layer	■ Eliminate regulatory arbitrage by redesigning the regulatory framework: 　■ Prevent risk mismatch and mislabeling 　■ "Formalize" banks' off-balance sheet lending to shadow banking institutions 　■ Improve risk management on bank related shadow banking products ■ Establish a credit "firewall" between commercial banks and non-bank shadow banking activities

		■ Prevent execution risk by prohibiting commercial bank employees' participation in non-bank shadow banking/financing activities ■ Clarify credit liabilities to avoid non-contract-binding risk spillover to banks via "guaranteed return"

Credit enhancement layer	■ "At the frontier of default," due to naturally higher risk of loans
	■ Relatively loose control over credit enhancement institutions (regulated under local government instead of CBRC)
		■ Enhance risk management capabilities:
		  ■ Regulations on capital requirements if credit enhancement institutions were to participate in lending
		  ■ Tight regulation and execution on credit enhancement institutions illegally participating in shadow banking activities
		■ Better coordinated policy setting, ultimately facilitating further industry consolidation

Non-bank lending layer	■ "Healthy" complement to financing via bank loans but very little oversight/regulatory control	■ Increase transparency in non-bank lending activities:
		  ■ Emphasize establishment of proper risk management to facilitate more rational pricing of credit risk
		  ■ Eliminate irregular practices to reduce moral hazard
		■ Regulate to enhance NBFI's risk management

*Off-balance sheet financing
Source: Expert interviews, FGI analysis, Oliver Wyman analysis.

7.3 FINANCIAL REFORMS – LOOKING BEYOND SHADOW BANKING

A pragmatic approach to addressing China's shadow banking problem requires a holistic review and understanding of its interlinkages with the formal banking sector and how they provide funding for the real economy. This review should be undertaken immediately but within the wider context of China's long-term financial reform agenda to promote efficient allocation of capital to meet the country's financing needs in a more sustainable and inclusive manner.

International experience shows that while crisis is an event, reform is a process that has four stages – diagnosis, damage control, loss allocation and changing the incentives. The proposed reforms can be grouped into immediate-term, medium-term and long-term measures.

7.4 IMMEDIATE-TERM REFORM PRIORITIES – DIAGNOSIS AND DAMAGE CONTROL

The reform agenda will require immediate-term measures at the diagnostic stage to assess the true size of losses or NPLs in the banks and shadow banks, specifically identifying the exposures of the corporate sector to inter-enterprise liability. Nine immediate-term measures are suggested:

1. It is recommended that an inter-agency task force be established at the State Council level, with experts from different agencies and regulators, to immediately look into the problem of inter-enterprise liability and their impact on bank and shadow bank credit. This can be undertaken through pilot studies that follow credit along the supply chain, examining where the vulnerabilities exist among the different credit providers. In many cases, this will involve on-site inspection and use of data analytics to examine interconnectivity and relationships between different borrowers. Ensuring credit accountability will help unwind the complex joint guarantees and intertwined credit risks that add moral hazard to the Chinese financial system. It will help improve the sound financing of the Chinese enterprise sector. This is an important part of the diagnosis phase to identify and measure the risks and losses inherent in the system.

2. There is urgency to clarify the responsibility for debt and therefore, implementation of the FSB's Legal Entity Identifier (LEI) initiative[2]

---

[2]The Legal Entity Identifier (LEI) is a 20-digit, alpha-numeric code, which connects to key reference information and enables clear and unique identification of participants in global financial markets.

will help to determine who owes what to whom in the Chinese financial system. By providing a unique ID for each single legal entity, LEIs enable consistent identification of all parties to financial transactions and ensure a consistent and integrated view of exposures. This will help improve the measurement and monitoring of systemic risk as the LEI serves as a standard to identify the ultimate borrower and will address the problem of evergreening, fraud and bundling of risks.

3. At different levels of government, the establishment of property registries to clarify property rights will help strengthen the credit culture in China, since all kinds of assets are now available as collateral for credit. Property registries will ensure that encumbered assets cannot be used for double or multiple collateralization, which is actually a form of fraud. Complementing the LEI, property registries identify who owns what and which properties are unencumbered and available for transfer or use as collateral.

4. As part of the effort to minimize immediate losses, there should be some effort to cap the excessive lending rates, especially if these are paid by state-owned enterprises (SOEs) and LGFPs, which have sovereign credit status. Exit and restructuring mechanisms should be established as a matter of priority, as the restructuring of failed or failing borrowers must be high priority to prevent the escalation of reckless borrowing, since that transmits further losses on the banking system.

   This will complement the establishment of a deposit insurance scheme to reduce the moral hazard associated with the widespread use (and abuse) of implicit government guarantees. It would also inculcate good corporate governance and discipline in the financial system. Speedy implementation of the deposit insurance scheme will ensure that it supports China's financial reform program and provides a safety net for depositors during a period of exiting and restructuring of non-viable financial institutions.

5. It is important to strengthen consumer and investor protection through greater investor education, outreach programs on financial literacy, credit counseling and debt management, as both investors and borrowers must take due care and diligence of their finances and promote the responsible use of financial products and services.

6. Once the LEI standard is established, credit monitoring can be improved via the creation of a nationwide credit bureau, formed with market input, to encourage financial markets to share credit information and develop transparent and objective assessment of

credit risk among borrowers. Over time, this will instill a strong credit culture in the Chinese financial system and minimize the moral hazard issues associated with recent cases in resolving wealth management product (WMP) defaults. At the same time, measures to strengthen corporate governance are equally important, including the inculcation of greater accountability and responsibility among the boards and senior management of financial institutions to ensure financial prudence and corporate social responsibility.

7. Restructuring/simplifying the regulatory supervisory model is important, with greater clarity in the roles of different regulatory agencies (including via legislative amendments) to enhance regulatory cooperation and close regulatory gaps and arbitrage opportunities.

8. Orderly financial liberalization, including deposit interest rates will also reduce the scope for regulatory arbitrage. In turn, this will reduce distortions and level the playing field for banks and shadow banks.

9. The time has come for China to establish a secondary mortgage corporation by adopting either the Hong Kong Mortgage Corporation or Malaysia's Cagamas model, to expedite asset securitization and deepen the capital market while promoting home ownership. Typically, these secondary mortgage corporations (SMCs) purchase portfolios of mortgage loans, secured by residential properties from approved sellers, which include banks, government bodies and their agencies, public bodies, and property developers. The SMCs then raise financing for their purchases of mortgage loans through the issuance of debt securities to banks, institutional and retail investors. And because of their AAA credit rating, they are able to raise funds at low cost, which in turn will enable primary lenders like banks to provide housing loans to house buyers at lower mortgage rates.

7.5 LOSS ALLOCATION – MEDIUM-TERM MEASURES

In addition to damage control, priority also needs to be accorded to the Third Plenum's[3] objective to complete a market-based exit mechanism for financial institutions (Table 7.2). As discussed in the previous section,

---

[3]A Plenum is a meeting of the Communist Party's Central Committee. Historically, Third Plenums have been important occasions where the top leadership can present a long-term vision and road-map for China's economy.

TABLE 7.2 Third plenum decisions on financial reforms

Key Points Regarding Financial Market Reforms

Open up the financial sector further both inwardly and outwardly. Authorize establishment of small privately owned banks and other financial institutions that meet certain conditions. Reform policy financial institutions.

Optimize multi-tier financial market structure. Reform equity issuance registration system. Promote equity finance via many channels. Develop and regulate bond markets. Increase the prevalence of direct finance.

Improve insurance industry's economic compensation mechanism. Develop mega-disaster insurance scheme.

Develop inclusive finance.

Encourage financial innovations. Diversify financial market strata and products.

Improve renminbi exchange rate formation mechanism through market forces. Accelerate interest rate liberalization. Improve the government bond yield curve to better reflect the market's supply–demand balance.

Open up capital markets both inwardly and outwardly. Further liberalize cross-border capital and financial transactions.

Establish and optimize a regulatory system for external debt and capital flows under a macroprudential regulatory framework. Accelerate renminbi capital account liberalization.

Steadily implement financial regulatory reforms and moderation standards. Improve regulatory coordination. Clarify financial regulation and risk mitigation responsibilities between national and sub-national governments.

Develop deposit insurance scheme. Improve the market exit mechanism for financial institutions.

Source: Jingu (2014).

a robust exit mechanism, together with a sound deposit insurance scheme, will become increasingly important as the re-regulation of the financial sector and the introduction of more market-based interest rates and exchange rates will have implications for the survival of the weaker financial institutions and their exit. Such reforms are essential not only to address the moral hazard and credit culture issues, but also to allocate losses incurred.

The resolution of financial system fragility requires deleveraging, which involves stock and flow options that are better suited to addressing the specific problems of non-performing loans (NPLs) in the SOE, LGFP, real estate and SME sectors. Speed, transparency and predictability in failed enterprise resolution are key.

7.5.1 Stock Approach to Bank Restructuring

Stock solutions involve the carve-out of debt, debt–equity swaps, or moving debt to asset management companies (AMCs). The aim is to put the banking and shadow banking industry on a clean slate and stronger footing to ensure that they continue to perform their financial intermediation role to support real economic activity. This could be done through government intervention in the case of the SOEs and LGFPs. China's earlier experience in managing the NPLs and restructuring of the four large state-owned commercial banks (SOCBs) via AMCs provides valuable lessons going forward.

A step in the right direction was the August 2014 requirement for the top four SOCBs to raise additional debt and equity to strengthen bank reserves. This will enhance the banks' capacity to address potential NPL problems while maintaining their financial intermediation role. Five local governments have also been granted permission to set up AMCs, or so-called "bad" banks, to purchase NPLs from local lenders and help to facilitate in cleaning up their balance sheets. In the process, the removal of NPLs by the AMCs will enable banks to focus on lending to support the real economy.

Successful bank restructuring requires a holistic approach to address both stock and liquidity problems, with solvency restructuring accompanied by operational restructuring and structural reforms to correct shortcomings in the accounting, tax, legal and regulatory framework. All these are necessary to resolve the fundamental causes of bank instability and get the incentives right.

7.5.2 Flow Approach to Bank Restructuring

Another resolution option is to allow the banking system to resolve its NPL problem through flow methods – widening net interest spreads and establishing proper exit mechanisms to address NPLs in the case of the property sector and the SMEs. The net interest spread will not increase if there is adequate provisioning for NPLs. This approach will require the formulation of procedures for the voluntary restructuring of NPLs, including write-offs where appropriate. An important step forward is the CBRC's plan to permit five local authorities, including in Shanghai, to establish local AMCs to purchase NPLs from banks at the provincial or city level.

A flow approach to enhance the credit culture would include:

1. Measures to redefine and strengthen the rules on loan classification, loss and interest in suspense to address the issue of evergreening. This is important to ensure that NPLs are recognized and resolved promptly, instead of postponing (and aggravating) the problem by continuously rolling over the debt to a future date.
2. Survey and review interlocking credit guarantees by enterprises and banks, especially in terms of strengthening the due diligence processes. Interlocking credit guarantees have created an opaque web that binds the shadow banking risks to the financial system. Untangling this web of interlocking claims is key to clarifying the risks and avoiding hidden, system-wide implications.
3. Establishing a main bank system to monitor credit of conglomerates and related enterprises. A main bank with the most exposure to a group of companies would be given primary responsibility not just for monitoring, but also resolution of problem loans and restructuring, including negotiations with other lenders. This is important to address the rapid expansion in inter-enterprise liability and ensure that it does not create undue risks.

At the institutional level, wider application of bankruptcy procedures for the orderly exit of inefficient entities and the recapitalization of banks affected by NPLs would be important. Although China enacted a comprehensive and modern bankruptcy law in 2007, including provisions for corporate restructuring, the law has yet to be tested, as the number of Chinese firms filing for bankruptcy remains low. Just over 1,000 bankruptcy filings were submitted in 2012, compared to an average of 800,000 companies that exited the market annually in 2005–09 (SCMP, 2013). In the U.S., there are more than 2 million bankruptcies annually. Continued outreach is important to correct public misperceptions and remove the stigma of bankruptcy by clarifying the role of bankruptcy proceedings in reviving troubled businesses and promoting efficiency.

In June 2014, the Basel Committee on Banking Supervision issued a consultative document, "Supervisory Guidelines for Identifying and Dealing with Weak Banks" (Basel Committee, 2014a). The document contained several guiding principles which may be relevant for the formulation of bank resolution policy in China:

1. Bank exits are a part of risk-taking in a competitive market environment. They help reinforce the right incentive structure and a credible resolution regime enhances market discipline.
2. A private sector solution – a takeover by a healthy institution – reduces the cost on taxpayers and minimizes distortions in the banking sector. Public funds should only be used as a last resort in times of acute financial market stress and instability.
3. Speed, transparency and predictability are key. Weak banks must be rehabilitated or resolved quickly. Assets from failed banks must be returned to the market promptly to minimize the final costs to depositors, creditors and taxpayers and to prevent the unnecessary destruction of value.
4. In any resolution via a merger, acquisition or purchase-and-assumption transaction, the acquiring bank must be selected via open competition. Any incentives to facilitate transactions should not distort competition or penalize other banks.
5. Resolution should ensure continuity of important banking functions and minimize market disruption.

7.6 MAPPING THE FUTURE OF CHINA'S FINANCIAL SYSTEM: A POTENTIAL LONG-TERM BLUEPRINT

As BIS General Manager Caruana (2014) suggested, it is time for the global economy to step out of the shadow of the global financial crisis and make the transition toward a more sustainable, less debt-driven growth and a more reliable financial system.

China is also undergoing profound change, as the economy and society transitions into a middle-income economy that is characterized by urbanized consumption and production that is not only more broad-based, but is technologically driven, mobile Internet friendly and more inclusive, and ecologically green. The present financial system was designed to serve largely a state-owned production environment and needs to reform to meet the changing requirements of a mass consumption-driven and market-led economy that has become more integrated with the world economy.

Indeed, Chinese banks and their regulators need to respond to the major shifts in the financial landscape, brought about by financial innovations and technological advances. In the new environment, banks and shadow banks are competing to offer new financial services as technology (the Internet of Things, cloud computing and big data analytics) opens up new market opportunities with the convenience of banking anytime, anywhere, via any mobile and Internet platform.

Just as the explosive growth in Internet finance and e-commerce reflect fundamental changes in Chinese supply chain production, distribution and consumption patterns, so do microfinance, moneylending and wealth management products reflect the increasingly complex, diverse and specialized needs of different segments of the market and society.

Of course, the explosive growth in new, opaque products gives rise to regulatory concerns of personal privacy, cybersecurity, moral hazard, fraud and systemic risks, which warrant closer regulatory oversight in setting prudential and consumer protection standards. A 2014 survey estimated that cybercrime costs the U.S. economy US$100 billion annually (Ponemon Institute, 2013). But there are also opportunities to address the genuine needs of the real sector and to reform the present antiquated financial structure and processes.

In bringing shadow banking into the light, it is also timely for China to take the opportunity to move towards a more holistic, long-term approach to financial reform. This is important to address structural weaknesses in the Chinese financial system that created the shadow banking problem in the first place. The aim of the long-term financial reform agenda is to diversify the financial system to address the structural (maturity and capital) mismatches in the economy; reduce the role of the state in the economy, particularly in reducing the resource allocation mismatches; and reduce the income disparities, including improving income transfers through the social security reforms.

The financial system is currently bank-dominated and biased towards short-term debt, without sufficient equity capital for enterprises to deleverage and absorb risks for long-term investments. The formulation of a comprehensive blueprint to diversify and reorientate the financial system to better serve China's changing needs as the economy transitions from an export-based to a domestic consumption-led growth model with knowledge-based and services industries includes the following elements:

1. Development of pension and insurance funds and equity/capital markets including funding for SMEs via private equity (PE) and

equity funds to inject capital into innovative enterprises and reduce leverage of borrowers. Currently, pension and insurance funds account for less than 5 percent of the assets of the Chinese banking system. In Australia, reforms of the pension schemes in the 1990s created a second "spare tire." During the GFC, the pension funds injected capital into the banking system and therefore strengthened the resilience of the overall financial system to the GFC shock. Developing pension and insurance funds will also address the maturity mismatch of bank lending and promote more efficient allocation of capital, financial inclusion and more balanced growth.

2. Use international standards to facilitate China's integration with the global economy and financial system. Ideally, adoption of global standards should be based on best fit to ensure that best practices are customized to China's circumstances.

3. Improve the management of state assets and separate the role of the state from ownership. Since China has a large amount of assets in central government and local government hands, improving the efficiency and liquidity of these assets would generate greater productivity and help drive growth. Some of the underutilized state assets can be leased (not sold) to private enterprises to improve their management. This will promote competition and efficiency in supporting innovation and resource allocation for long-term, inclusive growth.

4. Leverage on technology to restructure the financial services industry and enable China's economic restructuring process to leapfrog into the New Industrial Revolution.

5. Control and manage property market risks among local governments, including via reforms on fiscal revenue sharing arrangements, and the development of long-term municipal bond market and secondary markets.

The direction of reform with the market as the decisive factor needs to focus on:

1. Creating a level playing field for all players in the financial system, including equal treatment for financial services offered by technology providers, banks and shadow banks.

2. Leveling the playing field to ensure equal access to funding by the private sector (SMEs) and SOEs. This is key to more inclusive and balanced long-term growth.

3. Establish a competition commission to ensure that there is sufficient competition to promote innovation. The current system encourages entry (licensing), but not healthy competition and exit. Such a commission should encourage freer entry and exit and promote rules that do not obstruct competition and innovation.
4. The existing system also encourages herding (everyone wants to be a bank) and inhibits diversity. A sustainable and robust financial system requires diversity and more specialization of different banks and financial institutions to meet the specific needs of different sectors and industries.

Going forward, the realization of China's Dream requires more domestic consumption, more innovation and knowledge-based growth industries and green technology. Key elements of a financial sector blueprint to strengthen the financial system's effectiveness in supporting China's transition out of the middle-income trap toward a high-value, domestic consumption-led growth model include the following:

1. Promoting SMEs as China's main engine of growth, innovation and job creation. A major constraint to SMEs is funding. A revamped New Third Market/PE funds will deepen their access to capital and increase their capacity to invest and innovate for long-term growth.
2. Banks as a major mobilizer of savings will also need to devote more attention to equity funding. This will require a major review of the universal banking approach. The judicious use of foreign expertise and entry of foreign financial institutions to spur innovation in finance merits consideration.
3. The promotion of a vibrant private pension and insurance industry to meet China's need for long-term development funds as well as the needs of its aging population.
4. Investments in people, technology and infrastructure are key to build up a solid financial system, with deep and well-diversified capital markets to meet the changing needs of the real economy.
5. Improvements in corporate governance at the level of not just enterprises, banks, but also shadow banks and other financial intermediaries, along the lines suggested by the Basel Committee (2014b) consultation document on corporate governance principles.

The long-term financial reforms to develop the equity markets, insurance and pension funds will reduce overreliance on short-term bank lending and ensure a more diversified and resilient financial system that promotes efficient allocation of capital. To support China's financial reform agenda, more open communication via periodic dialogues and consultations with key stakeholders, including the top leadership and consumers, are important to garner support. Such interactions also provide useful feedback on the reform process itself, particularly on the orderly sequencing and pace of reforms.

It is also timely to undertake a comprehensive review of the relevant laws to clarify the roles and mandates of financial regulators, promote financial inclusion and consumer protection, and create a credit bureau to improve and inculcate a credit culture in China (Lei, 2014). Ultimately, success in financial reform will depend on China's ability to generate sufficient income and value creation to compensate for the expenditure and value destruction as the reform process gets underway.

At the structural level, China needs to address two fundamental imbalances. The first is to wean the large SOEs and local governments from their tendency to over-invest in low-yielding projects. Rationalization of SOEs and LGFPs engaged in loss-making industries and those suffering from overcapacity will reduce wastage and misallocation of resources, enhancing overall efficiency. This will also be in line with the move towards a more market-driven economy.

The second is to increase access to capital for the more productive SMEs that will generate growth, jobs and market innovation. Reducing the degree of financial repression will address inequities that are building up in the system. The PBOC is also engaging in targeted quantitative easing (QE) by channeling funds directly to the China Development Bank (CDB) to fund affordable housing in shanty towns. This is an example of financial innovation as a new channel for monetary and social policy.

In other words, interest rate liberalization cannot be divorced from simultaneous capital market reforms that will enable SMEs to deepen their capital base and resilience to make the market transformation from an export-led economy to a domestic consumption- and service-driven economy. The economy can only make the transition if value creation through innovation exceeds the value destruction through bad investments in obsolete excess capacity.

China needs simultaneously high-quality financial deepening and targeted financial austerity. The PBOC is attempting exactly that delicate balance between austerity for non-productive loans and providing adequate liquidity for the SMEs to access credit. The central bank has adequate resources and policy flexibility to slowly release the trapped liquidity in reserve requirements. A fine balance is required. If interest rates rise too fast, they will trigger asset price deflation. If too slow, continued financial repression adds to market distortions.

7.7 CONCLUSION AND SUGGESTIONS FOR FUTURE RESEARCH

To sum up, certain aspects of shadow banking can pose contagion and moral hazard risks, and continued vigilance and regulatory action is important to preempt shadow banking risks from triggering wider contagion effects. Time is of the essence, as the external environment has deteriorated in the course of 2015, with a "new mediocre" of slow and uneven global growth. But, more regulations and piecemeal reforms are not sufficient. Over the longer term, it is worth reiterating that China is undergoing profound change, as the economy and society move into middle-income, urbanized consumption and production that is not only more broad-based, but is technologically driven, more inclusive and ecologically sustainable. The present financial system needs comprehensive reforms to improve efficiency in the allocation of capital and accommodate China's economic transformation from a state-owned production environment to one that is more market-led and closely integrated with the world economy.

Successful reforms require innovations in the financial and real sector, so that growth in income and value creation exceeds growth in expenditure and value destruction. Here, the role of government is important in facilitating institutional, process and product innovation.

This chapter has attempted to provide an analytical framework, based on the national balance sheet and flow of funds approach, to shed some light on the complex interlinkages between the shadow banking and formal banking sector and the real economy, and their possible implications for policy. It provides a top-down, snapshot view of the situation at a point in time. There remain, however, four areas where further research may be warranted.

Firstly, it would be useful to develop a model to analyze the dynamic interactions and feedback loops between shadow banks and changes in the real economy. Such a bottom-up model would be highly data intensive and require the cooperation of the regulatory and government agencies to source the necessary data. Modeling the dynamics could be useful in predicting the possible outcomes in Chinese shadow banking in the event of a sudden shock such as a sharp economic slowdown or collapse in property prices.

Secondly, there is a need to assess the likely impact on NPLs from the weighted average interest rate burden on the various sectors of the economy. This is particularly important given expectations of a general rise in global interest rates in the long term.

Thirdly, no desktop analysis can substitute for on-site examination of the hidden connections and network of interrelationships and feedback mechanisms that link the banks, shadow banks and the enterprise/local government sectors. There is no substitute for hard work in uncovering such connections, which can be obtained either through on-site examinations or post-mortem analyses of failed enterprises through restructuring or bankruptcy proceedings.

Finally, further analysis of industries with excess capacity and the potential for real estate price adjustments is also useful to assess their likely impact on the NPL situation. In the process, such research would help to clarify the potential risks of NPLs arising from changes in these sectors.

REFERENCES

Basel Committee on Banking Supervision. 2014a. Supervisory Guidelines for Identifying and Dealing with Weak Banks (Consultative Document). Bank for International Settlements. http://www.bis.org/publ/bcbs285.pdf.

Basel Committee on Banking Supervision. 2014b. Corporate Governance Principles for Banks – Consultative Document. http://www.bis.org/publ/bcbs294.htm.

Borst, Nicholas. 2013. Shadow Deposits as a Source of Financial Instability: Lessons from the American Experience for China. Peterson Institute for International Economics Policy Brief. http://www.iie.com/publications/pb/pb13-14.pdf.

Caruana, Jaime. 2014. Stepping Out of the Shadow of the Crisis: Three Transitions for the World Economy. Bank for International Settlements, Annual General Meeting, Basel, 29 June. Speech. http://www.bis.org/speeches/sp140629.pdf.

FSB (Financial Stability Board). 2014. Report on Shadow Banking in Asia. Regional Consultative Group for Asia. http://www.financialstabilityboard.org/publications/r_140822c.pdf.

Jingu, Takeshi. 2014. China's Financial Reform Roadmap Unveiled at Third Plenum. Lakyara vol.185, Nomura Research Institute. http://www.nri.com/~/media/PDF/global/opinion/lakyara/2014/lkr2014185.pdf.

Lei, Wei. 2014. Policy Options for Mitigating 'Shadow Banking' Risks in China. *China Development Review*, vol. 16 (1). Development Research Center of the State Council, The People's Republic of China.

Ponemon Institute. 2013. 2013 Cost of Cyber Crime Study: United States. http://media.scmagazine.com/documents/54/2013_us_ccc_report_final_6-1_13455.pdf.

SCMP (South China Morning Post). 2013. Why Stigma Holds Back China's Bankruptcy Law. August 12. http://www.scmp.com/business/china-business/article/1295985/why-stigma-holds-back-chinas-bankruptcy-law.

CHAPTER 8

Conclusion

Andrew Sheng

8.1 INTRODUCTION

Our study has shown that shadow banks or non-bank financial inter-mediaries (NBFIs) are not fearsome, toxic creations which must be regulated out of existence. Globally, they form an integral part of the financial system, providing financial services to underserved sectors and actually exhibit transformations in the financial sector in response to major changes in the real economy. While advanced country shadow banks contributed to the Global Financial Crisis (GFC), those in China are smaller and less complex, with lower systemic risk. However, some Chinese shadow banks warrant closer scrutiny as they share the weak-nesses of their foreign counterparts in promoting opaque, usurious lending and cross-guarantees that bundle shadow banking credit risks into the formal banking system, with significant moral hazard issues.

Our conclusion is that China's shadow banks are unlikely to trigger a financial crisis as they are essentially a domestic debt problem without any direct global systemic implications, since China is a net lender to the world and very few foreigners hold Chinese shadow banking assets. This assessment is, however, based on the national balance sheet analysis, which provides a top-down, snapshot view of the situation in China and a review of current conditions. It did not attempt to forecast dynamic changes in the Chinese economy and its interactions with global condi-tions. Conditions could well change dramatically for the worse if growth falters or property prices collapse due to some unforeseen shock.

Any deterioration in shadow banking problems could undermine market confidence, with possible contagion effects on foreign holdings of China's bonds and securities. If not properly managed, a series of defaults by shadow banks or their clients can affect foreign banks and investors, as well as domestic confidence. As shadow banks are also driven by a rush for quick profits, they warrant closer regulatory oversight to curb exploitation and excessive risk-taking that do not serve the needs of the real sector.

China's NBFIs (for example, trust companies, moneylending and microfinance entities) served both depositors seeking higher returns, and small borrowers who had limited access to formal bank funding. At the same time, Internet financial platforms bridged the gap between logistics and e-commerce business and the payments function to enter into funds transfer, wealth management and, increasingly, lending business (e-finance). These two groups responded to fundamental changes in the Chinese supply chain production, distribution and consumption and savings patterns, whilst addressing the genuine needs of the real sector and exploiting regulatory and interest rate arbitrages not addressed by the official banking system.

While China's regulatory authorities have implemented preemptive measures to address the emerging shadow banking concerns, it is important to recognize that more comprehensive reforms to address processes and systems made obsolete by technology and market competition are both urgent and necessary. In the course of 2014–2015, the economy has slowed, property prices have peaked and the global environment has become more uncertain, with increased market volatility and downside risks.

Real sector and financial reforms are urgent and necessary because China is undergoing profound change as the economy and society moves into middle-income, urbanized consumption and production that is not only more broad-based, but is technologically knowledge-based and services driven, mobile Internet friendly, more inclusive and ecologically green.

The present financial system was designed to serve largely a state-owned production environment that relies on investment, and manufacturing and exports that have reached their limits due to excess capacities, pollution and reliance on cheap labor. China has reached its "Ford moment," when domestic consumption will rise as wages rise and the economy shifts away from quantity to quality of life for her people. The financial system needs to reform to meet China's changing needs as it rapidly shifts to a mass consumption-driven and market-led economy that is more closely integrated with the world economy.

This transformation will need higher levels of risk capital and long-term funds rather than short-term debt. This is because the phasing out of the excess capacity, polluting and energy inefficient industries will have large "deadweight loss" costs from creative destruction, whereas the requisite new investments in high tech, innovative industries will be investment intensive with higher risks. This transformation cannot be funded largely by short-term bank loans, even though interest rates will be kept low for both policy and global reasons. Excessively low interest rates have generated asset price bubbles that have heightened downside risks. All these considerations point toward the need for higher equity cushions to manage the transformation soundly.

It is now clear that a short-term debt-driven funding model is increasingly vulnerable to systemic shocks. Hence, the conclusion is that China needs to increase equity into its enterprise sectors in order for them to absorb risks during the transformation phase. This can only be done with the building up of the long-term pension, insurance and private equity funds relative to the banking system and the restructuring of existing, viable but undercapitalized enterprises. Both directions are structural and cannot be achieved overnight.

This is necessary on two counts. First, as the population ages and becomes wealthier, China must build up adequate pension and insurance funds to provide social security for the aging labor force. Second, given the higher risks in the transformation to an advanced economy, savers and investors must be rewarded by higher returns. To expect households to accept low deposit interest rates and to absorb the high transitional risks is to increase the level of inequality in the system.

At the same time, the banking system must embark on an active restructuring of its enterprise portfolio, away from the risk-shift of debt towards a risk-sharing framework to get the whole system out of over-reliance on debt and excessive leverage.

Hence, the strategy to improve equity and long-term pension and insurance funds is both a prudential and socially inclusive strategy. Similarly, prioritizing exit and restructuring of non-viable borrowers/enterprises (including SOEs in loss-making industries suffering over-capacity) aids structural transformation at the real economy and financial sector level.

8.2 SHADOW BANKING WITH CHINESE CHARACTERISTICS

Our review of shadow banking showed that there are differences between shadow banks in the advanced countries and shadow banks in China. These differences stem from the historical and institutional evolution of the Chinese financial system, which has been bank-based and designed to serve a manufacturing and industrial base, driven largely by investment and exports, rather than domestic consumption.

The Chinese characteristics of the financial system comprise four mismatches:

1. The system lends largely to the state sector and the foreign sector (in the form of large foreign exchange reserves), with a structural shortage of funding by the private enterprise sector.
2. There is a significant maturity mismatch, because the system is largely bank-dominated, with long-term institutional investors such as pension funds and insurance companies accounting for less than 3 percent of total financial assets.
3. There is a foreign exchange mismatch, because China's foreign exchange reserves amounted to about 9 percent of total financial assets. They impose a cost on savers, because they are funded largely by reserve requirements on the banking system.
4. The debt/equity mismatch is large, because the A-share market was open largely to SOEs, and private SMEs found it difficult to access capital from the stock market. The private equity market is still underdeveloped. It is the growing leverage of the SOEs, private SMEs and local government financing platforms (LGFPs) that has created fragility that must be managed.

There is much confusion about the potential risks in China's shadow banks, due to differences in definition, terminology and measurement. Current estimates of the size of Chinese shadow banking assets range from 14 to 70 percent of GDP. After netting out possible double counting, our study suggests that at the end of 2013, the scale of Chinese shadow banking risk assets was RMB 30.1 trillion or 53 percent of GDP and 27 percent of formal banking system credit assets. At this level, shadow banking in China remains less than half the global average of 120 percent of GDP. It has limited global systemic implications, since China is a net lender to the world and very few foreigners hold Chinese shadow banking assets. However, we cannot rule out the possibility that an escalation in the shadow banking problem could undermine market confidence and lead to contagion and crowded exits that would affect overall stability.

China's National Balance Sheet showed that at the end of 2013, China's public sector had net assets of RMB 103 trillion (162 percent of GDP), even after taking into consideration gross liabilities of RMB 124 trillion or 195 percent of GDP. With the economy still growing at 6–7 percent per annum, with low fiscal deficit and high savings rate, a financial meltdown is unlikely as China has adequate resources and policy flexibility to address what is essentially a domestic debt problem. Even if we were to exclude all its (less liquid) natural resource assets, the sovereign government's financial position remains solvent to avoid any potential liquidity problems.

Furthermore, because of the rise in land prices and high investments in infrastructure, Chinese real estate to GDP ratio is already high at 250 percent of GDP; comparable to that of advanced countries and the higher income EMEs. The good news is that China is still urbanizing at the rate of roughly 1 percent per annum, which means that 12–13 million people will need new urban housing and its related infrastructure each year. Moreover, the fixed investments per capita in China is still low at around US$10,000, compared with advanced countries like U.S. (US$90,000) and Japan (US$200,000).

There is, however, no escaping the fact that the splurge in investments in land and infrastructure since 2008 has created excess capacity in some second- and third-tier cities and industrial zones, with the emergence of "ghost towns." Because China is a continental economy, not all cities and regions will suffer downward land price pressures. But the largest single risk to the Chinese economy is a nationwide sharp drop in land prices, which will impact on the size of bank non-performing loans (NPLs).

Once we establish that there is little solvency issue at the domestic or foreign currency level, the next question is whether illiquidity could cause problems to surface. The answer is that sudden shocks in liquidity that lead to sharp rises in real interest rates and crowded exits could lead to financial crises. However, because a large share of Chinese savings are in lending to the foreign sector in the form of foreign exchange reserves, locked up in statutory reserves with the central bank, the central bank can easily release liquidity through relaxation of the reserve requirements.

Hence, the delicate balance in Chinese management of macroprudential stability is to release sufficient liquidity by the central bank without triggering inflation and without permitting wasteful investment in speculative activities. This requires close coordination between the central bank and the financial regulators to manage liquidity without disturbing macroprudential stability.

Our basic conclusion is that, barring any sudden shocks, the shadow banking risks are still manageable for the moment, and the Chinese authorities have the capital, solvency and tools to manage them.

However, rebalancing the four mismatches will require deft skills and strong determination. There are sufficient resources and administrative capacity to deal with this task, but the proper sequencing in the midst of rapid change in the external environment will not be easy.

8.3 UNIQUE OPPORTUNITY FOR REFORM

We therefore see the risks from the rapid growth in shadow banking as an opportunity to transform the financial system into one that will add efficiency, resilience and support for the real sector transformation. Getting this right will enable China to overcome the middle-income trap and advance into the ranks of the high-income countries.

The Third Plenum has correctly set out what should be done. Our only emphasis is one of sequencing and choice of priority areas.

First, the authorities must improve the *diagnosis* through more detailed studies and research into the complexities and risks of inter-enterprise debt and launch pilot projects on how to disentangle the bundling of risks between enterprises, local governments, banks and shadow banks. From an exposure point of view, inter-enterprise liability of RMB 51 trillion is even larger than enterprise loans from the banking system of RMB 39 trillion at the end of 2011. In other words, the rise in shadow banking credit represents another channel of funding for the private sector and local governments to fund their large investments in real assets, but at higher costs.

Second, from a *damage control* point of view, the priority is less on deposit insurance, but rather on the exit mechanism or debt restructuring. This is urgent because the longer the exit of non-viable borrowers or associated financial institutions is delayed, the larger the damage in terms of unrecognized NPLs and the greater will be the need for regulatory forbearance. Strengthening the bankruptcy law (especially its implementation) to allow corporate restructuring through Chapter 11-type debt-equity swaps will reduce the high leverage of the non-financial corporate sector and the bundling of risks between the shadow and formal banking sector and the real economy. The lack of clarity in credit accountability also raises moral hazard implications.

Third, in order to reduce the shadow banking and banking credit risks, it is important not only to price the risks properly (for example, use of more market-based interest rates), but also to deleverage their borrowers and therefore enhance their ability to absorb risks. In order to improve the pricing mechanism, the sovereign benchmark yield curve should be officially launched and a secondary mortgage market and municipal debt market be established. Key studies must be done on the impact of high interest rates on the borrowers, so that usurious rates and predatory behavior is avoided.

Fourth, *loss allocation* of NPL write-offs cannot be avoided through forbearance. By getting the banks to write off and also restructure the debt of their borrowers (enterprises), either using asset management companies or having in-house special restructuring units, this will change the behavior of banks from being passive lenders to actively managing their portfolio over the long term. Regulations on debt/equity swaps should be promulgated to ensure that the banks make best efforts to help resuscitate viable enterprises that are failing due to overleverage. However, those engaged in fraud should be weeded out of the system.

To inject equity into private sector enterprises, the government can consider establishing a domestic sovereign wealth fund and allowing pension and insurance funds to have a higher proportion of alternative assets to invest in more start-ups and innovative enterprises.

Fifth, to prevent recurrence of the present weaknesses in credit culture, credit standards such as the Legal Entity Identifier (LEI) and more transparent credit bureaus should be established to *change the incentives* for bad behavior that led to the current losses. Specifically, the tax bias between debt and equity issuance should be corrected. Currently, interest on debt and loan losses are both tax deductible, whereas dividends are subject to double taxation and capital losses are not deductible.

8.4 REFORM AGENDA GOING FORWARD

The greatest risks to the current financial system are a sharp slowdown in growth, spike in interest rates, social unrest and collapse of real estate prices. Given low global interest rates and fundamental domestic demand in China for residential and commercial real estate from continued urbanization, there is policy space to provide central bank liquidity and manage property prices through improving buyer affordability, as well as debt/equity swaps through project restructuring.

More regulation and piecemeal reforms are not enough as shadow banking highlights several structural mismatches in the Chinese financial system and economy. The problem is complicated, because the ultimate source of funding and the bulk of the risk exposure of shadow banking may lie with the formal banking system. This calls for immediate-term measures to bring shadow banking into the light as well as longer-term reforms to develop a modern financial system that is more diversified and resilient.

8.5 IMMEDIATE-TERM REFORM PRIORITIES

In terms of regulating the shadow banking sector itself, the reform agenda needs to be differentiated across the three risk layers in shadow banks, addressing the respective root causes, based on their interconnections with the formal banking system. Another immediate-term priority is on policy measures to address the lack of transparency and bundling of shadow banking risks with the financial sector, including putting in place the necessary mechanisms for a safety net and exit mechanism for failed institutions, address the moral hazard issue, resolve the inter-enterprise liability problem and improve credit accountability (via the FSB's LEI initiative and the establishment of a property registry and a credit bureau). Greater clarity in the roles of regulatory authorities, including through legislative amendments, is important to strengthen inter-agency cooperation and minimize supervisory gaps, while continued progress in orderly financial liberalization will reduce opportunities for regulatory arbitrage. More open communication, via dialogues with key stakeholders including the top leadership and consumers, will build support for the reform process.

8.6 LONG-TERM REFORMS: A FINANCIAL BLUEPRINT

Over the longer term, China's reform agenda needs to focus on measures to diversify away from the bank-dominated financial system to address the structural mismatches in the economy, including the maturity and debt–equity mismatches. This calls for a financial sector blueprint to develop the capital/equity market, and long-term pension and insurance funds, promote private equity and equity funds for innovative investments. The development of the long-term municipal bond market and creation of secondary mortgage markets will enhance market liquidity and financial resilience and help address the emerging property market risks. Measures to improve the management of state assets and separate the role of the state from ownership will promote greater competition and efficiency in spearheading innovation and efficient resource allocation for long-term inclusive growth.

Success in addressing China's shadow banking and financial issues rests on its ability to grow out of its internal debt problem. There may be little alternative to a debt/equity swaps for good enterprises that are currently overleveraged. This restructuring should be done at the bank level, since the lenders should bear the main risks and responsibilities of restructuring their failed borrowers. Of importance is the need to ensure sufficient liquidity in the financial system to support China's economic transformation. This can be achieved with the PBOC progressively releasing the liquidity currently frozen in statutory reserve requirements. Successful reforms also require innovations in the financial and real sector, so that growth in profits and value creation exceeds growth in losses and value destruction. Here, the role of government is important in facilitating institutional, process and product innovation. The role of regulators will be to promote financial innovation, including e-finance, while controlling the negative aspects of shadow banking.

In conclusion, China's shadow banking problem is a manageable, domestic debt issue, based on currently favorable conditions. Because the external environment is changing with a new mediocre of slower global growth and rising downside risks, prompt action is urgently needed to prevent any escalation of shadow banking risks and contagion effects. However, more regulations and piecemeal reforms are not enough. This is a golden opportunity for a holistic solution to address the structural imbalances in the Chinese economy and financial system, including the lack of transparency, corporate governance and credit culture and the hidden risks and moral hazard issues. Fundamental reforms are needed to ensure that the financial system meets China's changing funding requirements as the economy moves into middle-income, urbanized consumption and production that is not only more broad-based, but is technologically driven, mobile Internet friendly and more inclusive and ecologically sustainable.

Whilst this book has attempted to provide an analytical framework, based on the national balance sheet and flow of funds approach, to shed some light on the complex interlinkages between the shadow banking and formal banking sector and the real economy, the dynamic interactions between banks and shadow banks, and between the Chinese economy and the rest of the world are too complex and beyond the scope of this study.

In taking this study forward, further research in four areas may be warranted:

1. Modeling the dynamic interactions between banks, shadow banks and the real economy. Modeling such dynamics will be highly data intensive but can help to predict the possible outcomes in Chinese shadow banking under different scenarios.
2. Assessing the likely impact on NPLs from the weighted average interest rate burden on the various sectors of the economy. This is particularly important given expectations of a general rise in global interest rates in the long term.
3. Uncovering the hidden connections and network of interrelationships and feedback mechanisms that link the banks, shadow banks and the enterprise/local government sectors. This calls for on-site examinations or post-mortem analyses of failed enterprises through restructuring or bankruptcy proceedings.
4. Further analysis of industries with excess capacity and the potential for real estate price adjustments is also useful to assess their likely impact on the NPL situation. In the process, such research would help to clarify the potential risks of NPLs arising from changes in these sectors.

To sum up, time is of the essence, and this is a golden opportunity to transform the financial system to meet the changing needs of the Chinese economy.

APPENDIX A

EVOLUTION OF INTERNATIONAL FINANCIAL CRISES – LESSONS FOR CHINA

Li Sai Yau

A.1 INTRODUCTION

History does not repeat itself, but it is supposed to rhyme.

While no crisis is identical, Reinhart and Rogoff (2011) suggested that financial crises have occurred regularly in the last two centuries and shared some common themes. They noted that crises were preceded by a surge of capital inflows, introduction of innovative yet complex and highly risky financial products, a housing boom and/or financial liberalization/deregulation. In their research, current account deficits, rising housing prices and financial innovations are good indicators of potential banking and currency crashes. Credit and debt defaults were the common consequences of financial crises.

This Appendix compares developments in Chinese shadow banking with the international experience on the evolution of crises. Namely, the Asian Financial Crisis (AFC), U.S. Subprime Mortgage Crisis (SMC) and the Eurozone Sovereign Debt Crisis (ESDC). The aim is to draw lessons for China's management of its shadow banking sector, based on international experience. It should be noted that China does not have an external debt problem, as its shadow banking problem is essentially a domestic debt issue, and the authorities have the resources and policy flexibility to address emerging risks.

A.2 COMPARING THE EVOLUTION OF INTERNATIONAL FINANCIAL CRISES

Fundamentally, the AFC, SMC and ESDC share similar characteristics and initial triggers that led to a financial meltdown, including sudden reversals in investor sentiment and capital flows. Regulatory arbitrage and gaps in financial surveillance allowed the expansion of toxic financial products, while overreliance on credit ratings and lapses in market discipline resulted in excessive risk taking, leverage and off-balance sheet financing.

The **AFC** began when the Thai central bank stopped defending its exchange rate peg and floated the Thai Baht in July 1997. The widespread panic triggered runs on banks and massive reversal of capital flows, with negative consequences on the currency, property and stock markets. Financial liberalization enabled Thai banks to fund their lending operations (including to property and long-term infrastructure projects) via short-term foreign borrowing. This resulted in a twin currency and maturity mismatch, which became unsustainable when the Thai Baht came under severe depreciation pressure. The earlier surge in capital inflows inflated asset prices, and encouraged imprudent lending by weakly supervised non-bank financial institutions (NBFIs). Contagion effects spread to neighboring economies, including Malaysia, Indonesia, Singapore, South Korea and Hong Kong, which came under speculative pressure. The crisis was resolved when Thailand, Indonesia and Korea adopted IMF adjustment programs. The AFC was caused by corporate overleverage and poor governance, insufficiently managed by adequate macroprudential tools. One primary lesson was that fixed exchange rate regimes added fragilities to the system. A key component of the solution was the switch to more flexible exchange rates and build-up of stronger foreign exchange reserve positions.

The **U.S. SMC**'s 22-month distress officially started with Lehman Brothers' Chapter 11 filing on September 15, 2008. Investors' concern over short-term debts and defaults soared, and resulted in large-scale withdrawals from "high-yield" money market mutual funds and deposit-like funds, which were not protected by deposit insurance. Large losses and sudden pull-out from the money market created a systemic problem, freezing up the short-term financing markets and the turmoil spread to the interbank market. Coordinated G-20 efforts prevented the crisis from triggering a global depression. The U.S. authorities rescued Fannie Mae and Freddie Mac, and the UK government became the largest shareholder of Royal Bank of Scotland. Similar to the AFC, the U.S. stock and housing markets came under selling pressure, which was the SMC's final trigger. Between July 2007 and January 2009, the Nasdaq composite index fell by 43 percent, the New York Stock Exchange declined by 50 percent and Dow Jones Industrial Average dropped 47 percent. According to the Bank for International Settlements (BIS), the U.S. residential property price index fell 21 percent during the same period; and as of the end of 2013, the U.S. property price index was still 15 percent below the pre-crisis level.

The broad conclusion was that the housing and the financial sectors were overleveraged, without sufficient regulatory oversight over the complex, interconnected nature of shadow banking and the formal banking sector.

Under the shadow of SMC, the European interbank markets seized up due to concerns about their potential exposures to the U.S. subprime credit derivatives. The tipping point of the **ESDC** was in December 2009, when Greece's credit rating was downgraded after the government announced that its debt reached 121 percent of GDP and its budget deficit was 12.7 percent of GDP (four times higher than the Maastricht Targets). In May 2010, eurozone member states and the IMF announced a three-year €110bn rescue plan for Greece. Other eurozone member states, Spain, Portugal, Ireland and Cyprus, also came under contagion pressure, and Portugal's sovereign rating was downgraded to junk status by Moody's in June 2011. In August 2011, Standard and Poor's downgraded the U.S.'s sovereign credit rating below its triple-A status. Liquidity continued to tighten along with falling exports and domestic consumption demand. The eurozone's goods exports dropped 22.1 percent in 2009 (World Bank Data). According to the BIS, the eurozone's residential property price index dropped by 4 percent between July 2008 and March 2010 (see Figure A.1). In July 2008–Dec 2013, Spain's residential property price index fell by 30 percent, and Greece's residential property price index declined by 33 percent.

Although the trigger point for the European crisis was bank illiquidity from the subprime crisis, there were deeper problems within the eurozone structure; namely, a fixed exchange regime without a unified financial and fiscal structure. The result was a situation in which periphery countries ran current account balances which were unsustainable but these could not be adjusted through national monetary policy adjustments or devaluations. Thus, where periphery economies such as Greece, Ireland, Spain and Portugal allowed real estate bubbles to occur, the resultant

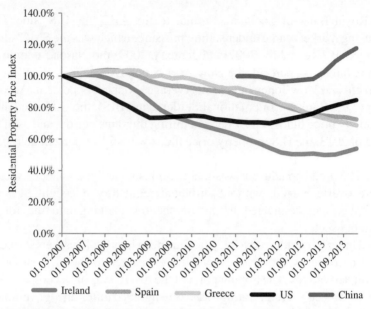

FIGURE A.1 Housing bubbles – the trigger points.
Source: BIS (2013).

losses required huge domestic deflation under the fixed exchange rate system.

The AFC, SMC and ESDC generated systemic contagion effects and required extensive official intervention, including coordination with international agencies, such as the IMF. The AFC was caused by poor sequencing of financial liberalization; and non-bank lending was also one of the key triggers. The ESDC reflected the inflexibility of a common monetary policy for individual eurozone member states and unsustainable fiscal and current account deficits. The SMC was due to regulatory arbitrage and lapses in banking supervision, which led to complex, highly leveraged, off-balance sheet financial innovations (see Table A.1).

The development of China's shadow banking activities in terms of off-balance sheet lending under a loose supervisory framework has similarities to the evolution of the SMC.

However, China's shadow banks are less sophisticated than their U.S. peers and do not involve highly complex toxic financial products. The problem is also a domestic debt issue, as external borrowing is not significant. This should minimize any contagion effects on the global

TABLE A.1 Comparison of recent financial crises.

	Asian Financial Crisis	Subprime Mortgage Crisis	Eurozone Sovereign Debt Crisis
Duration	March 1997–July 1999 (*2 years 5 months*)	Aug 2007–May2009 (*1 year 10 months*)	Oct 2009–Nov 2012 (*2 years 2 months*)
Initial Trigger	Collapse of Thai Baht	Lehman Bankruptcy	Greek Government Debt
Major Causes	*i) Formal and informal currency pegs* – discouraged lenders and borrowers from hedging	*i) Regulatory arbitrage* – investors bypassed restrictions placed on traditional deposits, investing in money market mutual funds and deposit-like funds which are not protected by deposit insurance, lack capital buffer and do not have access to the lender of last resort	*i) European interbank markets seize up* – due to fears of potential exposures to the U.S. subprime credit derivatives
	ii) Corporate sectors were highly leveraged – with large unhedged short-term external debt	*ii) Moral Hazard* – too-big-to-fail problem deepens under government interventions and bail-out rescue packages	*ii) Liquidity Trap* – euro members do not have independent authority over monetary policy

(*continued*)

TABLE A.1 (*Continued*)

Asian Financial Crisis	Subprime Mortgage Crisis	Eurozone Sovereign Debt Crisis
iii) *Surge of capital inflows* – helped fuel rapid credit expansion, which lowered the quality of credit assessment and led to asset price inflation	iii) *Large scale withdrawals from money market funds* – freeze up short-term financing markets	iii) *Tightened credit liquidity along with weak demand* – domestic consumption and exports declined significantly
iv) *Inflated asset prices* – encouraged further capital inflows and lending by weakly supervised nonbank financial institutions	iv) *Inaccurate ratings on toxic/junk financial products* – investors were buying junk assets and toxic products with high default risk but "structured AAA" ratings	iv) *Moral hazard* – European governments and IMF actively involved in bank rescues
v) *Insufficient banking supervision, financial stability surveillance and poor enforcement* – resulted in weak corporate governance and lack of market discipline allowing excessive risk-taking	v) *Complex linkages among credit and funding markets* – transmitted into broad-based financial sector, i.e. use of leverage and off-balance sheet financing	v) *Sovereign debt downgrades by credit agencies* - further reduced investor confidence

vi) Fiscal imbalances – Greece, Ireland and Portugal experienced huge fiscal deficits

vii) Political instability – change of governments due to elections

| **Final Trigger** | Housing Market Collapse. Asset quality and price slump, generating runs on the stock and property markets |

Source: IMF (1999), BIS (2009), Lin and Volker (2012), Bruegel (2014).

financial system in the unlikely event of a collapse in China's shadow banking industry. However, this does not preclude the risks of contagion via other channels. For example, if China's GDP growth were to falter significantly, this could have implications on the regional and global economies.

A.3 THE SUBPRIME MORTGAGE AND ESDC CRISES: LESSONS FOR CHINA

The SMC had global contagion effects, mainly in the U.S., the UK, eurozone and some Latin American economies. While Asia was not directly affected, the impact came through the trade channel, when world trade collapsed following a freeze of global trade finance. In contrast, China's shadow banking experience is more of a domestic debt issue as China is a net lender to the rest of the world and Chinese shadow banking credit is mostly domestic-based, with little or no global systemic implications. However, there are a number of similarities between the SMC and China's shadow banking situation.

Firstly, both subprime mortgage assets and shadow banking assets are off-balance sheet items, which make it difficult to estimate the actual size and scale of the risks or their implications on non-performing loans (NPLs). In addition to the lack of transparency, China's shadow banking problem is complicated by its bundling of risks with the formal banking system.

Second, the SMC and ESDC involved a moral hazard problem, as official support was needed to bail out the too-big-to-fail financial institutions. The shadow banks in China also present moral hazard issues as the public perception is that the commercial banks involved and/or the government will eventually intervene to cover any shadow banking losses. Most Chinese commercial banks are state-owned and have full government support. The U.S. and UK authorities "nationalized" the mortgage finance agencies and commercial banks, like Fannie Mae and Royal Bank of Scotland, during the SMC.

Third, during the SMC and ESDC, the quality of shadow banking collaterals declined significantly due to weak demand, falling property prices and overcapacity. China also suffers from overcapacity in old, polluting industries and property price corrections could affect certain regions, although a generalized property market collapse is unlikely.

Fourth, investor and consumer confidence fell considerably during the SMC and ESDC. In China's case, the Shanghai Stock Exchange Composite Index recorded a cumulative decline of over 30 percent since January 2010. The stock market turmoil in the summer of 2015 highlights the fragility of market confidence and the need for comprehensive measures to restore stability. China's PMI (manufacturing) index hit a 9-month low of 48 in April 2014 compared to 50.4 in May 2013. Moreover, China's exports as a percentage of GDP decreased by 2 percent in 2012 (World Bank Data).

In dealing with shadow banks, China has taken similar monetary measures in easing liquidity. PBOC raised its bank reserve requirement ratio to a record high of 21.5 percent in June 2011. In June 2013, shortly after U.S. Federal Reserve's announcement of a tapering plan, China experienced a temporary dry-up of liquidity, which is similar to what had happened during the SMC. At its height, China's Shanghai interbank offered rate (SHIBOR) increased by over 13 percent – almost five times the 12-month average. As liquidity tightened, several trust products, including one issued by Citic Trust Co. (a subsidiary of China's biggest state-owned investment company), failed to make principal and interest payments on time.

Both the SMC and China's shadow banking experience were the result of regulatory arbitrage as investors sought to circumvent the restrictions on traditional banking deposits to invest in higher yielding (and more risky) off-balance sheet financial products: money market mutual funds and financial derivatives in the case of the U.S., and wealth management products (WMPs) and trust funds in China. (See Key Events in Tables A.2 and A.3) China's WMPs' share of GDP is almost the same as the U.S.'s money market mutual funds share of GDP before the SMC (Borst, 2013).

A.4 INTERNATIONAL COMPARISON OF NONPERFORMING LOANS (NPLs)

The reported NPL ratios of the advanced economies, including the UK (3.7 percent), the U.S. (3.3 percent) and Germany (2.9 percent) are relatively higher than those in China (under 1 percent) (World Bank Data). Ernst and Young (2013) reported that the distressed loans on the balance sheets of U.S. banks accelerated to US$394 billion in December 2012 from US$9.7 billion in December 2007; whereas the eurozone's total NPLs as a percentage of banks' total loans rose from 5.6 percent in

TABLE A.2 U.S. subprime mortgage crisis: key events and stages.

Stage 1: Pre-March 2008	Stage 2: Mid-March to Sep 2008	Stage 3: 15 Sep 2008 to late Oct 2008	Stage 4: Late Oct 2008 to mid-March 2009	Stage 5: Since mid-March 2009
Use of leverage and off-balance sheet financing	Financial asset prices came under renewed pressure	Lehman Brothers filed for bankruptcy protection	IMF stepped in with a US$25 billion support package for Hungary	Volatility declined and asset prices recovered but confidence had not yet recovered in the global financial system
Losses from subprime mortgages exposed large scale vulnerabilities	Interbank markets failed to recover	Both the U.S. and UK authorities prohibited short selling of financial shares	U.S. Fed signed swap lines with Brazil, Korea, Mexico and Singapore	U.S. Fed announces plan to purchase longer-term treasury securities up to US$300 billion
Turmoil spread to interbank markets	Banks reluctant to lend to other banks	Central banks signed coordinated swap lines	U.S. Fed created a US$200 billion facility to extend loans against securitizations	U.S. Fed Open Market Committee authorized new swap lines with Select Five[1]
A severe liquidity shortage, e.g. Bear Sterns	U.S. authorities took unprecedented measures to support money market,	Mortgage lender and commercial banks began to be 'nationalized'	G20 pledged joint efforts	U.S. Fed's stress test reported that 10 banks had an overall capital

			shortfall of US$75 billion
		UK government became the largest shareholder of Royal Bank of Scotland	ECB decided to purchase euro-denominated covered bonds
injecting funds and purchasing troubled agency stocks			
Equity prices fell	Government offered capital injections to troubled corporate borrowers	The Irish authorities seized control of Anglo Irish Bank	Exports remained weak
Credit agencies downgraded credit ratings		Public–Private Investment Program was established to purchase troubled assets, up to US$1 trillion	
U.S. housing market collapsed			

[1] See FGI article: "Central Bank Currency Swaps Key to International Monetary System" by Dr. Andrew Sheng, April 2014. Available at: http://www.fungglobalinstitute.org/en/central-bank-currency-swaps-key-international-monetary-system

Source: BIS (2009).

TABLE A.3 China's shadow banking developments – key events.

2010	M2 growth decreased from 30 percent to 16 percent
June 2011	PBOC raised bank reserve requirement ratio to a record high of 21.5 percent
Mid 2012	Market survey showed that informal lending rate was as high as 21–25 percent in Wenzhou
As of end-2012	Financial Stability Board reported that non-bank financial intermediation in China rose 42 percent to US$2.13 trillion
	Exports as a percentage of GDP dropped by 2 percent to 27 percent
	Rise of thousands of peer-to-peer (P2P) Internet lending platforms, with about 20 defaults per month
	Informal lending annualized interest rates approaching 100 percent in several cities
	WMPs issued by banking institutions reached RMB 7.1 percent, up 55 percent year-on-year (YOY)
	There are 6,080 microlenders, 6,078 pawn shops and 8,538 financial guarantors registered with local governments under regulators' supervision
Mid 2013	Some trust funds begin to default on interest and principal
June 2013	U.S. Fed announced plan to taper
	SHIBOR spiked up to over 13 percent – almost 5 times the 12-month average
July 2013	PBOC allowed banks to determine their own lending rates
Sep 2013	China launched Shanghai (Pilot) Free Trade Zone with supportive policies on finance and banking
Dec 2013	PBOC allowed banks to trade deposits with each other at market-determined prices
As of the end of 2013	Total social financing reached US$2.8 trillion, up by 9.7 percent YOY

	Commercial banking NPL increased by 5 percent to US$95 billion, ending the NPL declining trend
	Banks' WMPs size accelerated by 39.4 percent to US$1.59 trillion
	Between 2012 and 2013 alone, the volume of lending brokered through nearly 1,000 P2P platforms tripled, reading 68 billion yuan (US$11 billion) (Zhu, 2014)
	Trust Fund scale reached US$1.65 trillion, up by 47.7 percent YOY
	Market analysts expect China's shadow banking assets can be as big as US$4 trillion, which is nearly double the FSB's 2012 estimate
	Since June 2010, PBOC signed US$426 billion swap lines with 21 central banks
Feb 2014	Tencent's Yu'E Bao (internet financial product) accumulated a fund size of over US$81 billion with over 81 million active investors. Yu'E Bao is now the world's 4th largest fund by size
March 2014	Nomura's estimated China's property price index fell by 3.8 percent YOY
April 2014	PMI (manufacturing) hit 9-month low at 48.0
	Shanghai and Hong Kong announced "through train" cooperative plan to allow investors to invest in both A and H shares directly
May 2014	RMB depreciated by over 3 percent since 1 January 2014
	Since 2010, Shanghai Stock Exchange Composite Index decreased by over 30 percent
	Mainland stock markets to resume IPOs
July 2014	PBOC announced that, in Jan–June 2014, there are 8,394 small-loan companies with an outstanding loans of RMB 881.1 billion (up 7.5 percent)

Note: Highlighted events are similar to those in the Subprime Mortgage Crisis.
Source: PBOC, various media reports and FGI compilation.

TABLE A.4 Bank non-performing loans in selected countries.

Country	2005	2006	2007	2008	2009	2010	2011	2012	2013
China	8.6	7.1	6.2	2.4	1.6	1.1	1	1	1
Germany	4	3.4	2.6	2.9	3.3	3.2	3	2.9	
Greece		61.8	53.7	4.7	7	9.1	14.4	23.3	31.3
Iceland	1.1	0.8			14.1	18.3	11.6	6.4	5.1
Ireland	0.5	0.5	0.6	1.9	9.8	12.5	16.1	24.6	24.6
Italy	7	6.6	5.8	6.3	9.4	10	11.7	13.7	15.1
Spain	0.8	0.7	0.9	2.8	4.1	4.7	6	7.5	8.2
United Kingdom		0.9	0.9	1.6	3.5	4	4	3.7	
United States	0.7	0.8	1.4	3	5	4.4	3.8	3.3	3.2

Source: World Bank.

TABLE A.5 Growth of commercial banking NPL ratio in selected countries, 2008–2013 (%).

	2009	2010	2011	2012	2013
China	−34.2	−28.5	−15	−1	5.3
Greece	48.9	30	58.2	61.8	34.3
Ireland	415.8	27.6	28.8	52.8	0
Italy	49.2	6.4	17	17.1	10.2
Spain	46.4	14.6	27.7	25	9.3

Source: World Bank, PBOC, FGI calculations.

2011 to 6.8 percent in 2012. PWC (2013) reported that NPLs in the eurozone reached over US$1.7 trillion in 2013.

Chinese banks' NPL ratios have also risen from 0.95 to 1.00 in 2013 (nearly US$95 billion), putting an end to the declining NPL trend (PBOC, 2014). Tables A.4 and A.5 show that the increase in China's NPL ratio is still relatively small compared to Greece, Ireland, Italy and Spain in the aftermath of the 2008 crisis. It should be noted that Chinese banks' provisions for NPLs exceed the NPL ratio by 280 percent, resulting in provisioning levels of roughly 4.6 percent of risk assets.

Figure A.2 shows the NPL ratios for different type of banks in China during 2005–2012. SOE banks' NPL ratio was only 0.99, and 0.81 for

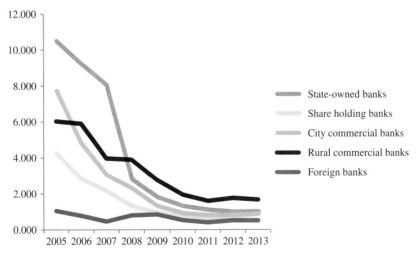

FIGURE A.2 NPLs of different classes of banks in China, 2005–2012.
Source: PBOC, CEIC.

TABLE A.6 Sub-sector NPL ratio for commercial banks, 2005–2012 (%).

	2005	2006	2007	2008	2009	2010	2011	2012
Farming, Forestry, Animal Husbandry & Fishery	46.3	46.1	47.1	7.5	4.5	3.2	2.4	2.4
Mining	4.8	3.7	3.3	0.7	0.4	0.3	0.3	0.2
Manufacturing	11.9	10.4	8.9	3.3	2.6	1.9	1.5	1.6
Electricity, Gas & Water Production & Supply	2.7	2.2	2.4	2.1	1.4	1.2	1.0	0.7
Construction	5.2	4.3	3.4	1.7	1.3	0.8	0.7	0.6
Transport, Storage & Postal Service	2.3	2.0	2.1	1.6	1.3	1.0	1.1	0.8
Info Transmission, Computer Service & Software	4.7	5.3	5.6	3.3	2.6	1.9	1.4	1.4
Wholesale & Retail Trade	20.5	17.3	13.9	4.1	2.7	1.6	1.2	1.6
Accommodation & Catering Trade	24.9	19.6	16.1	7.7	4.8	3.0	2.6	1.9
Real Estate	9.2	6.6	4.9	3.4	1.5	1.3	1.0	0.7
Leasing & Commercial Service	13.5	10.6	8.0	1.8	0.5	0.7	0.6	0.5

Source: PBOC, CEIC.

city commercial banks in 2012. But both rural commercial banks and foreign banks recorded double-digit increases of 10 percent and 26.8 percent respectively in 2012.

In the first decade of the 21st century, Chinese banks' NPL ratios declined rapidly due to faster GDP growth and a carve-out of bad loans. In 1999, China's Ministry of Finance established four asset management companies (AMCs) to acquire, restructure and sell bank NPLs to investors. Each AMC is aligned with one of the big four SOE banks in China: Agricultural Bank of China, Bank of China, Construction Bank of China and the Industrial and Commercial Bank of China.

In terms of NPL by sector, the "farming, forestry, animal husbandry and fishery," "wholesale and retail trade," "accommodation and catering trade" and "manufacturing" sectors have the highest NPL ratios for commercial banks during 2005 and 2012.See Table A.6.

Management of NPLs in the trust sector is likely to be crucial in resolving the potential shadow banking problem. The Bank of America Merrill Lynch (BoAML, 2014) has identified property developers, local government financing vehicles (LGFVs) and coal miners as the three major sectoral trust borrowers. See Table A.7.

As of end-2013, trust loans accounted for RMB 4.7 trillion out of the RMB 10 trillion of trust AUM, which is equivalent to only 6.1 percent of banking sector loans. Assuming a worst case scenario of 25 percent default ratio, and assuming the second derivative effect will triple the

TABLE A.7   Assessment of China's three main trust borrowers.

Sector	Risk	Size
Coal miners	Could see most default, as coal prices plummeted.	< US$32 billion (RMB 200 billion)
Property developers	Smaller developers with single-city operations in Tier 3, Tier 4 cities could be in trouble. Large national developers should be fine.	US$320–400 billion (RMB 2–2.5 trillion)
LGFVs	Have the most government support/intervention, and may see limited defaults.	US$240 billion (RMB 1.5 trillion)

Source: BoAML (2014).

impact, i.e. every RMB 1 of trust loan default would engender a RMB 3 default on bank loans/bonds, the potential size of bad debts would only be around RMB 3.5 trillion (that is only equivalent to 4.5 percent of bank loans). BoAML (2014) forecast that since banks will not be fully liable for all forms of off-balance sheet risk, banks' NPLs are more likely to be in the 4–5 percent range in the event of a default on trust loans.

A.5 CONCLUSION

The international experience in crisis evolution and resolution offers important lessons for China, in terms of the likely trigger points if a crisis were to unfold. In particular, closer attention is warranted to monitor developments in global long-term interest rates and their likely impact on the Chinese economy, including its property markets and industries with excess capacity. Early preventive action has proven always to be less costly than resolution measures after a crisis has erupted.

REFERENCES

BIS (Bank for International Settlements). 2009. The 79th Annual Report: 1 April 2008–31 March 2009. http://www.bis.org/publ/arpdf/ar2009e.htm.

BoAML (Bank of America Merrill Lynch). 2014. *The Coming Trust Defaults*, 13.

Borst, Nicholas. 2013. Shadow Deposits as a Source of Financial Instability: Lessons from the American Experience for China. Peterson Institute for International Economics Policy Brief. http://www.iie.com/publications/pb/pb13-14.pdf.

Bruegel. 2014. Euro Crisis Timeline. Prolegomenon. http://www.bruegel.org/fileadmin/bruegel_files/Blog_pictures/Eurocrisis_timeline/121130_Eurocrisis_Timeline.pdf.

Ernst and Young. 2013. Flocking to Europe: Non-performing Loan Report. http://www.ey.com/Publication/vwLUAssets/Flocking_to_Europe/$FILE/Flocking_to_Europe.pdf.

IMF (International Monetary Fund). 1999. Financial Sector Crisis and Restructuring. Lessons from Asia. Occasional Paper 188. http://www.imf.org/external/pubs/ft/op/opFinsec/.

Lin, Justin, and Volker Treichel. 2012. "The Crisis in the Euro Zone: Did the Euro Contribute to the Evolution of the Crisis?" The World Bank Policy Research Working Paper 6127. http://www-wds.worldbank.org/servlet/WDSContentServer/WDSP/IB/2012/08/15/000158349_20120815154113/Rendered/PDF/WPS6127.pdf.

PBOC (People's Bank of China). 2014. China Financial Stability Report 2014. http://www.pbc.gov.cn/publish/goutongjiaoliu/524/2014/20140429162156125254533/20140429162156125254533.html.

PWC (PricewaterhouseCoopers). 2013. Europe's Non-Performing Loans Now Total More Than €1.2 trillion. 29 October. http://pwc.blogs.com/press_room/2013/10/europes-non-performing-loans-now-total-more-than-12-trillion.html.

Reinhart, Carmen M., and Kenneth S. Rogoff. 2011. *This Time is Different: Eight Centuries of Financial Folly*. Princeton University Press.

Tsai, Kellee S. 2015. *The Political Economy of State Capitalism and Shadow Banking in China*. HKUST IEMS Working Paper No. 2015–25.

INDEX

Index compiled by Indexing Specialists (UK) Ltd